A REFLECTIVE JOURNAL

THE NEW ME

EXPLORING MY IDENTITY IN CHRIST

By Ralph Ennis, Judy Gomoll, Rebecca Goldstone,
Dennis Stokes, and Christine Weddle

NAVPRESS

NAVPRESS⬤

NavPress is the publishing ministry of The Navigators, an international Christian organization and leader in personal spiritual development. NavPress is committed to helping people grow spiritually and enjoy lives of meaning and hope through personal and group resources that are biblically rooted, culturally relevant, and highly practical.

**For a free catalog go to www.NavPress.com
or call 1.800.366.7788 in the United States or 1.800.839.4769 in Canada.**

© 2008 by The Navigators

ISBN-13: 978-1-60006-359-6
ISBN-10: 1-60006-359-4

Content Development Team: Ralph Ennis, Judy Gomoll, Rebecca Goldstone, Dennis Stokes, and Christine Weddle

Cover design by The DesignWorks Group, Jason Gabbert, www.thedesignworksgroup.com

Some of the anecdotal illustrations in this book are true to life and are included with the permission of the persons involved. All other illustrations are composites of real situations, and any resemblance to people living or dead is coincidental.

Printed in the United States of America

1 2 3 4 5 6 7 8 / 12 11 10 09 08

introduction	5
flawed	8
soul ugly	12
unlovable	16
disconnected	20
powerless	24
dirty	28
fragmented	32
unworthy/worthless	36
alone	40
numb	44
guilty	48
meaningless	52
undesirable	56
abandoned	60
futile	64
discontent	68
inadequate	72
ashamed	76
spiritually oppressed	80
in bondage	84
dishonored	88
unappreciated	92
dead	96
rejected	100
condemned	104
fearful	108
like a failure	112
disillusioned	116
depressed	120

introduction

The New Me interactive journal is a way to get to a real level, to experience how you *actually are* rather than how you *should be*. Used individually, it will help you see and honestly consider where the struggles and growing places in your life are. Used with others, it will offer a starting point to begin conversations about where you long for change, for new life, for tastes of God.

You are not locked into being what you've always been. There is hope and expectancy. That's because God always meets you where you are—not just where you think you should be. But becoming new isn't the result of a do-it-yourself effort, rather through the power of Christ you can anticipate discovery, change, and renewal. *The New Me* is simply meant to invite you into a new place of honesty as you begin.

You might be struggling with the tension of knowing you have a long way to go in this process of transformation. Christ promises to makes us new creations who are growing more and more like Him. So why is so much of the "old" still hanging on? In one sense you "already are" and in another sense you "are still becoming" like Jesus. That's okay. You aren't asked to have it all together—just be in the process of growing in His grace.

You may be thinking, "That sounds good, but how I *feel* about who I am doesn't always match what I *know* about who I really am in Christ! My head and my heart are out of synch." Once again, that's okay. On the journey of spiritual transformation, feelings often lag behind awareness and understanding. So be patient with yourself; God is passionate about transforming all parts of you, but He isn't pushy. Know that the journey is just as important as the destination, and God is eager to meet you along the way.

So how can you use this journal? You might use it as a journaling tool to work through emotions as you experience them. You can go in any order and skip around from topic to topic if you want to. Or you might choose to start at the beginning of the book and work through one topic a day.

You might find yourself using this journal in one of the following ways:

- As a parent helping a child navigate through these difficult feelings
- As a small group embracing the truth of your identity in Christ
- As a married couple learning to process feelings together
- As an individual to process through the more difficult emotions of life

You'll explore each topic in four pages—with lots of space for you to jot down your thoughts and questions.

- The first page introduces the topic through an image. Take time to gaze at the image even if it disturbs you.
- The second page invites you to identify with the experiences of people struggling with the same emotions and others bringing insight to that struggle.
- The third page offers the truth of God's Word to meditate on and anchor your soul in hope. These portions of truth aren't to be used as Band-Aids on your soul-wounds, but as an offering of hope. Acknowledge the disconnect

between what is and what should be, and invite the Holy Spirit into the gap.

- The fourth page challenges you to consider, wrestle with, and embrace who you are becoming in Christ.

Over time, those of you who are in Christ will be transformed through the power of His Holy Spirit and affirming connection to the body of Christ. You will continue to be changed into the *you* that you were created to be.

i may feel flawed

but by the power of His Spirit

i am becoming like Christ

haunted

When I let it get quiet, I can hear my science teacher's voice sneering in my head: "No one wants to work with you, so you'll do the rest of the labs this year with me as your partner. How does that feel?" He might as well just have come out and said it: You're a loser. You'll never be like the others. And somehow, even though I hated the man, I can't help but believe he's right, all these years later. I still just can't get it right.

> Another injury due to victimization is a deep, pervasive sense of being "all-bad," wrong, dirty, or shameful. No matter how affirming others are of their loveableness and their attributes, victims are convinced that, underneath it all, there is no good inside themselves. . . . They take on badness that isn't theirs. They begin believing that the way they were treated is the way they should be treated.
>
> —Dr. Henry Cloud and Dr. John Townsend, *Boundaries*

Whose voices have defined how you see yourself?

hope

And we, who with unveiled faces all reflect the Lord's glory, are being transformed into his likeness with ever-increasing glory, which comes from the Lord, who is the Spirit. —2 Corinthians 3:18

Dear friends, now we are children of God, and what we will be has not yet been made known. But we know that when he appears, we shall be like him, for we shall see him as he is. Everyone who has this hope in him purifies himself, just as he is pure. —1 John 3:2-3

More Verses: Psalm 51; 2 Corinthians 4:7-10; Philippians 3:20-21

I know about this flawed creation of Mine. I did not will it to be flawed, but I will allow it for a while. I must ask you to do the same—allow it for a while. It is part of my redemptive plan. You need not apologize, agonize, or pretend that brokenness does not exist. You were broken and I loved you. You still are not completely whole and still I love you. I have fixed you, redeemed you, but not perfected you. That will come later.

—RUTH SENTER, *Longing for Love*

What might Jesus have to say to you today about who you are and who you are becoming?

becoming

What parts of your life do you feel you just "can't get right"?

How do you feel about becoming like Christ? What does it do for your sense of personal dignity and worth?

i may feel soul ugly
but by the power of His Spirit
i am beautiful to God

dirty corners of my soul

Last night I ate dinner at the hotel restaurant alone. It's the price of travel-ing in this job. I could feel the bartender's eyes searching my face, and I made the mistake of meeting his gaze more than once. How can you not, when someone is watching you. And yet if he could see beyond the business suit, into the dirty corners of my soul, his eyes would turn elsewhere. He'd find someone with more to offer than this. I used to be flattered by one-night stands. But they each left when I let them really look into my eyes.

i feel really dirty. . . .
i could rip off my skin.
funny thing is, is that i know if i did i'd still feel the same.
i think it's just all in my head. but it isn't.
it's become so mental that i've found it like a physical dirty. so i'm Rachael. i like tearing myself up. i've noticed i do it a lot. but that's beside the point.
i know if i tore off my skin i'd still feel dirty.
my insides are dirty.
not my organs.
its deeper than that.
it's like my "soul" is dirty.[1]

[1] http://weblog.xanga.com/R4cH431/608010456/i-feel-really-dirty-not-in-some-perverted-way-tho
.html. [Note: NavPress is not affiliated with any comments that may be expressed on this blog.]

What are some things that make people feel ugly at the core?

hope

[He has sent me to] provide for those who grieve in Zion — to bestow on them a crown of beauty instead of ashes, the oil of gladness instead of mourning, and a garment of praise instead of a spirit of despair.
—Isaiah 61:3

He has made everything beautiful in its time. He has also set eternity in the hearts of men; yet they cannot fathom what God has done from beginning to end. —Ecclesiastes 3:11

Christ loved the church and gave his life for it. He did this to dedicate the church to God by his word, after making it clean by washing it in water, in order to present the church to himself in all its beauty — pure and faultless, without spot or wrinkle or any other imperfection.
—Ephesians 5:25-27 (TEV)

More Verses: Rahab story (Joshua 2 and 6); Psalm 139; Ezekiel 16;
1 Peter 3:1-6

What "ashes" in your life do you see God making beautiful (or do you wish He would make beautiful)? What "despair" is He replacing with praise?

becoming

What do you fear people might see when they look into your eyes?

Put words to a prayer asking Jesus to cleanse something particular about you, making you "pure and faultless, without spot or wrinkle or any other imperfection." If you're skeptical about all this, tell Him that, too.

not just broken windows

She said she'd forgive me for my past, and a small part of me sometimes believes it's true. But when I'm honest with myself, I can't imagine her being willing to love someone as broken as me. I see all the other guys she could be with, and sometimes I come close to asking her why she's with me. I feel like a window with a bullet through the corner, the broken lines radiating through the whole of me. She can see through me, and I am broken; I can't be what she wants.

Self-hatred is the enemy of humility. Where there is self-hatred, the addict must live behind a mask or false self, which has been constructed over many years in order to stifle the pain of his self-rejection. . . . The man with self-hatred is turned against himself because he is still in agreement with the negative messages that he received in his youth. He agrees that he is bad and contempt-ible, unworthy of love. He, therefore, experiences feelings of shame and self-pity that have nothing to do with the conviction of the Holy Spirit.

—CRAIG LOCKWOOD, *Falling Forward: The Pursuit of Sexual Purity*

What do you believe makes someone lovable? Would they still be lovable if those things were taken away?

hope

About Benjamin he said: "Let the beloved of the LORD rest secure in him, for he shields him all day long, and the one the LORD loves rests between his shoulders. —Deuteronomy 33:12

But now, GOD's Message, the God who made you in the first place, <u>Jacob</u>, the One who got you started, <u>Israel</u>: "Don't be afraid; I've redeemed <u>you</u>. I've called <u>your</u> name. <u>You're</u> mine. When <u>you're</u> in over your head, I'll be there with <u>you</u>. When <u>you're</u> in rough waters, <u>you</u> will not go down. When you're between a rock and a hard place, it won't be a dead end—Because I am GOD, <u>your</u> personal God, the Holy of Israel, <u>your</u> Savior. I paid a huge price for <u>you</u>: all of Egypt, with rich Cush and Seba thrown in! That's how much <u>you</u> mean to me! That's how much I love <u>you</u>! I'd sell off the whole world to get you back, trade the creation just for you. —Isaiah 43:1-4 (MSG, EMPHASIS ADDED)

More Verses: Romans 8:35-39; 1 John 3 and 4

Try reading Isaiah 43:1-4 again—but out loud. This time personalize God's words by putting your own name or saying "me" or "my" whenever you see an underlined word. Consider saying it more than once—yell it, whisper it, sing it—as many times as it takes to get inside of you.

becoming

What are some of the unlovable places you are afraid someone else might see? Do you usually keep these hidden or out in the open? What would happen if others saw them?

Take a minute and imagine bringing your unlovable parts to Jesus. See yourself "resting secure between his shoulders" (Deuteronomy 33:12). Talk with Him for a while from that place. Record what you say.

i may feel disconnected
but by the power of His Spirit
i am connected to the
body of Christ

soul cocaine

I felt . . . an anxiety, a loneliness, and a need for connection with someone. If no connection came, I would start to say things like "Life really stinks. Why is it always so hard? It's never going to change. . . . Who cares? Life is really a joke." . . .

My "comforter," my abiding place, was cynicism and rebellion. From this abiding place, I would feel free to use some soul cocaine—a violence video with maybe a little sexual titillation thrown in, perhaps having a little more alcohol with a meal than I might normally drink—things that would allow me to feel better for just a little while. I had always thought of these things as just bad habits. I began to see that they were much more; they were spiritual abiding places that were my comforters and friends in a very spiritual way; literally, other lovers.

—Brent Curtis and John Eldredge, *The Sacred Romance*

Somewhere deep down, we know that if we are to survive we must come together and rediscover ways to connect with each other, and with the earth that supports our collective life. We are social beings who need one another not just for physical survival but also for spiritual sustenance as we journey together.

—Jonathan S. Campbell with Jennifer Campbell, *The Way of Jesus: A Journey of Freedom for Pilgrims and Wanderers*

What are common reasons why people choose to disconnect or just somehow end up disconnected from others?

hope

He treated us as equals, and so made us equals. Through him we both share the same Spirit and have equal access to the Father. That's plain enough, isn't it? You're no longer wandering exiles. This kingdom of faith is now your home country. You're no longer strangers or outsiders. You belong here, with as much right to the name Christian as anyone. God is building a home. He's using us all—irrespective of how we got here—in what he is building. He used the apostles and prophets for the foundation. Now he's using you, fitting you in brick by brick, stone by stone, with Christ Jesus as the cornerstone that holds all the parts together. We see it taking shape day after day—a holy temple built by God, all of us built into it, a temple in which God is quite at home. —Ephesians 2:18-22 (MSG)

I am praying not only for these disciples but also for all who will ever believe in me through their message. I pray that they will all be one, just as you and I are one—as you are in me, Father, and I am in you. And may they be in us so that the world will believe you sent me. . . . I am in them and you are in me. May they experience such perfect unity that the world will know that you sent me and that you love them as much as you love me. —John 17: 20-23 (NLT)

More Verses: 1 Corinthians 12

Explore the idea of "belonging." When have you lacked a sense of belonging—or experienced true belonging anywhere?

Have you ever felt a sense of belonging in the body of Christ? How did that affect you?

becoming

A friend tells you, "After my experience with my last church, I don't need to connect with the body of Christ. All I need is Jesus." How would you respond?

How do you respond to God about His promise for heart and life connection among His people? Do you tend to feel cynical, afraid, hungry, angry, or something else about that possibility? Explain.

i may feel powerless

but by the power of His Spirit

i am empowered

at war with my weakness

Man, why did I do that? That was really stupid. I know better than that. I'm such an idiot! Why can't I just do what I know I should? Every time I get in that situation I mess up. Why do I have to be at war with myself! One part of me wants to do what's right. But the other part of me wants to do what I want, when I want to do it. If only I was stronger! Then I wouldn't be in this situation. I hate being weak! Weakness is like a poison that I can't get rid of. If I just try harder next time, then maybe I can beat this. Maybe I won't be such a fool. This is all my fault! At the end of the day, this falls on my shoulders because I'm not strong enough.

> Our enslavements and indulgences have not only developed into more distasteful appetites; they have also taken from us the power to change. Many confess a craving to change but find themselves helpless and powerless to do so.
>
> —Ravi Zacharias, *Deliver Us from Evil*

What are some things (both outside themselves and inside) that can make people feel weak or powerless?

hope

I was given a thorn in my flesh, a messenger from Satan to torment me and keep me from becoming proud. Three different times I begged the Lord to take it away. Each time he said, "My grace is all you need. My power works best in weakness." So now I am glad to boast about my weaknesses, so that the power of Christ can work through me. That's why I take pleasure in my weaknesses, and in the insults, hardships, persecutions, and troubles that I suffer for Christ. For when I am weak, then I am strong.
—2 Corinthians 12:7-10 (NLT)

For I can do everything through Christ, who gives me strength.
—Philippians 4:13 (NLT)

Instead, God chose . . . things that are powerless to shame those who are powerful. —1 Corinthians 1:27 (NLT)

More Verses: 2 Corinthians 4:7-10; 2 Peter 1:3-4; Ephesians 3:16

Do you really believe that God's power can change you and your situation? Why or why not?

becoming

Is power good or bad to you? Explain.

How can you rely on God's power in your place of feeling powerless?

mud-caked

During the summers at my grandparents' farm, my brother and I would play in the mud and we'd end up with more mud showing than skin. Grandma would make us stand on the concrete slab and spray us down with ice-cold hose water. We would laugh and shiver and watch the mud stream off until we were clean. But if Grandma could see me now, she'd cry. How did I get so far from those days? My friends tell me that everyone hooks up these days. But the next morning in the shower, I can never get clean. If only a garden hose could reach beyond my skin to my soul.

And I feel so DIRTY. Because it isn't natural to me, and how could I do something so disgusting and what is wrong with me and why am I so weird? And sometimes I feel so dirty. And sometimes I feel so hurt inside and I know that something feels good, but afterwards I feel so dirty. And sometimes I see scenes of others' hurt and lives, and it feels dirty to watch.[1]

1 http://weblog.xanga.com/climbingupthemountain/623863355/feelings.html. Posted: 10/27/2007 1:59 PM. [Note: NavPress is not affiliated with any comments that may be expressed on this blog.]

If someone looked into your soul, what dirt might they see?

hope

Purify me from my sins, and I will be clean; wash me, and I will be whiter than snow. —Psalm 51:7 (NLT)

I will cleanse them from all the sin they have committed against me and will forgive all their sins of rebellion against me. —Jeremiah 33:8

Don't you realize that this is not the way to live? Unjust people who don't care about God will not be joining in his kingdom. Those who use and abuse each other, use and abuse sex, use and abuse the earth and everything in it, don't qualify as citizens in God's kingdom. A number of you know from experience what I'm talking about, for not so long ago you were on that list. Since then, you've been cleaned up and given a fresh start by Jesus, our Master, our Messiah, and by our God present in us, the Spirit. —1 Corinthians 6:9-11 (MSG)

More Verses: Psalm 51

How is being forgiven like being washed clean? Have you or someone you know ever experienced that? Explain.

becoming

What "dirt" in your life do you long to have cleaned up?
(1 Corinthians 6:9-11) What might it take for that to happen?

Do you have enough faith to ask God to clean up that part of you? Why not ask Him anyway? Write a prayer about being clean.

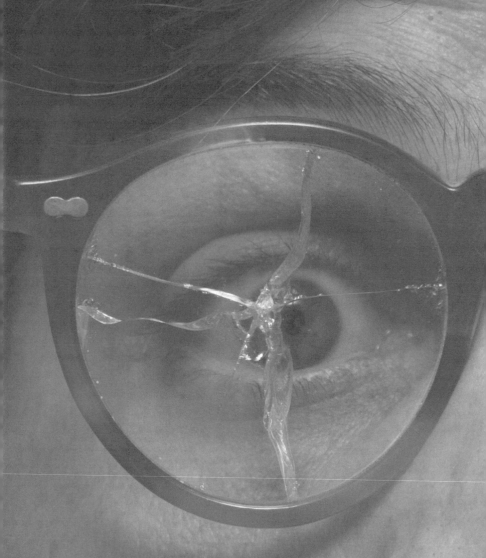

i may feel fragmented
but by the power of His Spirit
i am made whole

all my pieces

Who am I, anyway? I love my kids, so why do I yell at them all the time? I'm crazy about my wife, so how come I flirt with waitresses I don't even care about? The guys in my small group like it when I do some teaching, but if they could hear what comes out of my mouth on the basketball court . . . I love watching Monday night football, too. But if people knew what my eyes look at late on Tuesday night . . . I am tired and dizzy. My life has become a piece of shattered glass. Or maybe I'm Humpty Dumpty. Who can put me together again?

> Who am I? This or the other?
> Am I one person today and tomorrow another?
> Am I both at once? A hypocrite before others,
> And before my self a contemptible woebegone weakling? . . .
> Who am I? They mock me, these lonely questions of mine.
> Whoever I am, Thou knowest, O God, I am thine!
>
> —DIETRICH BONHOEFFER
> (As quoted in Jerry Sittser, *A Grace Disguised*)

What are some things people do that they really don't want to do? So why do you think they still do those things?

hope

I don't really understand myself, for I want to do what is right, but I don't do it. Instead, I do what I hate. But if I know that what I am doing is wrong, . . . And I know that nothing good lives in me, that is, in my sinful nature. I want to do what is right, but I can't. I want to do what is good, but I don't. I don't want to do what is wrong, but I do it anyway. But if I do what I don't want to do, I am not really the one doing wrong; it is sin living in me that does it. —Romans 7:15-20 (NLT)

So spacious is he, so roomy, that everything of God finds its proper place in him without crowding. Not only that, but all the broken and dislocated pieces of the universe—people and things, animals and atoms—get properly fixed and fit together in vibrant harmonies, all because of his death, his blood that poured down from the cross. You yourselves are a case study of what he does. At one time you all had your backs turned to God, thinking rebellious thoughts of him, giving him trouble every chance you got. But now, by giving himself completely at the Cross, actually dying for you, Christ brought you over to God's side and put your lives together, whole and holy in his presence. —Colossians 1:19-22 (MSG)

More Verses: Psalm 34:18; Psalm 51:17; Psalm 147:3; 2 Corinthians 4:16-18

What wrong things does the sin in you do that you really don't want to do anymore?

So why do you think you're still doing those things?

becoming

How have you tried to find wholeness in your own strength?

Draw a picture or diagram illustrating the fragments you struggle with or hide in embarrassment. Imagine for a moment God bringing you "over to his side and putting your lives together, whole and holy in his presence" (Colossians 1:22, MSG). Then write a prayer, inviting God into these pieces of your life.

i may feel worthless
but by the power of His Spirit
i am made worthy

not measuring up

But I still try to *deserve* Your affection—as though You might change Your mind about loving me if You find out what I'm really like. Human love withdraws when expectations aren't met; perhaps this is what I fear. If I'm not worthy, Your love will be transferred to someone worthier. Someone prettier. Wittier. Smarter. More loving. More patient. More self-sacrificing. It is a terrifying thought, this fear of losing love because I don't measure up.

—RUTH SENTER, *Longing for Love*

Stop trying to be perfect in order to deserve My love. You will never be "enough" of anything, anyway. I do not want your worth, your efforts, your gifts and credentials and produce. *I want you simply because you are you.* If tomorrow you should become anything other than what you are today, still I would want you.

—RUTH SENTER, *Longing for Love*

Think back to a time you felt unworthy. Express how you felt by filling in these blanks: "They/He/She should look for someone else besides me—someone more _____, someone _____-ier." Now finish the story. Did he/she/they choose you—or someone else? Explain.

hope

The son said to him, "Father, I have sinned against heaven and against you. I am no longer worthy to be called your son."

But the father said to his servants, "Quick! Bring the best robe and put it on him. Put a ring on his finger and sandals on his feel. Bring the fattened calf and kill it. Let's have a feast and celebrate. For this son of mine was dead and is alive again; he was lost and is found." So they began to celebrate. —Luke 15:21-24 (See Luke 15:11-32 for complete story.)

For you know that God paid a ransom to save you from the empty life you inherited from your ancestors. And the ransom he paid was not mere gold or silver. He paid for you with the precious lifeblood of Christ, the sinless, spotless Lamb of God. God chose him for this purpose long before the world began, but now in these final days, he was sent to the earth for all to see. And he did this for you. —1 Peter 1:18-20 (NLT)

More Verses:

> Jesus' family members: Luke 1:46-49; 1:42-45; Matthew 3:11
> Jesus' close friends and followers: John 13:8-9; 1 Corinthians 15:9;
> Romans 3:11-12

What do you think? Was the young man in Jesus' parable "worthy" to be called a son, or not?

How do you think his father would have answered that question?

becoming

What fears get stirred up in you when you conclude that you're not worth much?

Even Jesus' closest friends and family members didn't believe they "deserved" a place in His life. After reading about their feelings (see More Verses), describe how God stepped into their unworthiness.

Now pause to ask God to step into your unworthiness . . . and see what happens.

i may feel alone

but by the power of His Spirit

i am never alone

unseen tears

The kids are gone again this Christmas with their dad & his new wife. I will spend it alone. I tell everyone I'm fine—I'm lying. I'll be alone, crying. No one knows I cry.

—www.postsecret.blogspot.com Dec. 23, 2007

Mother Teresa once was asked about the worst disease she had ever seen. Was it leprosy or smallpox? Was it AIDS or Alzheimer's? "No," she said, "the worse disease I've ever seen is loneliness."

—LEONARD SWEET, *Out of the Question . . . Into the Mystery*

Surely this is the most primal fear of all—that we will end up alone.

—SHEILA WALSH, *Living Fearlessly*

Do you think most people feel more alone when they are by themselves or when they're with a group of strangers or friends with masks? Explain.

Do you feel alone or not alone in a virtual world? Explain.

hope

I can never escape from your spirit! I can never get away from your presence!

If I go up to heaven, you are there; if I go down to the grave, you are there.

If I ride the wings of the morning, if I dwell by the farthest oceans, even there your hand will guide me, and your strength will support me.

I could ask the darkness to hide me and the light around me to become night—but even in darkness I cannot hide from you.

To you the night shines as bright as day. Darkness and light are the same to you. —Psalm 139:7-12 (NLT)

Two people can accomplish more than twice as much as one; they get a better return for their labor. If one person falls, the other can reach out and help. But people who are alone when they fall are in real trouble. . . . A person standing alone can be attacked and defeated, but two can stand back-to-back and conquer. Three are even better, for a triple-braided cord is not easily broken. —Ecclesiastes 4:9-12 (NLT)

More Verses: Hebrews 13:5; Romans 8:39

Why might you actually want to get away from God's presence?

When you realize that's impossible because He's everywhere and will pursue you wherever you hide, what emotions does that stir up in you?

becoming

Sometimes being alone is refreshing and healthy. Do you often experience being alone and not being lonely? Explain.

When being alone leaves you feeling empty and lonely, how do you go about filling that void? What's life-giving about it? What isn't?

Which of your friends have you (or might you) feel safe enough to share your sense of aloneness with? How might God use that friend or others to meet your need for connection and companionship? (See Ecclesiastes 4:9-12.)

i may feel numb

but by the power of His Spirit

i am real

frozen tundra

I wish I could just say that life sucks, but then I would have to feel something. That's the problem. I don't. I watch people laugh and wonder if I will ever feel that spilling out of my gut like it did back then. Or watch a sad movie and feel the need to even blow my nose. Tissues are only for my sinus problems. Even though today shone through my morning window with all the energy of spring, my soul feels like frozen tundra, buried beneath feet of snow. An eternal permafrost. I wish I could feel something, but then I'm also afraid of what might come if the dam broke. Where could God be in all of this?

> Robert, a twenty-year-old artist who uses cigarettes to burn himself, articulates, "I have a hard time talking about what's going on inside me. When I start talking, all of the crap I'm saying sounds so lame. I like looking at the scars on my arms because I know that they're real. It's like I'm trying to say, I've suffered, man, just look."
>
> —quoted in JERUSHA CLARK with DR. EARL HENSLIN,
> *Inside a Cutter's Mind*

Have you been with someone who seemed emotionally numb? What was that experience like?

When you feel numb, what do you do? Do you have any idea what feelings or thoughts or fears you are trying not to feel?

hope

For this people's heart has become calloused; they hardly hear with their ears, and they have closed their eyes. Otherwise they might see with their eyes, hear with their ears, understand with their hearts and turn, and I would heal them. —Acts 28:27

And so I insist—and God backs me up on this—that there be no going along with the crowd, the empty-headed, mindless crowd. They've refused for so long to deal with God that they've lost touch not only with God but with reality itself. They can't think straight anymore. Feeling no pain [Having lost all sensitivity—NIV], they let themselves go in sexual obsession, addicted to every sort of perversion. But that's no life for you. —Ephesians 4:17-20 (MSG)

I will give you a new heart and put a new spirit in you; I will remove from you your heart of stone and give you a heart of flesh. —Ezekiel 36:26

More Verses: Romans 1; Hebrews 3:13

What are some things that used to touch you but you've become calloused to them now? Can you remember why you might have numbed that part of you?

becoming

What hope do you have that God will meet you in your numbness and give you a new heart that can feel again—both pain and pleasure? What part do you play?

How might others come alongside you, to warm you up, to surround you as your numbness comes to life?

i may feel guilty

but by the power of His Spirit

i am forgiven

nibbling at the edges of my heart

One of the curses of living away from the city is the critters. Mice are regular raiders of my pantry, no matter what I do to try to get rid of them. I find nibbled edges everywhere; bags with holes in them; gnawed places. They ruin things not by taking big pieces, but by eating at the edges and contaminating the whole thing. It's like they've taken lessons from my guilt. It has nibbled at the edges of my heart for so many years it feels like it's nearing the center. And I don't know which exterminator to call. Maybe this is the price I'll have to pay for the rest of my life.

> Picture Jesus standing next to that woman caught in adultery, surrounded by men ready to stone her for her guilt. Here Jesus invites anyone who was perfect to throw the first stone. All fell quiet. One by one, every single person dropped their rocks and walked away. Forgiveness stands beside me like that—until all the stones are back where they belong.
>
> —Sara Wevodau

What does the picture of "forgiveness standing beside you" stir up in you?

hope

God is sheer mercy and grace; not easily angered, he's rich in love. He doesn't endlessly nag and scold, nor hold grudges forever. He doesn't treat us as our sins deserve, nor pay us back in full for our wrongs. As high as heaven is over the earth, so strong is his love to those who fear him. And as far as sunrise is from sunset, he has separated us from our sins. As parents feel for their children, God feels for those who fear him. He knows us inside and out. —Psalm 103:8-14 (MSG)

At this, those who heard began to go away one at a time, the older ones first, until only Jesus was left, with the woman still standing there. Jesus straightened up and asked her, "Woman, where are they? Has no one condemned you?"

"No one, sir," she said.

"Then neither do I condemn you," Jesus declared. "Go now and leave your life of sin." —John 8:9-11

More Verses: Mark 11:25; Colossians 3:13; 1 John 1:9

How can "sheer mercy and grace" (Psalm 103:8, MSG) free you up from a life of guilt and hiding?

becoming

How do people in general deal with guilty feelings? How do you deal with your own guilt and guilty feelings?

When are you tempted to "stone" yourself with words or thoughts of self-condemnation? What do you think Jesus wants to say to you about that?

i may feel meaningless

but by the power of His Spirit

i am meaningful

floating

The goldfish died two days ago and I snuck out to buy another one that looked just like it. None of the kids have noticed, and that has gotten me thinking. Would anyone notice if I were gone; if someone went out and replaced me? Sure, I am this house's transportation coordinator, counselor, lover, nurse . . . but so what? I don't feel seen, except if I hit a glitch in any of my roles. Like when I was late for carpool twice in a row, and I got cursed out on my voicemail. Or when I burned the roast last night. I am a goldfish, floating randomly in a bowl of menial meaninglessness. Is there anything more?

Humans cannot easily sustain a world that's entirely random and plotless. . . . A French philosopher said, "We are condemned to meaning." There's an almost universal impulse to endow our joys and our sorrows, and our failures and our successes, with meaning.

—Martin Marty

Why do you think so many people feel that life is meaningless? What are some things people turn to in order to give meaning to their lives?

hope

"For I know the plans I have for you," declares the LORD, "plans to prosper you and not to harm you, plans to give you hope and a future."
—Jeremiah 29:11

Jesus replied, "The hour has come for the Son of Man to be glorified. I tell you the truth, unless a kernel of wheat falls to the ground and dies, it remains only a single seed. But if it dies, it produces many seeds. . . . "Now my heart is troubled, and what shall I say? 'Father, save me from this hour'? No, it was for this very reason I came to this hour." —John 12:23-27

From one man he made every nation of men, that they should inhabit the whole earth; and he determined the times set for them and the exact places where they should live. God did this so that men would seek him and perhaps reach out for him and find him, though he is not far from each one of us. "For in him we live and move and have our being." —Acts 17:26-28

More Verses: Ecclesiastes (especially chapters 1-3);
2 Corinthians 7:10-11; Colossians 1:15-18; 2 Timothy 4:8

What perspective on meaning do you think might have helped Jesus face suffering and even His own death? (See John 12.)

becoming

When in your life have you felt meaningless? Explain why.

When you're feeling meaningless, what do you wish God would say to you or do for you?

i may feel undesirable
but by the power of His Spirit
i am desired

another lifetime

I dusted the wedding album today, and then sneezed six times from the cloud that rose around my head. Against my better judgment, I opened it. Those pictures seem a lifetime ago. I thought that marriage would meet all my needs. What was I thinking? That's sure a crock. Things were great when there wasn't any conflict. But every time things got tough, he'd threaten to leave. A couple of times he has, but he has always come back . . . at least so far. The hamster wheel of this repeating cycle keeps getting squeakier and squeakier. His criticisms are different: I'm too fat, not neat enough, talk too much, spend too much money. But the foundation is the same: I know that I don't have what it takes to keep him. Next time he leaves it will be for good.

> Define yourself as one beloved by God. This is the true self. Every other identity is an illusion.
>
> —JOHN EGAN

In whose presence or in what situations do you tend to feel undesirable?

hope

On the day you were born, no one cared about you. Your umbilical cord was not cut, and you were never washed, rubbed with salt, and wrapped in cloth. No one had the slightest interest in you; no one pitied you or cared for you. On the day you were born, you were unwanted, dumped in a field and left to die. But I came by and saw you there, helplessly kicking about in your own blood. As you lay there, I said, 'Live!' And I helped you to thrive like a plant in the field. You grew up and became a beautiful jewel. Your breasts became full, and your body hair grew, but you were still naked. And when I passed by again, I saw that you were old enough for love. So I wrapped my cloak around you to cover your nakedness and declared my marriage vows. I made a covenant with you, says the Sovereign LORD, and you became mine. —Ezekiel 16:4-8 (NLT)

He [the Messiah] had no beauty or majesty to attract us to him, nothing in his appearance that we should desire him. He was despised and rejected by men, a man of sorrows, and familiar with suffering. Like one from whom men hide their faces he was despised, and we esteemed him not. —Isaiah 53:2-3

More Verses: Song of Songs; Isaiah 41:8-10; Isaiah 54; Ephesians 1:4; 2 Peter 2:9-10

There wasn't anything about Jesus' looks that made people desire Him. Can you identify with Him in some way? Do you think He desires you?

Can you identify with the baby/woman in Ezekiel 16 in any way? If so, how?

becoming

Reflect on a time when you were not chosen. Why do you think you weren't chosen? Do you think God rejects you on the same basis? Explain.

You have been set apart as holy to the LORD your God, and he has chosen you from all the nations of the earth to be his own special treasure.
—Deuteronomy 14:2 (NLT)

We all long to be desired by other people. What difference does it make to you (if any) that God desires you for Himself?

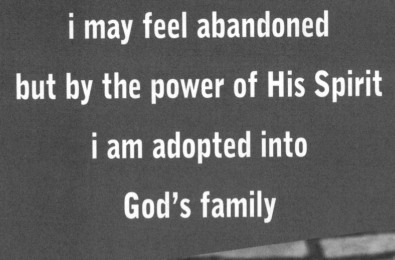

i may feel abandoned

but by the power of His Spirit

i am adopted into

God's family

the extra

It was eight years ago, on Christmas Eve, that my parents dropped the bomb: They had decided to part ways. They were getting a divorce. I was only sixteen. When Dad moved out, it left a gaping hole that I couldn't fix. I still don't know what I did so bad that he had to go.

Next month Rob and I want to celebrate our first anniversary with a romantic trip. But the closer it gets, the more paralyzed I feel. The pieces of my emotional world keep shifting and I don't know how they fit together anymore. I can rationally explain what has happened, but my heart is dying. And if I can't figure things out, I may become a casualty of divorce myself.

> I fear withdrawal—the agony of being ignored—that silent, invisible barrier that makes someone look at me without seeing me, transfer allegiance to one more favored, depart in spirit, as if to a far country. The longest distance is between two hearts.
>
> —RUTH SENTER, *Longing for Love*

What are several ways people are abandoned or rejected in our society?

hope

Yet they say, "My Lord deserted us; he has forgotten us."

"Never! Can a mother forget her little child and not have love for her own son? Yet even if that should be, I will not forget you. See, I have tattooed your name upon my palm." —Isaiah 49:14-16 (TLB)

Though my father and mother forsake me, the LORD will receive me. —Psalm 27:10

Even before he made the world, God loved us and chose us in Christ to be holy and without fault in his eyes. God decided in advance to adopt us into his own family by bringing us to himself through Jesus Christ. This is what he wanted to do, and it gave him great pleasure. —Ephesians 1:4-5 (NLT)

More Verses: Romans 8:14-16; Galatians 4:6-7; 1 John 3:1

When have you felt unwanted or abandoned?

Have you ever experienced God's embrace as His adopted child? Explain.

becoming

Being abandoned or rejected really hurts. Maybe you think you've gotten over it. Still, pause to invite Jesus to hold you in this place of hurt.

According to Ephesians 1:4-5, it gives God great pleasure to have you in His family. How does that make you feel?

i may feel futile

but by the power of His Spirit

i am useful in God's kingdom

grayscale

Today I couldn't get out of bed. I woke up at 7:43 and lay there until 11:07. It's Saturday, and I'm just marking time like an inmate scratching lines into his cell wall. Sure my life is full; I have tons of things to do. But why am I doing them? The paycheck never seems big enough, and now, losing her has turned my world into a grayscale. I am too tired, and there is a void I don't want to face. It all feels so pointless. Is this gray all there is?

> After a while you notice that your life has nothing at its core. It has no center. There is activity. There is opinion. There is busyness. But there's nothing to give real pleasure or deep meaning to the activity, nothing to ground opinions in truth and shape them into convictions, nothing to translate busyness into fruitfulness, nothing to convert selfish ambition into holy purpose. You realize you're stuck slow hearted on borderland. And you start to wonder if this is it, or were you made and called for something else?
>
> —MARK BUCHANAN, *Your God Is Too Safe*

What gets you out of bed when you're really tired? Does it have anything to do with meaning at your core?

hope

For we are God's workmanship, created in Christ Jesus to do good works, which God prepared in advance for us to do. —Ephesians 2:10

Because we know that this extraordinary day is just ahead, we pray for you all the time—pray that our God will make you fit for what he's called you to be, pray that he'll fill your good ideas and acts of faith with his own energy so that it all amounts to something. —2 Thessalonians 1:11 (MSG)

More Verses: Ecclesiastes (especially chapters 1 and 2); John 15:16

Do you have any idea of "what he's called you to be" or to do? Explain.

becoming

What parts of your life feel futile right now?

How might you put words to a prayer asking God to help you find meaning in that "futile" place?

i may feel discontent
but by the power of His Spirit
i am grateful

something more than more

The credit card bill came today with an offer to increase my credit limit. I am afraid of what might happen if I do, and of what will happen if I don't. I get so much satisfaction from my new toys at first, from seeing the eBay packages arrive in the mail knowing what a great deal I've gotten. I drag the outstanding balance around like a huge weight—yet I want even more. And the thrill of new stuff only lasts a moment. There's got to be something more than more.

> Contentment is wanting what we have, not having what we want.
> —*Kenton Beshore Jr., senior pastor, Mariner's Church, Irvine, CA*
>
> It's easy for us to fall into a mindset of viewing "our" world as "the" world, because it's all we generally see. We're constantly bombarded with images of the latest styles and models of everything, and it can easily leave us feeling like what we have isn't enough because we see people that have even more than us. But how does what we have compare to what most people in the world have? Maybe what we have is enough; maybe it's more than enough. Maybe God has blessed us with everything we have so we can bless and give to others.
>
> *http://www.nooma.com*

Most people in the world enjoy only a fraction of what we have in terms of money and things and living conditions. What might they teach us about true contentment?

hope

Yet true godliness with contentment is itself great wealth. After all, we brought nothing with us when we came into the world, and we can't take anything with us when we leave it. So if we have enough food and clothing, let us be content. But people who long to be rich fall into temptation and are trapped by many foolish and harmful desires that plunge them into ruin and destruction. —1 Timothy 6:6-9 (NLT)

Not that I was ever in need, for I have learned how to be content with whatever I have. I know how to live on almost nothing or with everything. I have learned the secret of living in every situation, whether it is with a full stomach or empty, with plenty or little. For I can do everything through Christ, who gives me strength. —Philippians 4:11-13 (NLT)

More Verses: Matthew 6; Hebrews 13:5-6

What are some messages from advertising or the culture around us that feed our discontent with what we have—or don't have?

becoming

Wanting more is a real struggle. What are you pursuing "more" of? What do you hope the "more" will provide or give you?

The idea of fasting is an age-old practice to help us remember contentment. What would happen if you fasted for a day from food or technology or work or something else?

i may feel inadequate
but by the power of His Spirit
i am adequate in Jesus

echoes

Math was never my thing. Art, on the other hand, is my passion. One night, when I should have been studying for a geometry test, I was drawing. My dad walked into my room, took one look at me, and said, "What the hell are you doing that for? You'll never be able to support a family if you don't get a grip and learn some real skills." I barely brushed against him in the hallway as I rushed past him, needing to escape outside. It was dark, and snowing, and my scream echoed off the frozen clouds, and still echoes as I lie awake in the middle of the night. Will I ever have what it takes?

> Everything inside me wanted to scream, to punch a wall, to throw something and hear it shatter, see it break. It was all too much. The shame I felt, the anger I could never express. It was like a volcano started to erupt in my mind. Raging thoughts assault me in every imaginable way: *You idiot! You'll never be good enough. Did you really think you could make him happy? You're nothing but a fat, worthless failure.*
>
> —JERUSHA CLARK with DR. EARL HENSLIN, *Inside a Cutter's Mind*

What messages about being inadequate or "not enough" have you heard from the media and advertising? From your family? From your own heart?

hope

But by the grace of God I am what I am, and his grace to me was not without effect. No, I worked harder than all of them—yet not I, but the grace of God that was with me. —1 Corinthians 15:10

Not that we are competent in ourselves to claim anything for ourselves, but our competence comes from God. —2 Corinthians 3:5

More Verses: 1 Corinthians 1:18–2:5; Philippians 3;
    1 Corinthians 1:26-29

How does God's evaluation of your adequacy differ from the way the world sizes you up?

becoming

How can you hold on to God's words of acceptance when your own or others' criticism blares in your mind?

What are two to three things you feel inadequate about right now? Listen to God's voice. What do you hear God saying to you about those things?

i may feel ashamed
but by the power of His Spirit
i am unashamed in
God's mercy

playing it safe

I have learned the safe thing is to not want anything from anyone. It's safer that way. The only one I couldn't get past this with was my big brother Tre—the cool, smart, and athletic one. It felt so good when he noticed that I did good on a test, or made the wrestling team. He rarely noticed me most of the time, but on the rare occasion he would want to hang with me, I always felt so honored.

I've never said this to anyone, but I can't pretend anymore. One night it was just the two of us. After hanging out all day together Tre offered to teach me how to masturbate with him. What was I thinking when I said yes? Since that moment I have felt dirty and desperately confused about what we did to each other. And I have hated both myself and Tre.

> Shame is the raincoat of the soul, repelling the living water that would otherwise establish us as the beloved of God. It pre- vents us from receiving grace and truth where we need them most. . . . For some, the roots of bad shame go deep. They reach back to early abuse and abandonment, to long-stand- ing tendencies like addiction and homosexuality, even back to centuries-old expressions of cultural and ethnic shame. . . . Bad shame . . . forms a "shame coat" causing us to conclude that we are unworthy of love and honor. The emotion of inferiority, bad shame expresses . . . invites the soul to turn on itself rather than to welcome mercy. Bad shame bars us from life.
>
> —ANDREW COMISKEY, *Strength in Weakness*

Which type of shame do you think most people experi- ence—shame over bad things they have done, or shame over bad things others have done to them? Explain.

hope

Fear not; you will no longer live in shame. Don't be afraid; there is no more disgrace for you. You will no longer remember the shame of your youth and the sorrows of widowhood. For your Creator will be your husband; the LORD of Heaven's Armies is his name! He is your Redeemer, the Holy One of Israel, the God of all the earth. —Isaiah 54:4-5 (NLT)

Let us fix our eyes on Jesus, the author and perfecter of our faith, who for the joy set before him endured the cross, scorning its shame, and sat down at the right hand of the throne of God. —Hebrews 12:2

More Verses: Ezra 9:6-7; Psalm 44:13-16; Isaiah 50:6-9; Hebrews 11:16

> On the cross God in Christ endured the ultimate humiliation. For our weaknesses and shame, God allowed himself to become weak and full of shame. God was strung up naked before a mocking, jeering public. He subjected himself to the worst kind of exposure in order to make a way for us, his creation, who have been subject to the exposure of sin and shame ourselves.
>
> —ANDREW COMISKEY, *Strength in Weakness*

Jesus experienced great shame though He was sinless, so He can relate to your shame. What difference does that make to you?

becoming

Deep down, do you believe that God is ashamed of you? Why or why not?

As you stop and listen to God, what words of mercy and peace does He have for you in the midst of your shame?

Through the heartfelt mercies of our God, God's Sunrise will break in upon us, shining on those in the darkness, those sitting in the shadow of death, then showing us the way, one foot at a time, down the path of peace. —Luke 1:78 (MSG)

i may feel

spiritually oppressed

but by the power of His Spirit

i am delivered from

Satan's hold

just some game

I can't get the voices out of my head . . . telling me I'll never have what it takes to be a real man. But what the hell does that mean, anyway? I've found things that quiet the voices for a while, but then they come back with a vengeance. Playing video games makes me feel like one of the guys. But they also make me feel sick—all the killing and all the blood. What a wimp I am. It scares me even more when I start enjoying it. The games with demons are even worse. I tell myself that it's just a game—nothing is real. Recently I've let myself check out some of the porn sites that make me feel excited and sick at the same time. What is happening to me? Sometimes I feel that something dark and evil has its hooks in me. And that it won't ever let go.

> I am staggered by the level of naiveté that most people live with regarding evil. They don't take it seriously. They don't live as though the Story has a Villain. Not the devil prancing about in red tights, carrying a pitchfork, but the incarnation of the very worst of every enemy you've met in every other story. Dear God—the Holocaust, child prostitution, terrorist bombings, genocidal governments. What is it going to take for us to take evil seriously? Life is very confusing if you do not take into account that there is a Villain. That you, my friend, have an Enemy.
>
> —John Eldredge, *Epic*

What do you imagine when you think of spiritual oppression?

hope

For he has rescued us from the kingdom of darkness and transferred us into the Kingdom of his dear Son, who purchased our freedom and forgave our sins. —Colossians 1:13-14 (NLT)

Yes, and the Lord will deliver me from every evil attack and will bring me safely in to his heavenly Kingdom. All glory to God forever and ever! Amen. —2 Timothy 4:18 (NLT)

You, dear children, are from God and have overcome them, because the one who is in you is greater than the one who is in the world. —1 John 4:4

More Verses: 2 Corinthians 1:10; 1 John 2:14

Where are you in your awareness of Satan in the world and in your life?

becoming

In what areas do you long for freedom? What do you long to
have Jesus deliver you from? What might His deliverance look
like for you?

Satan can have a stronger influence when we're isolated or
alone. Who can you invite into your struggles with prayer and
support?

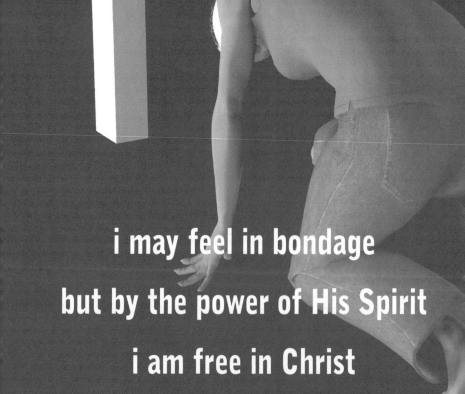

i may feel in bondage

but by the power of His Spirit

i am free in Christ

wasted

These walls are closing in on me. I am suffocating. Last night was one more on a string of nights that have blurred into a permanent twilight. I'm being wasted by the very thing that once made me feel so alive. Each time I fall back into old habits, I hate myself more. And the more I hate myself, the more like a slave I feel. I might as well be wearing leg irons for all the freedom I have found this life to bring.

> Sin is ruled by the law of diminishing returns. . . . Each time you sin, you receive a decreasing amount of pleasure and fun from the act. So, in order to receive the same amount of fun, you have to escalate the sin or else sin more frequently to achieve the same level of pleasure. . . . In the end, the law of diminishing returns turns what started out as outright fun into outright slavery.
>
> —Richard Wagner, *Christianity for Dummies*

In your opinion, what makes people feel free? How do people generally use their freedom?

hope

Jesus said to the people who believed in him, "You are truly my disciples if you remain faithful to my teachings. And you will know the truth, and the truth will set you free."

"But we are descendants of Abraham," they said. "We have never been slaves to anyone. What do you mean, 'You will be set free'?"

Jesus replied, "I tell you the truth, everyone who sins is a slave of sin. A slave is not a permanent member of the family, but a son is part of the family forever. So if the Son sets you free, you are truly free.
—John 8:31-36 (NLT)

It is absolutely clear that God has called you to a free life. Just make sure that you don't use this freedom as an excuse to do whatever you want to do and destroy your freedom. Rather, use your freedom to serve one another in love; that's how freedom grows. . . . Love others as you love yourself. That's an act of true freedom. —Galatians 5:13-14 (MSG)

More Verses: Romans 7:7–8:17

What has you in its clutches—a shameful habit, an addiction, a fear, or something else?

becoming

If God were to free you *from* whatever has you "chained up,"
what might He be freeing you *for*?

Sometimes our own choices enslave us. Is there an area in
your life where you think you've traded in your own freedom
for some form of bondage? Talk with God about how it feels to
be in bondage again.

i may feel dishonored

but by the power of His Spirit

i am honored in His eyes

never enough

Just because I'm Asian, my boss expects twice as much from me as he does from my other teammates. He always tells me that I'm so reliable. But when he called me in to work on New Year's Day, I slammed the office door so hard it broke. What's going on inside of me? I can just hear my wife's voice telling me that I've done this to myself by refusing to say no. But I keep hearing my father's voice telling me that it is my job to keep the family's honor. Why do I feel so dishonored when I've worked so hard all my life to maintain and show honor to others? How is it honorable to work twice as much—for half the pay the white guys get? When will I have done enough to satisfy them? To satisfy myself?

What does it mean to honor someone? To dishonor them?

Write about a time when you felt misunderstood or dishonored. When you go back and read what you wrote, what do you see? How does this affect you?

hope

Because he has set his love upon Me, therefore will I deliver him; I will set him on high, because he knows and understands My name [has a personal knowledge of My mercy, love, and kindness — trusts and relies on Me, knowing I will never forsake him, no, never]. He shall call upon Me, and I will answer him; I will be with him in trouble, I will deliver him and honor him. — Psalm 91:14-15 (AMP)

Who dares accuse us whom God has chosen for his own? No one — for God himself has given us right standing with himself. Who then will condemn us? No one — for Christ Jesus died for us and was raised to life for us, and he is sitting in the place of honor at God's right hand, pleading for us. — Romans 8:33-34 (NLT)

More Verses: Psalm 8; Isaiah 40; Isaiah 54

When have you been honored or felt respected? What did it feel like, and how did it change you? (If it's easier for you to remember being dishonored, then describe that experience instead.)

becoming

In your day-to-day life, what kind of honor do you find yourself seeking out? What does this show that you believe about the source of your worth?

What might be obstacles to receiving honor from God? Talk to God about them. Ask God to remove any barriers and listen to His words of honor for you.

i may feel unappreciated
but by the power of His Spirit
i am delighted in by God

lost and losing

I asked for this deployment. What in God's brown desert was I thinking? I remember Grandpa telling stories of being in the war, of guarding prisoners in Africa, and the time he got shot in the shoulder by one who died trying to escape. I had already imagined the stories that I would tell my own grandkids, and they were nothing like this: wounded in the third week by my own stupid carelessness, sent to do boring filing until my foot heals. Captain Grink has wasted no opportunity to remind me of just how useless I am. There will be no glory for this soldier. I am a loser of the first rank. No one seems to appreciate the sacrifices I've made just to be here.

> What would it be like to experience for yourself that the truest thing about his heart toward yours is not disappointment or disapproval but deep, fiery, passionate love?
>
> —JOHN and STASI ELDREDGE, *Captivating*

Think of a time when you felt unappreciated. Describe what that felt like at the time, and how it impacted you later on.

hope

He brought me out into a spacious place; he rescued me because he delighted in me. —Psalm 18:19

The LORD delights in those who fear him, who put their hope in his unfailing love. —Psalm 147:11

The LORD your God is with you,
*   he is mighty to save.*
*   He will take great delight in you,*
*   he will quiet you with his love,*
*   he will rejoice over you with singing.*
*   —Zephaniah 3:17*

More Verses: Numbers 6:24-26; Psalm 36:7-8; John 15

Have you ever imagined or experienced God delighting in you? Describe that experience—or lack of it.

How does God's delight in you change your perspective?

becoming

Who do you delight in, and why?

What words do you expect God to have for you most of the time? Are they words of delight or disappointment?

Knowing that God says He delights in you, what do you wish God would say to you? If you are having trouble with that, ask God to silence the voices of disapproval and replace them with whispers of delight.

missing in action

No one ever told me not to express my feelings as a kid. From day one I just knew not to. I'm like my dad that way. I never had an identity, not really, and because I don't, what I do is meaningless. I never realize the consequences of my actions, whether it's not paying my bills, or binge eating, or getting involved with rotten men. I'm never aware of the reality until it's literally hitting me over the head, like when the IRS closed my bank account. It's like I don't exist. I feel as if I could disappear from the earth and no one would ever notice.

> The greatest loss in life is not death. It's what dies inside while you['re] alive.
>
> —JERUSHA CLARK with DR. EARL HENSLIN, *Inside a Cutter's Mind*

What are some different ways people can be dead (while still living)?

hope

I tell you the truth, those who listen to my message and believe in God who sent me have eternal life. They will never be condemned for their sins, but they have already passed from death into life. And I assure you that the time is coming, indeed it's here now, when the dead will hear my voice—the voice of the Son of God. And those who listen will live. The Father has life in himself, and he has granted that same life-giving power to his Son. —John 5:24-26 (NLT)

I came so they can have real and eternal life, more and better life than they ever dreamed of. —John 10:10 (MSG)

"For this son of mine was dead and is alive again; He was lost and is found." So they began to celebrate. —Luke 15:24

More Verses: 2 Samuel 14:14; John 1:4; Romans 3:12-13; 2 Corinthians 4:10-12; Ephesians 2:4-6

From Luke 15:24, in what sense was the son "dead" before? How is he "alive" now?

becoming

Does anything in you feel "dead"? Do you remember when the feeling began? What would it be like to simply invite God to stir up that place in you again?

As we live in the reality of death all around us, what hope (if any) do you find in Jesus' promises for a full life now and for eternal life forever?

i may feel rejected

but by the power of His Spirit

I am accepted as i am

getting real

I was never one to need counseling, until I got diagnosed with post-traumatic stress disorder after my second tour. I was afraid that I'd gone soft and tried to push myself to be more of a man and "tough it out" like my father always used to tell me to do. It didn't work. It started with the panic attacks in the middle of the night, and then one time I woke up with my hands around my wife's throat. She was crying, and I was sick that I came so close to hurting her. I agreed to get help. But my buddies say that real men take care of their own problems. So what does that make me?

Acceptance often starts "movement" in someone's spiritual growth. In an environment of no condemnation, people are honest about issues they haven't felt safe to reveal before. When they find that it's okay to confess one problem, they fire up the back-hoe and they dig deeper into the dark parts of their souls. As acceptance increases, so does confession, and with confession come intimacy and growth.

—Dr. Henry Cloud and Dr. John Townsend, *How People Grow*

When is a time you experienced acceptance from others? What was that like for you?

hope

Can anything ever separate us from Christ's love? Does it mean he no longer loves us if we have trouble or calamity, or are persecuted, or hungry, or destitute, or in danger, or threatened with death? . . . No, despite all these things, overwhelming victory is ours through Christ, who loved us. And I am convinced that nothing can ever separate us from God's love. Neither death nor life, neither angels nor demons, neither our fears for today nor our worries about tomorrow—not even the powers of hell can separate us from God's love. No power in the sky above or in the earth below—indeed, nothing in all creation will ever be able to separate us from the love of God that is revealed in Christ Jesus our Lord. —Romans 8:35-39 (NLT)

Accept one another, then, just as Christ accepted you, in order to bring praise to God. —Romans 15:7

More Verses: Romans 14:1; Acts 10:34-35; 1 Corinthians 1:30-32; James 5:16; 1 Peter 2:4-5

Do you feel acceptable to God, whatever that means to you?

If not, what do you think would make you acceptable? What does God say makes you acceptable?

becoming

Very few of us escape the pain of rejection or disappointment in relationships. Have you ever had love withheld or withdrawn? What impact did that experience have on you?

People in Jesus' day rejected Him, and millions more still do today. As you struggle with your own experiences of rejection, what do you think Jesus is saying to you about that?

Are you rejecting someone else? How might that impact your own sense of being rejected?

i may feel condemned

but by the power of His Spirit

i am not condemned

desperate

No one knows what has haunted my waking hours every day since it happened: the dancing and the strobe lights, the cool martini glasses, the guy who kept meeting my eyes across the room. How I thought the flirting was harmless, the drinks less potent than they really were. Feeling sick, and trying to find a place to lie down. How he followed me into the room, calling two of his friends to join him. Strong, rough hands that did not hold me like I've always longed to be held. The sound of tearing fabric, the feel of tearing skin. Trying to call out; the smell of cologne on the hand cupped over my mouth. Not remembering exactly when I blacked out; the taste of dried blood when I awoke. Hearing my mother's voice say, "I told you so." I wonder if their own voices are condemning them like my voices are condemning me? I can't meet anyone's eyes anymore. If they look at me, they'll see what I fight to hide every day.

> Jesus caught this woman (see John 8) in the place where everyone else would throw her away—the place of her sin and shame. But he takes her by the hand and leads her to freedom. . . . Jesus does not turn away. He steps right into the mess we have made and offers us not another stone of condemnation but, of all things, MERCY. . . . Out of this place where we have been loved in our shame, we come to know ourselves as women [and men] worthy of love. And this love changes everything.
>
> —PAULA RINEHART, Sex and the Soul of a Woman

Have you ever received mercy or pardon when you expected or deserved punishment? Or have you ever received condemnation and blame when you expected sympathy and understanding? What was that like for you?

hope

Therefore, there is now no condemnation for those who are in Christ Jesus. —Romans 8:1

Who dares accuse us whom God has chosen for his own? No one—for God himself has given us right standing with himself. Who then will condemn us? No one—for Christ Jesus died for us and was raised to life for us, and he is sitting in the place of honor at God's right hand, pleading for us. —Romans 8:33-34 (NLT)

This is the only way we'll know we're living truly, living in God's reality. It's also the way to shut down debilitating self-criticism, even when there is something to it. For God is greater than our worried hearts and knows more about us than we do ourselves. And friends, once that's taken care of and we're no longer accusing or condemning ourselves, we're bold and free before God! We're able to stretch our hands out and receive what we asked for because we're doing what he said, doing what pleases him. —1 John 3:19-22 (MSG)

More Verses: John 8:1-11

From these verses, what has God done to end the withering pain of condemnation?

becoming

Whose voices condemn you, and what do they say?

Throughout history, people have stoned those they condemned. What stones of self-condemnation can you lay at the feet of Jesus, where they belong? Now what words of mercy and grace can you reach out to receive from Jesus?

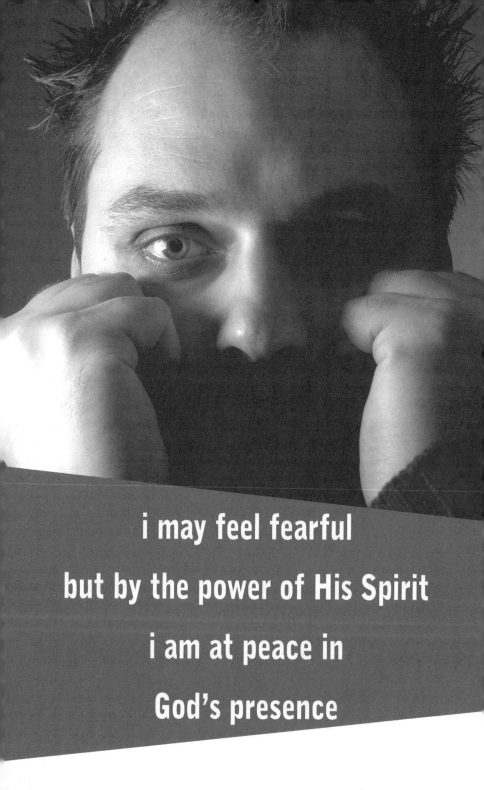

i may feel fearful

but by the power of His Spirit

i am at peace in

God's presence

forecast uncertain

My boyfriend and I talk about the future all the time. He's says he wants to have kids, too. But I'm scared. I mean, who wants to bring kids into a world as messed up as this one? Terrorism, diseases (especially STD's), wars, suicide bombers, global warming, sexual predators—it's everywhere and just getting worse. Seriously, I worry about this constantly. And then after talking like this, he won't talk about getting married. Maybe I'm most scared that he'll bail out on me and leave me to sort out my life alone. He tells me to just enjoy today. How can I when I don't know what's coming?

It is early in the morning and my joints ache. The bed is damp from fear as I look into my future. My night terror is the looming specter of crippling arthritis. I am forty years old and already my neck cracks with the dead sounds of a dry limb. . . . I am going to be crippled, confined to an earthly hell while my family and friends go skiing, play tennis, or stroll along a well-lit street in downtown Denver on the way to a delicious Italian meal. I am a crustacean, a distant memory that provokes sadness, a burden that engenders pity and labored patience. I feel loneliness, then fury. How can this happen? My fury glides into envy. Then I round the corner into stark, naked terror.

—Dr. Dan B. Allender & Dr. Tremper Longman III,
The Cry of the Soul

What do you think makes people really afraid? What puts people at peace?

hope

I will lie down and sleep in peace, for you alone, O Lord, make me dwell in safety. —Psalm 4:8

So do not fear, for I am with you; do not be dismayed, for I am your God. I will strengthen you and help you; I will uphold you with my righteous right hand. —Isaiah 41:10

Peace I leave with you; my peace I give you. I do not give to you as the world gives. Do not let your hearts be troubled and do not be afraid. —John 14:27

More Verses: John 16:33; 1 John 4:18

Why do you think God repeatedly reminds us to "fear not"?

becoming

What tends to make you most afraid? What obstacles to peace do you encounter?

How has God's presence brought you peace?

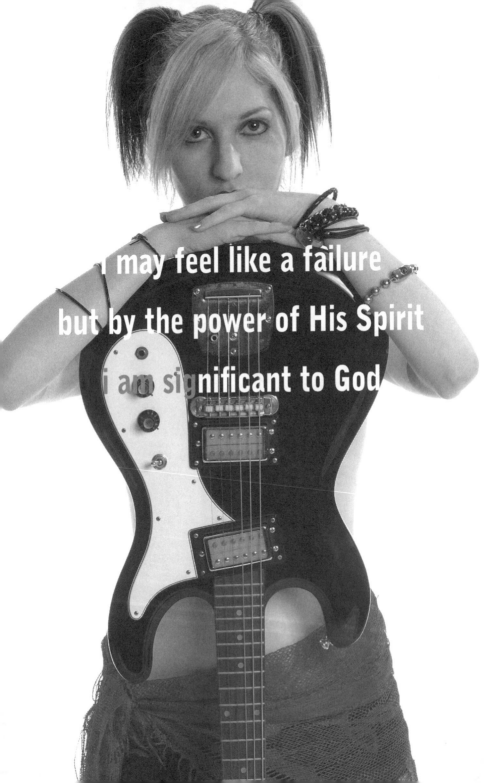

i may feel like a failure
but by the power of His Spirit
i am significant to God

what it takes

I remember standing in the math hallway, listening to the wrestling coach praise my younger brother for making the team he was taking to state. He went on and on about what an honor that was and all that needed to be done to be ready. I don't even know if he realized I was there. That was, until he glanced at me, wrinkled his forehead in concern, and said, "Too bad you don't have what it takes to hang with us, big guy." I didn't realize it then, but he was confirming what I had begun to suspect: I don't have what it takes. And what really has changed?

God dreams that you would discover your destiny and walk into the reasons he placed you on this earth. God has a ticket of destiny with your name written on it—no matter how old, how broken, how tired, or how frightened you are. No matter how many times you may have failed, God dearly longs for the day when he gets to hand you that ticket, smile, and whisper into your ear, "You have no idea how long I've waited to hand this to you. Have a blast! I've already seen what you get to do. It's better than you could have dreamed. Now hurry up and get on that train. A whole lot of folk are waiting for you to walk into your destiny and into their lives.

—BILL THRALL, BRUCE MCNICOL, and JOHN LYNCH, *TrueFaced*

When is a time you have felt like a failure? When have you felt significant? Describe both.

hope

What is the price of two sparrows—one copper coin? But not a single sparrow can fall to the ground without your Father knowing it. And the very hairs on your head are all numbered. So don't be afraid; you are more valuable to God than a whole flock of sparrows. —Matthew 10:29-31 (NLT)

Remember, dear brothers and sisters, that few of you were wise in the world's eyes or powerful or wealthy when God called you. Instead, God chose things the world considers foolish in order to shame those who think they are wise. And he chose things that are powerless to shame those who are powerful. God chose things despised by the world, things counted as nothing at all, and used them to bring to nothing what the world considers important. As a result, no one can ever boast in the presence of God. —1 Corinthians 1:26-29 (NLT)

More Verses: 1 Corinthians 12:1-31; Romans 12:6-8; Ephesians 4:11-13; Philippians 3:7-9; 1 Peter 4:10-11

Why do you think God deliberately chooses the "foolish . . . powerless . . . despised . . . nothings"?

becoming

How might God be inviting you to appreciate the unique way
He has designed you?

Sit with God in your disappointment with yourself or with
your pride of self-accomplishment. What does He say to you?
Receive whatever He says about your significance to Him and
write it here.

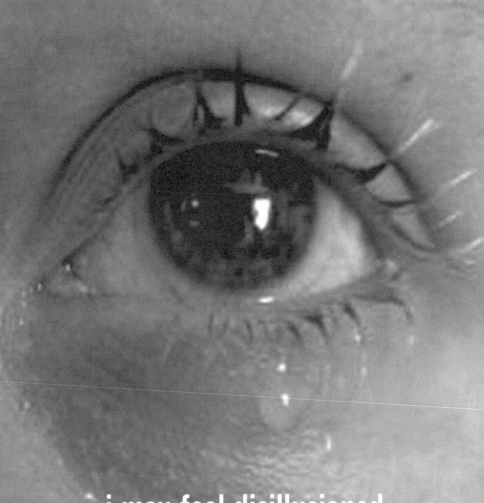

i may feel disillusioned

but by the power of His Spirit

i am hopeful

as if

So we went to check out another rental house today. I called to make sure it was still available, and when the landlord invited us to come look, my wife came too. We have until Friday to find a new place to live. The landlord looked surprised when he opened the door, and stalled us with small talk in the entryway. Finally I asked to see the house and he said that he had made a mistake, and it was already promised to someone. His smile was so sticky it could have been made of maple syrup. I've heard that before. Translation: the hypocrite just didn't want a black family disrupting their suburban paradise.

> Hopelessness steals our sense of purpose. Once we lose hope, we lose vision. Our destiny becomes clouded by the events of the past. Our eyes are darkened, and we become blind to our future. We turn a deaf ear to the encouraging words of our friends. Our senses are shadowed by our distorted reasonings and perceptions. The encouraging words we read in Scripture mean little, if anything to us.
>
> —MIKE FEHLAUER, *Finding Freedom from the Shame of the Past*

What are some things people in general feel disillusioned with or cynical about?

hope

The LORD is the everlasting God; he created all the world. He never grows tired or weary. No one understands his thoughts. He strengthens those who are weak and tired. Even those who are young grow weak; young men can fall exhausted. But those who trust in the LORD for help [who expect, look for, and hope in Him—AMP] will find their strength renewed. They will rise on wings like eagles; they will run and not get weary; they will walk and not grow weak. —Isaiah 40:28-31 (TEV)

May the God of hope fill you with all joy and peace as you trust in him, so that you may overflow with hope by the power of the Holy Spirit. —Romans 15:13

More Verses: Hebrews 6:18-19; Romans 5:5

How does this process of trusting God move us a few steps from disillusionment toward hope?

becoming

What does hope feel like to you?

Do you feel hopeful about your future? If you invited God into any part of your disillusionment, how do you think He would meet you there?

i may feel depressed

but by the power of His Spirit

i am comforted

walking through mud

I am exhausted, and yet I lie here, unable to sleep. I watch the moonlight play shadows across my walls, and think about yesterday, how it feels like I'm walking through a field of knee-high mud, no fences in sight. Nothing is easy anymore. And tomorrow promises to be more of the same. I don't know if others hear it, but when I laugh, it sounds like an echo. My life is like staring into a steamed mirror; nothing is in focus. Nothing is clear.

> I wake up in the morning to shades of grey and brown and long lists of things to do and not enough time to do them all and an endless repetition of last week's cycle. Same old news on the radio, just wrapped in a different broadcast set on a different continent. You [God] are here, easing me through it all, but You can be as gray to me as the sky. As brown as the winter grass. As uneventful as the news.
>
> —RUTH SENTER, *Longing for Love*

What things do people turn to for comfort when they are sad or depressed?

hope

Their insults have broken my heart, and I am in despair.
If only one person would show some pity;
if only one would turn and comfort me.
But instead, they give me poison for food;
they offer me sour wine for my thirst.
—Psalm 69:20-21 (NLT)

"I have seen his ways, but I will heal him; I will guide him and restore comfort to him, creating praise on the lips of the mourners in Israel. Peace, peace, to those far and near," says the LORD. "And I will heal them." —Isaiah 57:18-19

All praise to God, the Father of our Lord Jesus Christ. God is our merciful Father and the source of all comfort. He comforts us in all our troubles so that we can comfort others. When they are troubled, we will be able to give them the same comfort God has given us. For the more we suffer for Christ, the more God will shower us with his comfort through Christ.
—2 Corinthians 1:3-5 (NLT)

More Verses: Isaiah 53:3; Psalm 77; Psalm 88; 2 Corinthians 7:5-7

For a few minutes, listen to Jesus talk about His emotional struggle (see Psalm 69:20). How can He relate to you?

How does it feel knowing that Jesus can relate to your deep sadness?

becoming

Where have you turned for comfort? Has it been genuinely healing or just distracting? Explain.

How has God used others to comfort you in your depression? Why do you think He chooses to comfort us through others?

about the authors

RALPH ENNIS is the Director of Intercultural Training and Development for The Navigators. Ralph and his wife, Jennifer, have ministered with The Navigators since 1975 in a variety of areas, including at Norfolk military bases, Princeton University, Richmond Community, Glen Eyrie Leadership Development Institute, and with The CoMission in Moscow, Russia. Ralph has a Master's degree in Intercultural Relations. Some of his publications include *Searching the Ordinary for Meaning; Breakthru: Discover Your Spiritual Gifts and Primary Roles; Successfit: Decision Making Preferences; An Introduction to the Russian Soul;* and *The Issue of Shame in Reaching People for Christ.*

Ralph and Jennifer currently live in Raleigh, North Carolina. They have four married children and nine grandchildren.

JUDY GOMOLL is Director of School Agreements as a National Training Team Associate. Before joining The Navigators, Judy was an educator with a specialty in curriculum development. Judy and her husband, George, served with The Navigators as missionaries in Uganda and Kenya for fifteen years, where they helped pioneer ministries in communities, churches, and at Makerere University. Judy led in leader training and designing of contextualized discipleship materials and methods.

In her current role with the National Training Team, Judy is assisting in the research, development, and field testing of spiritual transformation training tools and resources. She also directs our partnerships agreements with seminaries and graduate schools.

Judy has an MA in Curriculum and Instruction, and an MA in Organizational Leadership. She and George live in Parker, Colorado.

DENNIS STOKES is Director of National Training and Staff Development. Dennis has been serving with The Navigators since 1980, ministering with the Collegiate Mission, as well as being a collegiate trainer and training consultant. Dennis has designed, developed, and led seven Navigator summer training programs, and was the Training Coordinator for The CoMission project. Dennis has done gospel ministry in Lebanon, Russia, Ukraine, Mexico, Canada, England, Cyprus, Egypt, Jordan, Syria, and Israel. He is ordained and speaks at training events, conferences, and in church pulpits both in the U.S. and overseas. In his role as the National Training Director for the U.S. Navigators, Dennis leads in strategic planning, leading, and implementing all national initiatives for staff training and development.

Dennis and his wife, Ellen, live in Boulder, Colorado, and have three children, Christopher, Cheryl, and Amy.

CHRISTINE WEDDLE is Associate Director of National Training and Staff Development and has been on staff with The Navigators since 1997. She first connected with The Navigators when she joined the CoMission Training Team. In this role she assisted in the planning and organization of staff training events in the U.S., Russia, and the Ukraine.

Since moving to Colorado Springs in 1998, she has directed numerous national training and staff development events. She specializes in developing adult learning environments and visual resources.

REBECCA GOLDSTONE is a National Training Team consultant for The Navigators. Before joining The Navigators, Rebecca was a consulting partner with The Navigators in training and developing The CoMission project staff and leaders from the former Soviet countries. After leaving The CoMission Rebecca pioneered and developed a crosscultural urban ministry in Santa Ana, California. She is a training consultant, life coach, and serves on the faculty of Hope International University. Her role on the National Training Team consists of creating and editing resources related to spiritual transformation and strategic tools to equip leaders ministering to the millennial generation.

Rebecca and her husband, Marc, live in Irvine, California. They have two children, Ryan and Joshua.

Connect Even More!

The CONNECT series is designed to help you discover and embrace the truth Jesus spoke of in a holistic way. By using the series in a small group, you will find encouragement, trust, and support from others as you travel together on this spiritual journey.

God: Connecting with His Outrageous Love
Ralph Ennis, Judy Gomoll, Dennis Stokes, Christine Weddle
978-1-60006-258-2
1-60006-258-X

This study presents a foundational biblical principle for primary relationships in life: receiving God's love and loving Him in response.

Identity: Becoming Who God Says I Am
Ralph Ennis, Judy Gomoll, Dennis Stokes, Christine Weddle
978-1-60006-259-9
1-60006-259-8

Discover who God says you are and learn to live out your true identity by loving God, others, and yourself.

Soul: Embracing My Sexuality and Emotions
Ralph Ennis, Judy Gomoll, Rebecca Goldstone, Dennis Stokes, Christine Weddle
978-1-60006-262-9
1-60006-262-8

Find out how growing in your love for God, for others, and for yourself will help manage your personal life in ways that honor Him.

Relationships: Bringing Jesus into My World
Ralph Ennis, Judy Gomoll, Rebecca Goldstone, Dennis Stokes, Christine Weddle
9-781-60006-261-2
1-60006-261-X

Receiving God's love and in turn loving others is God's plan for us. But loving others as ourselves is not always easy. Learn how to reach out in love to family, friends, and others who may be more difficult to love.

Life: Thriving in a Complex World
Ralph Ennis, Judy Gomoll, Rebecca Goldstone, Dennis Stokes, Christine Weddle
978-1-60006-260-5
1-60006-260-1

Explore important areas—time, money, decisions, commitment, work—that play a role in living life well with Jesus.

To order copies, call NavPress at 1-800-366-7788, or log on to www.navpress.com.

Playlist

This One's For the Girls- Martina McBride

ME! (Featuring Brandon Urie)- Taylor Swift

Fireflies- Owl City

I Gotta Feeling- Black Eyed Peas

Storm Warning- Hunter Hayes

I'll Be There For You- The Rembrandts

Deep End- Daughtry

I Won't Give Up- Jason Mraz

Your Body is a Wonderland- John Mayer

Maroon- Taylor Swift

My Universe- Coldplay x BTS

Feels Like Home- Chantal Kreviazuk

I Want Crazy- Hunter Hayes

CONTENTS

1. Cortney   1
2. Dylan   9
3. Cortney   21
4. Dylan   30
5. Cortney   40
6. Dylan   47
7. Dylan   54
8. Cortney   56
9. Dylan   66
10. Dylan   81
11. Cortney   83
12. Dylan   91
13. Cortney   98
14. Dylan   109
15. Dylan   116
16. Dylan   118
17. Cortney   127
18. Dylan   132
19. Cortney   137
20. Dylan   146
21. Cortney   151
22. Dylan   159
23. Dylan   162
24. Cortney   168
25. Dylan   177
26. Cortney   182
27. Cortney   185
28. Cortney   194
29. Dylan   198
30. Dylan   203
31. Cortney   207
32. Dylan   211
33. Cortney   218
34. Dylan   223

35. Cortney   225
36. Dylan   227
37. Cortney   232
38. Cortney   241
39. Dylan   242
40. Cortney   249
41. Dylan   255
42. Cortney   266
43. Dylan   273
44. Cortney   279
45. Cortney   284
46. Dylan   289
47. Cortney   295
48. Dylan   301

Mother Pucker Sneak Peek   305
Also by Jenni Bara   317
Dear Reader   319
Acknowledgments   321
About the Authors   325

Dedication

To my girls. I love that we celebrate each
other wins and are there for the rough times.
We may be all over the country but
I'm so blessed to have found you all.
And if we ever need to momcom...

I promise to Dylan the house up!

Cortney

1

A mid-season initiation. That was the only explanation for this.

I narrowed my eyes, taking in the four-story…let's call it a house. *Dilapidated money pit* was a mouthful.

I chuckled. Did the idiots I played with every day really think I'd be dumb enough to believe Beckett Langfield lived in this dump? No freaking way the grouchy asshole who owned the team would be caught dead in here.

The large front window announced *Happy… Day*. A word was obviously missing between *Happy* and *Day*, but maybe it was fitting for the brownstone which seemed to have a mixed holiday vibe. A Christmas wreath hung on the blue front door, while a huge Easter bunny sat off to the right of the brick steps. The railings were adorned with white ghosts and part of a skeleton. None of it would be that weird if it weren't almost July. At least the red, white, and blue stars on each one of the zillion windows actually made sense.

Chalk drawings and tic-tac-toe games covered the sidewalk and steps like a preschool stopped to have recess in front of the house.

I pulled out my phone to snap a picture, because, fuck, they went all in for this prank. Life was too short to not laugh.

My finger hadn't even left the little red button before the shower started. A zipping sound and a ping, then rubber balls smacked against my chest. Then my ear and my cheek and my forehead. Jeez, a true Nerf sharpshooter. Something I'd appreciate more if I wasn't the target.

I zeroed in on the screenless window, where a small kid with a shaved head stuck the upper half of his body out. His tutu was navy; the gun was orange and white.

"Gets off my sidewalk."

Squinting at the kid, I grunted. I was pretty damn sure that sidewalks were public property. But did I really want to argue with a child? Drunk? Maybe. But sober? Less appealing.

The kid climbed through the window, and like a monkey, he flung himself through the air and landed on his feet on the porch a foot and a half below. Holy shit. He's lucky he didn't break his neck.

"Bossman says it's up to us guys to potect this house and the one *zillion* annoying girls in it."

I smirked at the kid. Between the shaved head, the camo pants, and the navy ballet tutu, he stood out. Had to appreciate that this kid's parents let him *do him*.

Before I could tell him why I was here, he fired again, and the neon orange ball bounced off my forehead.

"Ouch, what the hell?" Rubbing the spot, I shot him a glare.

The kid, who couldn't have been more than five, might be a good shot, but shit, didn't his parents teach him rule number one in Nerf battle? *Don't aim for the face.* He could leave someone blind, and I, for one, needed to see.

"Hey, Huck, you better not be shooting the mailman again." The front door opened, but it was too dark in the foyer to see who finally came for this kid.

"No, it's an invasion of tall guys with weird ponytails." The kid stomped his Timberland boot on the landing of the brownstone and aimed again.

I threw my hands into the air in surrender. "I'm just here for my socks." Ridiculous but true. According to my teammates, the punk-ass teenager who'd stolen my lucky socks lived here.

But with every minute that passed, it became more obvious that this was a setup.

"Miller?"

Holy shit. Beckett Langfield.

My broody, dark-haired boss stepped out of the shadows and onto the top step.

How the hell had the team gotten *him* to go along with this prank? Beckett *had* brought a bunch of kids to the game earlier in the day—some kind of publicity stunt that helped smooth things over after all the crazy press lately—but to get in on a team prank was on a whole other level.

"Don't shoot." Beckett held one arm out to the kid. "If you hurt him, my team's going straight back into the toilet."

Hell yeah, they were. Beckett might not like me, but since my arrival a few weeks ago, his team was winning. He and I both knew he needed me calling the pitches. But to do that effectively, I needed my lucky socks.

"Why are you here?" Beckett still held his hand out to the young boy to his left, but his attention was trained on me. The cocked head and pursed lips implied that he wasn't expecting me, so either he was a good actor, or this wasn't a joke.

"Good to see you too, Bossman." I smirked, falling into my role as the shithead Beckett would expect.

His father and mine had been friends for a long time. The Langfields focused on baseball and hockey empires, while the Millers dominated the real estate and racing worlds. Both families were respected and liked across the board. None of that meant Beckett and I got along.

"Don't be a d—" The curse died on his tongue. Swallowing

it back, he cut a glance at the kid still training his Nerf gun on me.

I surveyed the brownstone again. Although the foyer lights were off, all the windows of the second floor and the basement were lit up like the Fourth of July night sky. The noise coming from inside the open front door spilled out into the quiet summer day.

"Is this your house?" I couldn't not ask the question. Just like I couldn't hold back the shit-eating grin that overtook my face. If Beckett Langfield lived here, then the world needed to know.

Beckett rolled his eyes. "It's complicated."

"No, it's not," the kid said. "You love Mom, and Mom lives here, so that means we get you."

Beckett smiled down and rubbed the little guy's head. "You're right, Finn."

Ah. That's right. Beckett had recently married the head of the team's PR division, Olivia Maxwell. I still couldn't believe it was true. Beckett hated everyone. He and love didn't mix in my brain. Yet he'd fallen for a single mom with a couple of kids? Mindboggling.

My team's owner sighed. "What do you want, Cortney?"

"Some punk-ass kid stole my socks." I shrugged, going for chill, like I wasn't freaking out over the possible loss of luck.

Being rational didn't matter to me, but playing ball did. I wasn't twenty-five anymore, and I wasn't ready to lose my spot on the team I had only just been traded to. My unexpected trade had rocked the baseball world. I had been with the New York Metros for almost ten years, and there hadn't been even a whisper before I was called into the office and informed of my new status as a Boston Revs.

As much as billionaire Beckett grated on my nerves, the last thing I wanted was another trade. Bonding with a team took time and work, and I was too old to start again next year. Hell, according to some, I was too old to be playing, period. During every game, I had to prove I still had what it took to crouch behind the plate. Sure, I was known for being one of the smartest catchers in the league and for getting the pitchers winning games, but my hips and knees felt older than my thirty-five years.

Beckett's ever-present scowl was still in place when I pulled myself out of my thoughts, so I cleared my throat, ready to explain and get the hell out of here.

"Heard I could find the sock thief here. Damiano said the redheaded kid you brought to the game swiped them from my locker."

"Demon Spawn," he muttered.

"Don't worry, I won't tell the moms," the kid warned. "Auntie Dylan hates when you call him that."

Beckett looked at me for a long minute before he blew a long breath out of his nose. "Come in. We'll find the ducking socks."

Ducking?

"Use the door. Medusa gets mad when you climb in through the window." Beckett headed back into the brownstone.

I ran up the steps behind him, equally curious about how this would play out and desperate to get my hands on my lucky socks. If I didn't get them back before the long road stretch the team was about to leave on, I'd be fucked.

Inside the foyer, I stopped to let my eyes adjust to the darkness. Once they did, I scanned the space, catching sight of a hole in the ceiling—two, actually—and wires that stuck out in place of a light fixture. Part of the floor was nothing but plywood. Damn. The inside of the house looked worse than the outside.

"*Don't* ask." Beckett gritted out, his jaw clenched. "If you want the socks, keep your mouth shut and look pretty, Man Bun."

Without thinking, I ran my hand over my hair and the bump of my bun. These days, I was known for my hair as much as my ability to call pitches. It was my trademark and the reason my agent received constant endorsement calls.

Beckett shot me the side-eye, confirming that I wouldn't open my big mouth. I was tempted, but I wanted to keep my job and leave with the damn socks, and I still wasn't 100 percent sure this wasn't a prank.

He tilted his head and strode off, so I followed him into a large family room. This space was somewhat finished, with lights, a full ceiling, and finished floors. It could have used an update, but it wasn't a construction zone. The only aspect that jumped out as odd here was the large brick fireplace. The handles of the screen were linked together with what looked like wire. Or maybe it wasn't a fireplace screen. Could that be a wired-shut gate? Almost like they were trying to lock something inside.

A dark-haired kid on the sofa peeked back quickly, then did a double take. "Oh, wow." It was almost a whisper. His brown eyes were wide as he looked from me to Beckett. "He's going to teach me to play baseball?"

Beckett crossed his arms. "I thought you wanted to play hockey, Iceman."

"I'm not picky." The kid spun until his knees were planted on the cushion and his elbows were propped on the back of the sectional.

"I'm working on the hockey thing." Beside me, Beckett uncrossed his arms and pounded a fist against the wall twice. A sprinkle of plaster dust from a crack above him fluttered down and coated his brown hair. With his jaw clenched, he banged again and yelled into the air conditioning vent. "Team meeting. Let's go, crew."

The house erupted before Beckett had even finished his directive. What sounded like a stampede of horses echoed above us, and a moment later, a horde of kids made their way into the room. Twin girls with matching blond French braids appeared, along with another girl who looked to be about the same age as the dark-haired kid on the sofa. The kid in the navy tutu reappeared as well. Just as I began to think this house was like a clown car and people would keep popping up until the place was bursting at the seams, a tiny girl toddled in. Her hands were covered in a slimy yellowish substance.

She wobbled over to Beckett on her chubby legs and yanked on his pants. Without hesitating, Beckett lifted the kid and propped her on his hip.

Grinning, she opened her hand and offered Beckett what looked like mashed banana.

"I'm good, Little One." Beckett shook his head, wearing a surprisingly chill expression even as the little girl shoved the mashed food into her mouth, then wiped her dimpled hand on Beckett's Revs jersey. "Livy, we need a wet paper towel."

"Got it," came a familiar voice. A moment later, the team's head of PR rounded the corner and stepped into the room. At the stadium, Liv was always the picture of perfection, so this woman, the one sporting a messy bun and a handprint on her leggings, was almost unrecognizable.

I opened my mouth to greet her, but truthfully, I didn't know what to say.

What the hell was going on right now? I wasn't sure whether the house itself was the most whacked-out part of this moment or if it was the sight of Beckett and Liv—two of the most put-together people I knew—inside it. Either way, I was getting major *what the fuck?* vibes.

Liv went straight for Beckett's jersey with the paper towel, but he held up a hand.

"I'm not worried about me," he said, holding the little girl's hand out. "Get this wiped off. We don't need Junior gnawing through wire for a taste of mashed banana *again*."

"It only happened once," Liv said, chuckling. "But Raccoon-gate and watching you jump around in your boxers to escape her was definitely the highlight of my year."

"The stuff I put up with for you." Beckett shook his head.

I was floored, because the expression on his face didn't scream anger or annoyance. No, when he looked at Liv, he wore a goofy expression that was reserved only for men who had been flat-out knocked over by love.

I shook my head. *Poor schmuck.*

"Where are the rest of them?"

"The rest?" I sputtered.

Beckett's only response was a frown.

"Bro, this is enough."

I knew Liv had kids, but not an army of them.

Beckett's frown deepened, and his face turned a darker shade, but before he could respond, the reason I was distracted enough after the game to let my socks go missing stepped into the room.

Willowy, porcelain skin, auburn hair, and eyes that sparkled like gold. Just like when I spotted her across the team room after the game, her presence alone knocked the air out of my lungs. And I almost fell to my knees when her full pink lips lifted into a smirk that said *I've got your number.*

And damn if I didn't want her to have it.

Dylan

2

Normally, *team meetings* were just a way for Beckett to rant a bunch of new over-the-top rules to our family. As much as I loved to mess with Liv's husband, I tried not to judge him too harshly.

The four of us, along with our seven kids, were a lot to handle under one roof. Especially for the grumpy billionaire who'd lived alone until a few months ago. In Beckett's world, less was more, even when it came to people. But it looked like he was adding to the party tonight.

Maybe the universe was giving me a present in the form of a hot blond. Damn, he was the definition of man candy. I'd seen the tall catcher at the game earlier today, and his smirk said he'd noticed me too, and wouldn't mind seeing a lot more of me.

My friends and I had made a pact last year. We'd committed to living in this brownstone and raising our kids together. It had gone great for a few months before Liv had fake married her boss.

In the beginning, she didn't see how it could be real, but she and Beckett had always been written in the stars. Liv had never been as happy as she was when she was with her new hubby, so we all agreed he could stay, and our unique family adopted a billionaire.

What Liv didn't know was that Beckett had other plans. Some half-baked idea to pawn Delia, Shay, and me off on other guys so he could move Liv out of this house. He thought he was being sly about it, but I knew what he was doing.

Still, if he was putting Cortney Miller up for grabs, then I was in.

For a night anyway.

Maybe even *to*night. With it being Father's Day, Liam's dad had picked him up after the game. My kid-free nights were few and far between, but my fifteen-year-old was out of the house, and I intended to take advantage of it.

"Do I needs to be here for this?" Liv's son, Finn, said, flopping onto the couch. "I didn't do it. Can I go have a tea party?" He aimed his Nerf gun at the fireplace and sent one bullet after another pinging against the mesh screen.

"Team meetings are for everyone." Beckett tipped his chin, trying to keep Adeline's pigtail out of his mouth as she rested her head on his shoulder.

"Liam isn't here," Finn announced.

Next to him, Kai fought hard not to smile.

Beckett chuckled. "Liam isn't home."

"Dyl, you forgot your smoothie."

Shay trotted into the room and held the green goop out with one tiny arm. She still hadn't learned that if she made something that looked like cat vomit, then she shouldn't use a clear cup.

"No, I didn't forget." I shook my head. "It's more of an Anja crisis."

Blinking, she tilted her head, causing her straight black locks to fall over one eye. The uneven cut was gorgeous. She still had that cool Cali vibe, even though she'd been back in

Boston for six months. My thick, messy mop could never look that chill.

She cleared her throat. "What does having a crisis with your third eye have to do with your smoothie?" Shay was still holding out the glass like she really expected me to take it.

Ignoring the proffered drink, I tilted my chin. "I can no longer in good conscience support putting things in my body that taste like someone else puked them out of theirs. I checked with my pendant." I lifted the thin silver chain holding my rose quartz charm from under my shirt. "Smoothies are now a big no."

Letting the pendant fall against my Revs T-shirt, I held my palms out and shrugged. It wasn't that Shay was a terrible cook, she just decided somewhere along the way that she could forgo taste for health. And I decided—starting ten minutes ago—that happiness was most important. After letting my pendant hover over the cup sitting on the counter, it became clear that the yucky green goop was blocking my energy flow.

"So, unfortunately, I'm going to have to object to that smoothie and any you make in the future. According to the universe, it's bad for my third eye."

"Me too!" Beckett blurted out from across the room.

That earned him a frown from Liv.

"Really, Livy. Exactly what she said. I had one of those universe come-to-Jesus, kumbaya moments too. And we all know how important third eyes are."

I raised a brow, but before I could call him a dumbass, Cortney jumped at least a foot in the air and yelled. "Is that a raccoon? *In the house?*"

Junior hissed as another Nerf bullet hit the mesh screen separating the animal from the rest of us.

"I will come out and steal every bullet if you keep shooting at me and my babies," Junior called. The threat was followed by a strange not-so-raccoon-like hiss.

Cortney jerked back, wide-eyed, and scanned the room,

looking for the source of the voice that very obviously didn't belong to the raccoon.

The kids laughed at my Junior impression. They'd heard it a hundred times but still found it hysterical. I was eight when I'd learned to talk without moving my lips. By ten, I could throw my voice, and in my teens, I'd mastered the art of mimicking.

Shay shook her head, but her lips lifted in a smirk. She loved me because I made her laugh. After losing her husband to cancer, she needed more laughter in her life. Since he died, she lived her life as a ball of *nevers*. Never going out, never eating anything unhealthy, never letting Kai out of her sight, and never relaxing. Her stress was constant.

"You know she doesn't like that." I walked over and took the gun from Finn as he lined up another shot. "She worries about her babies."

"I can't believe we're about to have four ducking raccoons," Beckett grumbled.

"Four?" Cortney scoffed and shuffled closer to the foyer like he was ready to bolt at any second.

"With the way she's nesting, it's going to be any day. I read that sometimes when a raccoon has a litter that big, they need help." I smirked at Beckett's wide-eyed panic.

"Help?" He darted a glance at Junior.

Liv took a deep breath in and let it out slowly, then did it again, probably counting in her head. I'd tell her I was kidding later. If I didn't, she'd stress.

"Why is it…" Cortney shook his head, his man bun bobbing a little. "Why is it *in* the house?" His wide blue eyes flicked from Junior, who was much happier now that she wasn't being shot at, to me, and then to Beckett.

"Are you suggesting my babies and I be homeless?" Junior asked.

Cortney scanned the room again, still trying to pinpoint the source of the voice.

"I know when I'm not welcome in a team meeting. *Humph.*"

"Although it seems unbelievable, she's harmless." Liv let out an odd, high-pitched chuckle as she cautiously watched Junior disappear deep into the fireplace.

"But—"

Beckett growled. This was just one more thing he would happily pay to fix if only we let him. "I told you not to ask questions, Man Bun."

Man Bun. No, that didn't fit him. I'd go with something like—

Before I could decide, Delia walked in, her heels tapping on the hardwood floor. Shay handed *her* the green goo.

"Oh, you made these *again*. Swamp sludge." The last bit Delia muttered under her breath as she plastered on a fake smile and brushed her long blond ponytail over her shoulder.

How did she wear that slicked-back ponytail twenty-four seven and never get a headache? Some days, just looking at it gave *me* a headache. I swore she had it so well trained that she didn't even need gel. Like her hair knew better than to fall out of line. Just like how her feet knew better than to hurt in the heels she shoved them into every day.

My feet would have rebelled ten minutes into wearing four-inch stilettos. Barefoot worked best for me. It helped to channel the clear energy of the earth. When forced into something, my feet preferred sandals. My style fell somewhere between artsy and boho chic. As long as it made me smile when I put it on, then I'd wear it.

Delia, on the other hand, was more business-meeting formal. If I didn't know better, I'd wonder if she slept in a suit.

She grimaced at the cup in her hand, likely brainstorming ways to get out of drinking it, then surveyed the group. When she caught sight of Cortney, her grimace turned to a scowl, and she slammed her free hand onto her hip. Uh-oh. New angry man-hater vibes had taken over. Delia didn't believe any woman needed a man, even for orgasms. No matter how many times I assured her that a man who knew what he was doing was better than a toy, it wouldn't change her mind. Delia's pretty red aura turned a muddy burgundy any time she was near a guy. Didn't matter how friendly or good-looking the guy was. His existence alone was enough to ignite her rage.

She pursed her red lips. "What is he doing here?"

"I think Beckett's auctioning him off to the highest bidder." I shrugged. "That's why he called the team meeting."

Liv glared at her husband.

"I am not," Beckett assured her. Then he turned to me and shot me the exasperated scowl I constantly got from him. "Don't start trouble, Dippy Do."

Me? If anyone was starting trouble, it was Beckett. He'd tried to be subtle when he questioned Shay and Delia and me about what we liked when it came to men, but the look in his eye when he was fishing told me exactly what he really wanted. He had a plan, but I'd let him run with it. Mostly because it seemed like fun.

"I love trouble." I was down for anything that made life worth living.

Cortney smirked at my statement.

"But does he *belong* to you, Beckett?" Delia asked, glaring at the baseball player.

"No." Cortney scoffed.

At the same time, Beckett said, "Yes."

"The fuck I do," Cortney sputtered.

Delia's daughter Phoebe cleared her throat and stuck one finger in the air. "Excuse me, Mr...."

"Miller," Liv finished. She surveyed the room with a frown like she was planning which impending disaster to deal with first: the raccoon, the baseball player, her husband's schemes, my unpredictability, or the twins. She finally just shut her eyes and started her deep breaths again.

"Yes. Mr. Miller." The eight-year-old's blond braids bounced as she nodded. Although her body was young, her soul was old —way older than me. "The fine for bad words in this house is currently one thousand dollars. We take cash." She crossed her arms and lifted her chin, not taking her focus off him.

I cleared my throat to get her attention and lifted my brow when she looked at me.

Phoebe sighed and rolled her eyes. "We also take Venmo and Zelle."

Cortney reared back, clearly confused.

"But," her twin sister added, "we charge a fee for electronic payments. Five percent."

He rolled his lips together and crossed his arms over his broad chest. "Five percent," he parroted. The glint in his eye made me think he was trying not to laugh. In all fairness, we were ridiculous as a group, so most people *would* find us funny. But the twins were very serious about their electronic curse jar.

"Do you need the QR code to send the payment?" Collette asked. "Our society is almost completely cashless these days, so I understand that you might not carry ten hundreds with you."

Most eight-year-olds didn't know the meaning of the word *cashless*, but Delia's twins were far too smart. I'd spent the better part of the last five months attempting to channel all that energy into good instead of evil. I never wanted to snuff out anyone's fire, but I'd worked to help center them and open them up to becoming positive members of the universal *we*. It was something all kids needed, but especially Collette and Phoebe, who seemed determined to take after the girls in *The Shining*.

Delia sighed next to me.

"Don't worry," I angled in to whisper. "The fees go into the 529 account. Think of how it will benefit their education." I tapped my green nail against my lips. "Unless their college experience is anything like ours, because…" I chuckled. "Then it will just be beer and frat boys."

She and I had met Liv and Shay when we were assigned the same suite for our freshman year at Boston College. Fifteen years later, we were still thick as thieves. There was no way time would dull the memories of all the shit we got into back then. And while the fun got us into trouble from time to time—especially my surprise pregnancy and the eighteen months of awfulness that followed Liam's birth—our instant connection and bond had kept us close all these years.

"Curse jar money won't help with trash cans of jungle juice and horny teenage boys." I shrugged with a giggle.

Delia groaned.

Cortney chuckled, pulling my attention to him, and when our eyes met, a smile ghosted across his lips. Had he heard me? Maybe. But most people didn't get me, so it was rare that they laughed. More often than not, I got confused blinks in response to my random thoughts.

Something about the way he watched me, though, sent a kaleidoscope of butterflies taking flight in my stomach. It wasn't simply the piercing blue eyes or the Herculean frame. The man was gorgeous. There was no question. It wasn't the way his gaze trailed down my body like he was planning every detail of what he'd do when we were alone either. Although that was hot. The thing that got to me was the understanding that shone in his gaze.

Beckett cleared his throat, and Cortney winked before looking away.

My heart stuttered. That blue-eyed wink had affected me just as much at the stadium that afternoon. I'd been intrigued by the Viking. He'd started to make his way over after the game, but before he could get across the room, Beckett had ordered us out.

I wasn't sure whether it was because the twins' forecast of the drop in the third baseman's batting average had freaked the guy out, or because Finn's snake had escaped and scared the crap out of one of the pitchers. Maybe it was because Adeline had thrown up in the middle of the room. Whatever the reason, Beckett was set off, and he'd shooed us all out quickly.

He was overly dramatic like that.

"Okay." Cortney uncrossed his massive arms. Seriously, it was like a mountain range of muscle ran along his body. The flat stomach could be the planes of the earth. I couldn't see his ass from here, but I bet it looked just as good in dark-washed jeans as it did in baseball pants.

Delia elbowed me in the side, startling me back to reality.

"You might be drooling," she teased.

"No might about it," I whispered back. "He's hot. You know baseball is my favorite trope. All those guys know exactly how to hit a home run."

That got me an eye roll that looked a lot like her daughters'. Delia really needed to get over the idea that men were the enemy.

Cortney glanced around before chuckling. "You all had me going. This has got to be a top-ten prank."

"Pranks are defined as practical jokes." Phoebe stomped her little foot. "Something like putting a lobster claw in a person's bed or pretending to be the voice of a ghost. This is a bad word fee."

I really tried to hold it back, but a giggle slipped out of me at the seriousness of Phoebe's tone. Cortney Miller was known for his intelligence, his ability to read batters, and his ability to call the pitch. He wasn't dumb, but listening to an eight-year-old mansplain to him might have been the highlight of my year.

Collette frowned at me. "Auntie Dyl, it's not funny. She's right. It's a fee. If you want to use bad words, then the house charges a fee. Same as the fee to drive fast."

"The fee to what?" Shay's hair fell into her eye again, and she tucked it behind her ear.

"Auntie Shay." Phoebe sighed. "You know how Mom says

she just pays a fee to go faster than the speed limit? Well, Mr. Miller will pay a fee if he wants to use bad words."

I loved the creative way Delia explained breaking rules to her two little geniuses, but Shay frowned like she didn't approve. Shay was probably going to stress every time Delia was behind the wheel after that comment. Or worse, she'd insist on driving. Delia's head would explode if that happened. Even I would have trouble keeping my chill while Shay drove down the highway like we were in a school zone with children present.

"Enough." Beckett tossed his free hand into the air. "Man Bun's bank account doesn't support a thousand-dollar fee."

"*What?*" Cortney shook his head and frowned. "Don't be a prick. You pay me more than that for each pitch I call."

Now things were getting interesting. A pissing contest loomed on the horizon between the two men as they glared at each other. It was the definition of high entertainment. The aura around each man became a clash of color.

Beckett's reds signaled anger, ego, or drive. They were always bright and intense.

It was interesting the way they meshed with the cool yellows and blues that surrounded our new guest. If their auras could blend to a purply green that made them both empathetic and wise, we'd all be better off.

As much as I loved men, I'd deemed very few wise.

Before the madness could begin, Cortney's cool colors took over. He shook his head and turned away. That simple action calmed the room *and* Beckett almost instantly.

"I apologize for the foul mouth," Cortney said to the twins. "A QR code would be great. AirDrop it to me."

The way he spoke to them, like they were adults, made both twins smile. Looked like he hadn't found himself on their shit list. He had no idea how lucky he was.

While Cortney waited for the QR code, he turned back to Beckett. "I'm here for the lucky socks the redhead stole."

This interaction became less amusing in that instant. Beckett hadn't concocted some scheme to get him here, and he wasn't here to hunt me down. No, his presence in our house was because my son had stolen his stuff. Liam was one of those kids who had a good heart and very bad ideas. Why he'd swiped the catcher's dirty socks was a mystery. Maybe I'd spent too much time telling him to listen when the universe spoke. Was that why he thought every harebrained idea that floated through his mind was meant to happen?

I spun and stalked out of the room.

Our crazy, unique family worked because we all had roles to fulfill. Pretty quickly after moving in, I had taken on the stay-at-home mom role, so laundry was one of my things. But once Beckett came around, things changed. After I turned one—*just one*—of his shirts pink, he'd had a coronary and taken over. Now, instead of two piles of clothes—dirty and clean—he'd instituted a militaristic system the rest of us tended to ignore. Poor Beckett would probably be mostly gray before the end of the year.

The laundry room was ridiculously organized. Signs around the space designated where each grouping of laundry should be deposited. He'd even included photos for the little ones who couldn't read yet: whites, colors, darks, and special care. Then bins in each section were designated by family name, along with a photo of said family.

As much as I'd love to tease him about the system and his type A personality, we always had clean clothes, and he hadn't had any mishaps or ruined any items. I'd never once heard him say, "It doesn't matter whose shirt it is. It's the only clean one." He'd even found a special plant-based, dye-free laundry detergent that Shay approved which actually worked. The man understood how to handle laundry. Apart from one thing—underwear.

I smirked at the sign that read *unmentionables*. The realization that living with four grown women, not to mention a handful of girls, meant a ton of bras and panties, had hit Beckett like a wrecking ball. Liv was deliriously happy with Beckett, and I was thrilled for her, but boy was he weird about underwear.

Next to the panty bin was a lost and found. Basically, anything Beckett couldn't home. And inside was a pair of clean navy socks folded together neatly. It was odd that my son hadn't hidden the contraband, but who was I to look a gift horse in the mouth? I set Finn's Nerf gun on the counter and grabbed the socks, then headed down to my room. I wasn't interested in getting sucked back into the chaos of the team meeting that would probably last another hour, so I'd sneak out the window. I could leave the socks on Cortney's car, then have a guilt-free night out.

Cortney
3

I shut the door, still entirely unsure of whether this was a prank. I half expected Damiano or one of the other Revs' starting pitchers to jump out and yell *gotcha*. Because what I'd just witnessed in that house was too ridiculous for even reality tv. My wallet was a thousand dollars lighter, but I *had* discovered a few things I could use to forever torture Beckett. Even so, this trip had accomplished almost nothing. Initiation or not, my socks were still missing. Beckett swore they'd be with us on the plane tomorrow, but unease still churned my stomach. I didn't do well with changes in my routine. Especially not now, when I was still settling in from the unexpected overhaul of my life.

Although he told me he was certain he'd find them, he didn't look so confident when he walked into the family room empty-handed.

According to him, the teenager who'd stolen them was out with his dad, so they couldn't ask him, but every adult in the room assured me it would be fine. I might have hung around, but my socks aside, there was only one reason I cared to be in the brownstone, and she had disappeared twenty minutes earlier without a word.

I seemed to be the only one who noticed her absence, though in the middle of a circus like that, it was probably easy for someone to go missing for days. Especially when that damn raccoon made another appearance and drew the attention of everyone in the room again. The thing didn't talk this time, at least. But why hadn't someone called animal control to remove her from the fireplace? And was she really having babies? I couldn't be sure if that was a joke.

Racking my brain for a topic to focus on that didn't include obsessing over my fucking socks, I headed down the porch steps. Yes, a pair of socks was a pair of socks. I knew that. But much like my left leg guard *had* to go on before my right—and they had to be clipped from ankle to thigh, not the other way around—I wore the same socks all season. My sister had drawn a shamrock on the right heel every year since I was a freshman in high school.

Absent-mindedly, I turned left and headed down the sidewalk. When I reached my Dodge Charger, I palmed the roof, resting my hand on the warm purple steel, and stared at my feet. My Alexander McQueen white leather sneakers always had the emerald green heel and my number in the same shade. The Cortney Miller NY Metros shoes. After my trade, my agent had them switch to a sapphire color to represent the Revs and keep the sponsorship deal. Shoes in size eighteen were hard to find, and these sneakers were comfortable, so I tried not to stress about the slight changes, but now my socks were missing too. The shoe change wasn't to blame for the missing socks. My heart pounded, and I took a long breath.

I'd be fine. "What's the worst that could happen if I don't have my lucky socks tomorrow?"

"You lose," a voice behind me answered. "But the universe has other plans."

I spun to discover a ball of navy fabric soaring toward me. Instinctively, I caught it. Only, the damn socks were no longer my focus. Because I was staring at *her*. She had changed from the cut-offs and Revs T-shirt into something gold. The shimmering fabric tied around the back of her neck and clung to her every curve. I had no idea what the one-piece shorts thing was, but fuck, she looked hot. Her auburn curls were piled on top of her head with just a few red tendrils framing her almost makeup free face. Just like the moment I'd seen her at the stadium, and again when she stepped into the living room inside that circus tent masquerading as a house, she was my sole focus.

"You okay?" she asked, lifting her sunglasses to the top of her head.

Probably because I was gawking like I'd never seen a woman before. Why did she have this effect on me? Joking and flirting typically came easily. But her presence instantly caused my brain to misfire. *Gorgeous woman, gorgeous woman, gorgeous woman* ran on repeat, chasing off every other thought.

She tilted her head to the side, and a silky curl brushed against her bare shoulder. I lifted my hand from the hood of the car, intending to touch her, to wrap her hair around my fist, to feel the soft skin of her shoulder against my palm or press my lips against the hollow of her throat—

"I know how important luck is to athletes." A small crease formed between her brows. "I hope we didn't jinx you or throw you off your game."

I blinked, but I couldn't control the way my eyes trailed down her body. "You have legs?"

What the fuck, man?

I was the smart-ass, the guy with the snappy responses. And even if I didn't fuck around during the season, *flirt* was my default setting when I was in the presence of a gorgeous woman. Yet I'd asked this one if she was in possession of a basic part of her anatomy as my *opening line*?

She tucked her chin and surveyed her long, pale legs. I

couldn't help but do the same. From mid-calf to ankle, she was wrapped in some kind of gold rope that hooked to her sandals.

"Yup." She lifted her head up and nodded. "They're still there. It's nice when they stay attached like that."

The melody of her laugh was contagious, and I couldn't help but chuckle as she mocked me.

"I'm Dylan." She stepped into my space, instantly engulfing me in her soft coconut scent.

She held out her hand, which I quickly wrapped in my own. The stacked rings on her middle finger clinked against one another as I squeezed gently. She was exactly as soft as I'd known she would be.

My stomach tightened almost instantly, and images of her hands moving over my body flooded my consciousness. Shit. I gritted my teeth, fighting the surge of desire rushing through me before I acted like a dumbass in front of her again. My reaction to her was visceral. No sex during the season be damned. In that moment, I was certain my rule didn't matter. Tonight needed to end with her red hair spread across my sheets.

"I should be easy to remember as the one with the legs that stay attached."

Maybe if I stopped acting like a dumbass, she'd stop teasing me. I cleared my throat. "Cortney."

She nodded, and the curls loosely hooked to the top of her head bounced. "I'm pretty sure most of the world knows that, but I've decided Samson would fit better."

I had no idea what she meant or how to respond to that. So I remained in character—whoever the hell this awkward, mute asshole was—and silently fought a frown as she pulled her hand away from me.

"Good luck on your road trip."

"Yeah, thanks." Look at that. Two words strung together. I was making progress.

With a smile, she lowered her sunglasses, then she turned and took off down the sidewalk.

My entire being rebelled against the idea of her walking away from me. "Are you going out?" I called after her. Again with the stupid questions. I'd smack myself in the face if it wouldn't make me look like more of dumbass in front of this goddess in gold.

She peeked over her shoulder at me. The glasses had slipped down the bridge of her nose, and the gold flecks in her iris sparkled in the setting sun. "Yeah."

"Can I buy you a drink?" I stuttered. But hey, my sentences were getting longer. So I went with it, and before I could think my words through, I added, "You know, to make up for the whole sock thing."

She chuckled and spun around to face me. "*My* son stole *your* socks, and you want to make up for that?"

Huh.

Her son was the thief? I supposed it made sense. They were both redheads. Did I want to get involved with a single mom? I barely had time for myself during the season, let alone a woman who would want a good deal of my attention. And throwing a kid into the mix? There should have been a million red flags flying at me after witnessing the clusterfuck that was this woman's home, but the sight of her alone was enough to make my heart clench. She was special. I just couldn't put my finger on what continued to draw me to her like I was a moth and she was a flame.

She lifted a hand to her throat, almost like she was about to grab something, but she stopped herself and dropped her hand again. "I feel like I should be the one buying the drinks."

"Sounds good. We can figure out who buys later."

A small crease appeared on her forehead, confusion marring her otherwise flawless skin. I was not the type of guy to argue with a woman over who was paying. We both knew I could afford all the top-shelf drinks she wanted. Money, I had. What I wanted, though, was some of her time. If the only way to get it was to let her pay, then my ego could handle that.

I clicked the remote start button on my key fob, then opened the passenger door and held out one arm.

"I see my purple magic chariot awaits." She practically skipped toward me, sending that same soft scent into the air. My stomach clenched as her shoulder brushed my chest when she climbed in. Before I could shut the door, she tilted her chin up and hit me with another smile that knocked me in the teeth. I should have been concerned about the grip this woman I barely knew had on me, but for now, I wasn't interested in dissecting the weird connection between us.

By the time I was around the car and sliding into my seat, Dylan's sunglasses were in my cup holder and she was playing with the touchscreen on the dash.

"What are you doing?" I pressed the brake and tapped the ignition button, taking the car from the remote start setting to on.

Without giving me a sideways glance, she took over my sound system like she had every right. "Every epic night needs an anthem."

"ME!" blasted through the speakers as I put the car in gear. I chuckled. Teammates and friends liked to tease me for being a Swifty. Too often, her songs echoed in my ear while I worked out, and even more of them were loaded onto my cleaning playlist. Who wouldn't want to do dishes to "Gorgeous"?

"Glad you approve. Would've wrecked our vibe if you hated on T Swift," Dylan informed me, even though I hadn't said anything. It was eerie the way she seemed to read my mind.

"Seems like the perfect anthem." I turned onto the main road and hit the gas, letting the engine roar. Much to my father's disappointment, I was not actively involved in the racing world with my family, but I loved cars, and suping this one up had been fun.

"Where we headed?"

"My place."

She tapped her green nails on the armrest for a beat. "Bold move."

Tossing my head back, I laughed. "Just a pit stop. Then we can go wherever you want."

I expected a game of twenty questions to ensue—most women I'd met were full of questions—but Dylan just shrugged a delicate shoulder.

"Cool."

Ten minutes later, I was tossing my keys to the valet and pressing my palm against the bare skin of Dylan's back. I swore she fought a shiver as I guided her into the building. Maybe it was wishful thinking, that she might have half the response to me that I had to her, but I wanted to make her shiver, squirm, scream my name. Any and all of the options would make my night. But I was patient, and I could wear her down slowly if that's what it took.

My penthouse was on the top floor of a high-rise along Boston Harbor, so my guests' reactions were always the same. The view of the harbor was breathtaking.

When the elevator door dinged and opened into my apartment, I waited for the gushing amazement from the woman beside me. Waited for her to scurry to the floor-to-ceiling windows, squealing all the way.

Instead of taking in the view, Dylan did the damnedest thing. She took three steps and *shut* her eyes. Taking a deep breath, she spun in a circle.

When she stopped, her eyes were still closed, but she was wearing a smile so bright that just looking at her made my chest ache. "It's perfect."

What the fuck was perfect? She was *missing* the view. And at this time of night, it was at its most spectacular. When the sun hit the horizon behind us, the colors reflected off the bay, creating an almost watercolor image in a 180-degree view outside the floor-to-ceiling windows.

The gold fleck of her irises sparkled when she finally opened her eyes and focused on me. But she ignored the million-dollar view. "The energy in here is like the best kind of hug."

How the *hell* did I respond to that? Was the energy attached to the place? Or had I brought it with me when I moved in? Fuck if I knew.

"I liked the feel of it the moment I stepped inside for the first time." I held my breath, because so far, everything out of my mouth so far had been a train wreck and I wasn't sure if this was any better.

"Makes sense. Totally flows with your blues."

I dipped my chin and surveyed the white untucked button-down I wore religiously on game days, confused. But she didn't elaborate about what blue she was referring to. Her goddess-like sandals barely tapped against the wooden floors as she headed deeper into my apartment, moving on like she hadn't just confused the hell out of me.

"Oh, a pool table." She clapped, almost bouncing on her feet. "I love to play."

Finally, an easy response. "Me too." Yup. Nailed it. God, I was destined to always be a moron around her.

She ran her fingers along the dark wood of the pool table set up in the middle of the dining room. Stools lined the bar that looked into the kitchen, so there was little need for another seating area.

Still stunned by what I could only assume was the spell she'd put me under, I tracked the sway of her hips as she moved around the pool table. She turned the corner, and the sight of the silky skin of her bare back flanked by the gorgeous reflection of the sunset on the water was etched into my memory in an instant. The sparkle of the gold shorts clinging to her heart-shaped ass would haunt me for a lifetime.

She spun to face me, resting her palms on the crimson felt. Now it was the gold of her eyes that twinkled in the sunset. "Wanna play?"

I cleared my throat. "I thought I'd just do my hair really quick and we could head out."

Tilting her head to one side and pursing her lips, she assessed me. "This is the second time in the last hour I've totally read you wrong." She smirked. "Usually, I'm better with people. But I nailed the nickname."

"Uh" was my eloquent response.

She blasted me with a smile as she giggled. "Go channel your power, Samson. I can entertain myself for a bit."

Her words were lost on me. Dissecting and analyzing conversation with her might become my new favorite type of puzzle. So far, I'd discovered that I had no idea what the fuck she was talking about most of the time. Regardless, every interaction, every word, every smile she flashed my way lit me up from the inside out. Almost like she spoke directly to my soul or some other nonsense. I'd known her for all of twenty minutes, but her presence alone relaxed me and made those twenty minutes feel like years. I was known for overanalyzing every aspect of my life, but if there was a woman in the world who I was willing to say fuck it and dive into the deep end with, it was this one.

Dylan

4

With his attention fixed intensely on me, he raked his long fingers across the blond hair he had pulled into a bun. Was he reconsidering the idea of fixing his hair? Or was he judging whether it would be wise to leave me unattended in his house?

He had nothing to worry about. I didn't need to peek through cabinets or rifle through drawers to get a read on him. Everything I needed to know, I learned two steps into this massive penthouse.

The vibe of his space was exactly like him. A calm honesty blanketed the air, mixing lightly with the creative energy that zinged through me each time I got close to him. It was the kind of place where people naturally wanted to spend time.

"Nine ball?" His eyes danced as they slowly moved down my romper.

I'd be damned if every time he gave me a once-over like that —and he'd done it at least a handful of times since I found him on the sidewalk outside my house—it didn't feel like a caress across my skin. My stomach tumbled.

With his teeth pressed firmly into his plump bottom lip, he

brought his attention back to my face. Staying in tonight might be the best kind of dangerous. "Or are you more of an eight-ball woman?"

"Nine ball."

The corner of his mouth lifted in a smirk. "But."

His blue eyes narrowed.

"For every ball I sink, you have to answer a question."

He cleared his throat and studied me for a long moment. "Deal." He nodded. "As long as I get one for every ball *I* sink."

"I'm all about equality." I snagged the triangle from where it hung along the side of the table, ready to rack the balls, but when I turned back, my breath caught and my heart seized.

Cortney pulled his button-down over his head, leaving him in a fitted T-shirt. Damn, it was cliché, but he could totally pass for Thor—a huge blond God of the elements. Just like his ethereal counterpart, he had a massive chest and shoulders, and they molded to the fabric of his shirt like a second skin. His biceps strained against the sleeves like they wanted to burst through the material.

"Damn, dude. Trying to kill me? Warn a girl before you go stripping off clothes like that."

"All things equal." He chuckled. "You've been killing me since the second you smiled at me across the team room."

That moment our eyes met, I swore the universe was pointing a huge flashing arrow above Cortney's head that read *this guy.* Yeah, I'd listen. The universe rarely steered me wrong. That was why I didn't hesitate to don a sexy outfit and put myself in his path. I had zero complaints about how the night had gone so far or about the way we were dancing around each other.

The balls snapped against the wooden triangle as I locked them into place, curving my fingers to shape the balls into the classic nine ball diamond. "I'm breaking."

He reclined against the black barstool, resting his ass against the cushioned seat. "It's always ladies first." His words vibrated through me with a husky promise that hinted at something other than the game of pool we were starting. But I loved games, and flirting was the best kind.

Pool cue in hand, I moved to the end of the table and tilted at the hips to line up my shot. I couldn't help the smile that pulled at my mouth as he groaned from behind me. The smooth wood of the cue slipped between my fingers and connected with the cue ball, sending it careening across the felt and scattering the balls to all corners of the table. The telltale *plunk* of the resin dropping into the leather pocket had me smiling.

"Lucky shot," he rasped from behind me.

"Better to be lucky than good." I joked, spinning to face him.

His relaxed posture suddenly went rigid. He pulled his shoulders back almost imperceptibly, but the tightness of each of his muscles was hard to miss in that painted-on T-shirt. It was the first time I'd seen him look uncomfortable. That was nuts in itself, because he'd been in my house, and that place made *everyone* uncomfortable.

"Do you believe in luck?" he asked me, though his attention was fixed on the view of the harbor behind me. The energy in the room had gone from light to so weighted that it felt like a heavy cloud of anxiety had settled around us.

"I'd like to think I'm open-minded about just about anything. Luck, energy, karma, religion. We all have beliefs."

He finally focused on me, searching my face. For what, I wasn't sure.

"No one granted me the ability to judge who's right and who's wrong."

His brow was furrowed, and he was wearing a frown for the first time since I'd met him. The expression was full of questions, doubts, and wonder, but he didn't respond to my statement.

Disliking the prickle of unease that coursed down my spine, I tried to lighten the heavy vibe. "What I do know without a doubt, though, Samson, is that I sank a ball, so you're answering the first question, not asking it."

He chuckled, and his shoulders lowered. Yeah, I was getting a read on him. He needed a bit of ridiculous to get him out of his head. And I was happy to provide that.

"How tired are your legs after a game?"

He blinked twice, his mouth going slack. "Tired?" he parroted.

"I've heard the rumors about catchers and hip issues, so if I needed you to squat"—I waggled my brows—"what are the chances you'd do it without issue? Or are you more of a *flat on your back, let your partner do the work* on game night kind of guy?"

He threw his head back and laughed. "You don't have a shy bone in your body, do you?"

I shrugged. People were often shocked and amused when they realized how nonexistent my filter was. But my "way with words" could grate on people after a while. Even so, I had little interest in apologizing for my personality these days. It was why I no longer sought a long-term relationship.

And with Cortney, I wasn't getting a vibe that my desire to keep this casual and short would be an issue.

"The key to leg fatigue is motivation." He cocked a brow and took me in unabashedly. That attention had my core clenching with need. With every minute that passed, my body was more eager to feel more than just his baby blues caressing my skin. "Something tells me motivation won't be an issue tonight."

"Then I'm glad we're staying in." I needed tonight.

A year ago, I was living in New Jersey near my father and brother. I taught at and co-owned a preschool. Although I loved my job at Little Fingers, balancing the behind-the-scenes aspect of childcare, teaching a class of three-year-olds, and parenting on my own had been rough. When Liam was expelled for the second time, I added homeschooling my teenager to my list of jobs.

During our annual girls' weekend, my best friends and I each opened up about how much we were struggling with the single mom thing: Shay had lost her husband to cancer. Liv was going through a divorce. Delia had recently been fired from her fancy law firm. We all needed help, so we'd made a pact. We'd move to Boston and raise our kids together.

Moving to Boston and agreeing to be the stay-at-home mom to my besties' kids was the best decision I'd ever made. Living in a home so full of support and love soothed my soul immediately, and together, we'd created the kind of energy kids thrived in. But since I'd taken over the role, I had only managed one night away from the chaos of all the people under five feet tall.

Tonight, I wasn't Mom or Auntie Dyl. Tonight, I was just Dylan. Cortney's proximity alone made me feel alive, and the attention he'd given me already had me vibrating with an energy that had been missing from my life lately.

"Want a beer?" His deep voice echoed off the high ceiling as he headed into the kitchen.

I lined up my next shot and tapped the cue ball, sending it smacking into the solid yellow one, which fell into the far-left corner pocket. "Whatcha got?"

"I feel like I got off easy with that question." He returned, holding up two brown bottles. "Which would you prefer?"

"Ooh. Cherried Out is perfection in a bottle. I love the All Out brand." Although Knocked Out, the heavy IPA he'd also brought out, was good, cherry-flavored anything was my go-to. "But that didn't count as my question for you."

He cocked one brow as he popped both bottles open with the bar key. "You picked the rules. Sink a ball, ask a question. That's what we just did."

With a shake of my head, I scoffed.

He rounded the counter and stopped just inches from me.

Close enough that I could feel the heat of his body through my thin romper. His hand brushed mine as he handed me the Cherried Out, sending a ripple of goose bumps coursing up my arm.

Leaning in closer, he tucked a loose curl behind my ear. His callused palm barely brushed against my shoulder. His full lips were so close to mine in that moment, the thought of his mouth against me had my core clenching. But then he turned slightly and inhaled deeply through his nose. Like he needed a piece of me inside him, even if it was just the scent of my hair.

"You should be more clear about your rules." His warm breath danced off my ear. And just when I was convinced he'd press his lips to my neck, he stepped back, taking the soft cedar scent of his cologne with him.

Damn, I wanted him. I wanted his hard body pressed to mine. His hot skin moving along mine. Strong hands guiding, dominating me.

The bright blue of his irises danced as he watched me watching him. The unspoken words, *yeah, me too,* floated between us, stronger than his cedar scent. The awkward guy who'd approached me on the street had faded away, and in his place was a confident man radiating nothing but pure sexual energy. A man who knew how to play the flirting game. I had mastered the skill years ago, and if he wanted to play, then it was game on.

I lifted my beer and took a sip, letting the crisp cherry flavor invade my senses, and dragged my tongue across my lower lip, grabbing the single drop of beer that escaped.

Cortney homed in on my mouth for an instant before he cleared his throat and focused on the felt table in front of us. "Got a third shot in you?"

"I can go all night." I gave him a little shimmy.

Rubbing a hand down his gorgeous face, he groaned. But he quickly pulled his shoulders back and schooled his expression. He tilted forward along the table, eyeing the balls. His Knocked

Out sat on the edge of the wood, and his fingers skimmed along the glass bottle.

The sight sent a shiver down my spine. If only those fingers were skimming over my breast, down my stomach...

"You've got no shot on the two."

His words jerked me back to reality. The line on the two was blocked, but if I banked off the far edge, I could hit it without an issue. I wouldn't pocket it, but I'd hit it. Being up by two gave me an edge. Even if Cortney was known as one of the smartest players in baseball, it was unlikely that he could run the table in one turn. So I took the good enough and then let the smarty pants take over the table.

"The thing I like about baseball," he said, rounding the table and setting himself up, "is that you don't win on a single pitch. You set yourself up to win all game long." He tipped forward, bending farther than ninety degrees to line up his shot. With a quick flick, the cue nailed the blue ball and sent it rocketing into the side pocket. "In a long game, what really matters is the follow-up." He turned and rested his hand on the felt. Then he sank the red ball into the far pocket, spinning the white cue ball back to him. Another adjustment, and the purple four dropped into the leather pocket. "That's three." With that, he trained those intense blue orbs on me. "You and your son's father. What's the deal there?"

The deal was a bullet hole I'd covered with a Band-Aid. Not that I'd give this guy the details. I'd learned long ago not to give that much of myself to anyone. "Haven't been together for fifteen years. His dad is a three-times-a-year kind of parent."

"Fucker," Cortney spat out. "That's not a parent. Sounds more like a sperm donor."

His sentiment was pretty damn accurate, but years ago, I'd realized that spreading negativity was like slowly poisoning myself day by day. So I embraced life for what it was.

I shrugged. "Brett and I are fine. His relationship with his son is exactly what he wants, so no complaints from any of us."

Cortney ran his hand over his chiseled jaw. "I'd end him if I were you."

I laughed. "You sound like Delia."

"The blond?" he asked.

Taking a pull from my beer, I nodded. "The house we all live in actually belongs to Delia. She inherited it from her great-aunt."

"Is there a reason you picked that—" He cut himself off and cleared his throat. "It seems like a work in progress."

To put it mildly. "It's supposed to be, but we've had trouble finding contractors who are willing to stick around and get the work done."

With a frown, he turned so he was facing me head-on. "What kind of people have you been hiring? They seriously quit and left you guys in that mess?"

His righteous indignation on our behalf was cute, but the man had no idea what Delia was like. The place was Delia's dream house, and she had very specific plans for it. That, unfortunately, made her seem demanding and difficult to work with.

She had high standards, yes, but her requests were only sometimes unreasonable. We just hadn't found the right contractor yet. "Mostly, they don't like ghosts." I set my beer on the bar and wiped the condensation from my hand. "But someday, the universe will send us the right man for the job."

I had no doubt about that, but Lord help us all if Delia and the universe didn't agree on who the right man might be.

"No way your house has ghosts." Wearing a smirk, he leaned on his pool cue and took another sip of his beer.

The supernatural might not be for everyone, but there was nothing I appreciated more than an open mind. "You sound like Beckett," I huffed, swatting at a rogue tendril of hair brushing against my cheek. "Anything *is* possible."

In an instant, his teasing expression morphed into an annoyed glower. "You *all* live with Beckett?" Although our conversations today had started out awkward, he'd been nothing but laid-back since the game began. Now, though, he sounded like he was chewing on nails as he spoke. Either he didn't like the idea of us living with Beckett, or he didn't like the man himself.

"Try again," I scoffed. "Beckett lives with us."

His eyes narrowed. "What does that mean?"

"Liv, Delia, Shay, and I moved in together five months ago. We created a mom community support system. We promised to stay together and raise our kids. Beckett..." To say we'd welcomed him with open arms wouldn't be strictly true, but there was one thing that was impossible to deny. "Beckett decided he couldn't live without Liv, even if it meant dealing with the rest of us. But in the end, the four of us are besties. We're each other's ride or die."

"Tell me about them," he prompted, bending over the table. He sank the orange ball next. Four in a row, and the damn man had set up shot five. He had a direct line on the six ball now.

When I didn't start talking, he turned to me with raised brows.

"You're going to run the table in one turn, aren't you?" I laughed, crossing my arms and sinking onto the stool.

He grinned, and wow, it took my breath away.

"Your friends?" he prompted, pointing at the pocket the orange ball had just fallen into.

Right. I owed him this answer.

"I guess I'd sum them up like this: If I needed to knife a guy, I'd call Delia. She wouldn't hesitate to do it for me. Shay would do everything in her power to convince us it was a bad idea and remind us that someone might get hurt. And Liv would be the one bailing Delia and me out when we did it anyway."

Cortney laughed. The sound echoed through the open space

and hit me directly in the solar plexus. Damn, it was a beautiful sound.

"Delia's the fire of the group. Shay's the voice of concern. Liv's the practical one who cleans up the mess."

He sank the six ball, then focused his blue eyes on me.

"And what are you?"

I paused for a second before the universe gave me the answer. "Happiness. The person who shows them life doesn't always have to be hard. I remind them that it can be fun too."

"So you're their own personal sun?"

"Oh, gosh no. That would be far too much responsibility to take on." I chuckled. "More like the fireflies. Like the surprise that comes out just when life seems too dark to give you a reason to smile."

Cortney

5

I sucked in a breath so hard I almost choked. No statement could describe the woman better than the one she'd casually tossed out. There was something about her that lightened a space, and I really liked having her in mine.

"Most people probably wouldn't want to be called a bug." She lifted a shoulder in a simple shrug and grinned. "But they're kind of magical, so I'm good with it." With that, she brushed past me and sauntered toward the living room. Maybe she was finally going to check out the view, and this was an exceptional time for it. The harbor at night was almost as good as the sunset.

But I was stuck on her statement. Magical was the perfect way to describe her. Like my own happy fairy gracing me with her presence for one night.

"You puzzle?"

Her voiced jarred me back to the moment and made my stomach drop. Shit. That was a secret hobby of mine. It definitely wasn't the kind of thing I'd advertise to impress this woman. But no part of my plan when I left for the game this morning included entertaining company, so the puzzle still sat on my coffee table.

"Is this an old-school Ford engine?"

Fewer than half of the three thousand pieces of the gray-scale motor were put together, but the woman was spot-on. Yep, there was definitely some magic inside her.

Before I could formulate a coherent response—looked like I was back to being a bumbling idiot—she plucked a couple of pieces from the box.

"I-I should put that away," I sputtered out, darting across the room. With dread growing in my gut, I gripped the edge of the green mat the in-progress puzzle lay on and started to roll it up so I could save what I'd completed thus far.

I was mid-roll when she splayed a hand over my heart, stopping my movement. The feel of her warm palm snagged my attention instantly, and my body tightened. Awareness of her proximity scorched through me, and my mind flooded with the image of her slipping her delicate fingers under my shirt. What would her silky skin feel like against my chest or my back? My cock?

All the blood in my body rushed south as my dick swelled against the press of my jeans. With a deep inhale, I willed my body to fight the impulse to maul her. I lifted my hand to cover hers, and her sweet coconut scent flooded my brain.

"They're fun." She tipped her head back and waited for me to respond. Her face held no mocking or judgment. She tapped my pec and then slipped her hand from underneath mine. The loss of her warmth was instant and acute. "I've tried to get Shay into puzzles. She struggles with overthinking too." This close, the gold flecks in her amber irises sparked like fireflies in the night sky. Yes, definitely fireflies. Damn, this woman was magical and insightful and calming *and* alluring all at once. She was so much more insightful than she appeared at first glance.

Long ago, I'd learned how to hide my inability to shut off my thoughts. Anxiety had been my constant companion for as long as I could remember, but it didn't fit with the image of the Thor-like athlete that sponsors liked. I used games, puzzles, and crowds of people to slow my thoughts. Activity helped keep my worries from creeping in. But alone, without something to focus on, my thoughts could spiral.

It felt weirdly good to be seen for who I really was, but I didn't necessarily want to talk about it. I tensed, ready to shut down the twenty questions I had no doubt she was devising.

She popped in two puzzle pieces, then skipped back to the pool table. "It's still your shot, Mr. I Don't Miss." Slapping her hands onto the dark wood of the billiard table, she spread her arms wide. "Although I don't see how you'll make this one. Even if you bank it off the far rail, the cut on that pocket?" She shook her head. "Rough."

She was right. There was no way I was making the shot, so I did the next best thing and left her with a piss line on the eight ball. She didn't seem the least bit discouraged, though. No, she took her time studying the table, then she wailed on the white cue, sending the balls flying. And amazingly, the black resin dropped with a *thunk* into the far pocket.

"That's why no one should hate on luck. That really was an impossible shot." She curtsied dramatically.

I couldn't hold back a genuine laugh. Not only was she gorgeous, but she was so damn cute.

"Do you like Boston? Or are you hoping to get back to New York real quick?"

I took a long sip of my beer while I collected my thoughts. Shit, the answer to that question was a complicated one. My father's corporate office, which my older brother, Jamie, helped run, was in the city. Not to mention the Miller Foundation. My sister, Taylor, led that endeavor. I loved my family, but putting some distance between us had its benefits. Family expectations had always been high, and choosing baseball over the family business had been a sore subject since the day I was drafted. Here, though, the conflict wasn't so in my face. But not finishing my career with the team I assumed I would always play for was a hard pill to swallow. Facing the realization that I was aging and had become replaceable was like a punch to the gut. Especially since the Metros had always treated me like an essential part of their organization.

"Can't say I loved being part of the most shocking trade of the season, but Boston has its perks."

I was currently looking at one.

She nodded. "Liam was pissed when he heard. He's been a Metros fan his whole life. Pretty much since my dad and brother taught him that was the only acceptable way to be."

Liam. Her son, I guessed. With another pull from my beer, I let the idea of her with a kid float around my mind again. I didn't have a problem with kids, but I didn't have much experience with them outside charity events for the team. My siblings didn't have kids yet, and besides a small handful, most of my friends and teammates didn't either. Strangely, I wasn't put off by the idea that she had a son. Even so, I wasn't sure exactly what to say about him.

"What about you? You a fan?" I asked.

"Only of your ass in baseball pants."

With the bottle poised at my lips, I laughed. Here I was, stressing over every word I said to her, while she was brave enough to say anything that popped into her head.

"My butt is quite the topic lately."

"It's those black almost see-through…" Her head tipped. "I don't know what to call them. Pants seems like a stretch."

Pressing my lips together to hide a smile, I set my empty bottle on the bar. "It's the Sideline athletic girdle I wear under my uniform."

She clapped. "Oh good. Now every time I see you squat behind the plate, I'm going to think about that Rolling Stone cover." She fanned herself dramatically and took another swig of her beer. "I bet a solid 70 percent of your fans think that same thing."

I rounded the bar back and opened the fridge. "Yeah." I grabbed another beer. "My brother thinks it's hilarious. Last time I saw him, he gave me a magnet with a bee on it. It says *don't make me turn my butt on.*"

"No way." She laughed so hard her eyes filled with tears, and she brought the back of her hand up and swiped under one eye.

Damn. For the first time, the story didn't irritate me. All because it made her laugh.

I grabbed the stupid bug off my fridge and headed back around the bar as she lined up her shot and sank the striped ball into the corner pocket.

"Nice shot, but I still win, five to four." I set the magnet on the table edge.

"Winning is all about perspective." She leaned her cue on the cutout of one of the barstools.

Silently, I took her in. Winning had always seemed pretty cut and dried to me, but I was beginning to wonder if that was really the case.

She picked up the bee magnet and studied it. "It's a sign." She smiled and set it back on the lacquered edge of the billiard table.

I shrugged and ducked my head, uncomfortable at how easily she got me to open up to her. "Nah, I think of it as one more way my brother has found to harass me over the years."

"No," she urged quietly, shaking her head. "It's the universe's sign." Her delicate fingers wrapped around my wrist, stopping me from lifting my beer.

Little sparks of electricity rocketed up my arm at her touch, but she didn't react as she took my beer from me with her free hand. My heart thudded in my chest, and I couldn't look away as she wrapped her lips around my bottle. Leaning to one side, she set it on the counter behind me. Her chest brushed against mine as she did.

I swallowed past the lump that had formed in my throat at her proximity and the serious expression she wore when she squared her shoulders with mine.

"It's not a bee." She tilted her chin and watched me, her face only inches from mine. "The creature that brightens the sky when the world feels dull. The magic. It's a firefly."

She lifted onto her toes and pressed her plush lips against mine.

The soft touch rocked me instantly. I needed more. Instinctively, I cupped her face with both hands and held her in place as I ran my tongue along the seam of her lips.

She sighed into my mouth and opened for me. Her tongue tasted like beer and cherries, the perfect combination of sweet and spicy.

I spun and pressed her against the pool table so I'd have leverage to devour her mouth, then trailed one hand over the soft skin of her jaw and along the contours of her neck. She whimpered as my fingertips danced along the swell of her tits. I was tempted to pause there and take my time, but I was on a mission. With both hands now, I cupped her perfect ass and set her on the wooden edge of the table. Bending my knees, I lined myself up with her core so my cock could rock into the apex of her thighs.

The goddess in my arms did exactly what I knew she would. Without hesitation, she thrust right back.

I wanted this, wanted her, but in a moment of clarity, I pulled back, resting my forehead against hers, intent on full transparency.

Her harsh breath bounced off my lips as she caught her breath, and I wanted nothing more than to dive straight back in.

"First thing tomorrow, I'm headed out on a ten-day road trip." God, I wanted this woman more than anything, but she needed to know where I stood. "During the season, I have zero time for a relationship."

"I watch seven kids every day and manage a house of twelve people." She ran her fingers through the short hairs that had fallen out of my bun. "I don't have time for this to be more than tonight, Samson."

That was all I needed to hear.

Dylan

6

A deep groan vibrated in his throat as he claimed my mouth. And just like the first time, the moment his lips touched mine, the world fell away. All that remained was the feel of his hot mouth. The pressure of his hand around the back of my neck. The bite of his fingers digging into my waist. His thighs between my legs as they dangled off the pool table. As if Cortney and I were the only two souls in existence. A thrill shot down my spine, leaving a throbbing need in its wake.

The desire radiating through me left my heart pounding and my breasts heavy. My nipples tingled, and a longing settled deep in my core, along with a burning need for *more*.

More of his hands on my skin, more of his lips on my body. More of *him*.

Deepening the kiss, he plundered my mouth with his tongue. An ache to feel his lips run down my neck, along my breasts, across my stomach, on my pussy, grew with every beat of my heart.

I threaded my fingers through his hair and pulled out the tie, letting it fall down around his shoulders. The cedar scent hit me hard as I gripped the soft strands to anchor myself to him.

Nipping and teasing, he made his way down my throat in the exact way I'd been so desperate for. I dropped my head back and let my eyes flit shut, savoring his hot breath against my skin with each of his heavy exhales.

I released his hair and skimmed my hands over his broad shoulders. Every part of him was solid muscle. The biceps that held me close, the wall of his chest that pressed against my breasts, his tight abs, even his ass.

Especially his ass. And for one night, this masterpiece of a man was all mine to enjoy.

He nipped at a sensitive spot behind my ear, forcing a whimper from me.

"I need this off." He panted, pulling at the tie around my neck that held my romper in place. With a firm tug, he loosened the straps, and the gold material fell to my waist. He stepped back and raked his gaze over me. His irises were blazing with the heat of twin blue flames.

If he wanted a show, I'd give him one. I tipped back and planted my palms on the felt behind me. His pupils blew out, and he pressed his teeth into his lower lip. At his sides, he clenched his hands into fists, only to release them and do it again. The attention he gave my bare breasts during his perusal made me shiver in anticipation.

"Fucking perfect," he mumbled, stepping between my legs again. Once more, he trailed his fingers down my neck and along my collarbone. A groan rumbled from him, this time deep in his chest. "You're softer than I thought possible. Your skin is like silk." The pad of his thumb ran slowly over the crest of my breast, and of its own accord, my body arched into his touch. "So responsive." His words were barely a whisper. His attention was focused solely on the hard peak of my nipple. He pinched it between his fingers, and desire shot straight between my thighs.

"Cortney, please." I moaned and rocked against his thigh.

He chuckled darkly, his eyes hooded. "I know exactly what

you need, and I'll give it to you as many times as you can take it."

A shiver rocked down my spine at the vision that came to me with those words.

Slowly, he skated those callused hands over my ribs and down my stomach. Goose bumps peppered my skin, and a flame ignited in my core, roaring to an inferno almost instantly. He kept his eyes locked on mine, even when he slid both hands under my ass and gripped it, lifting me against him. Through his pants, his cock pressed against my pussy, hard and ready. The perfect fit.

"It's like your hands were made to hold my ass. They're the perfect size." I chuckled.

"From your lips to God's ears, Dylan." To emphasize his response, he squeezed, his fingers biting into my cheeks for an instant before he adjusted and yanked the romper off my body. In one quick move, I was naked before him and my clothes were a golden puddle at his feet. Then my bare ass hit the felt again.

"Holy shit," he muttered, stepping back. His eyes locked on the apex of my thighs.

Feeling bold, I separated my legs just a bit. The groan that escaped him at the move only bolstered my courage. I rested back on my palms again and arched my back, letting his examination burn against every part of me.

"The shorts are thin, and I always have a stupid panty line." Tilting my head, I spread my legs a little wider.

"You like teasing me." Finally, he blinked and dragged his attention away from my pussy. With one arm, he reached behind his head, and in one yank, his T-shirt was over his head and on the floor with the romper. Damn. He was all defined chest, ripped arms, and washboard abs.

"It wasn't a tease." My eyes met his blazing blue ones. "It was an offer."

"Good." He shot me a wicked smile and pressed one massive

hand to my chest. "Lay back. Get comfortable." He smirked. "Might be awhile. I'm gonna worship every inch of this gorgeous body."

I lay back against the soft felt. Cortney kicked off jeans. When he sauntered back up to the table and stood between my thighs, I couldn't pull my eyes off him. I could lie like this for days and not get tired of the view. Even the smaller details. The light dusting of blond hair on his arms and chest and the V that dipped below the band of his boxer briefs. When I took in the pattern on the fabric still covering his thick erection, I couldn't help but chuckle.

"Yeah." He dipped his chin and shook his head. "The boxers make it pretty clear that this wasn't my plan for the night."

"It's what's under the Ninja Turtles that matters." I giggled at the Ninja Turtles holding pizzas dotted all over the navy-blue cotton.

"Don't worry," he said, caging me in with those thick arms. "*That* will not disappoint." He ran his nose along my cheek and over my jaw and to my neck. "You smell like heaven. And you feel just as good." Inhaling a deep breath in, he tensed. Then his body relaxed and he sank just a little closer as the air left his lungs. "I don't know how I got so lucky, but I promise you will leave here feeling as happy as I do right now." His lips skimmed down over my collarbone. "Such pretty tits. I can't wait to taste them."

I shivered as he kissed down my chest until he pulled my nipple into his mouth.

"Cort." I arched up in response.

He sucked and nibbled, and I writhed against him when he pulled it deep into his mouth. Then he released me with a pop. I almost sobbed in desperation for more. Before I could beg, though, he moved to the other nipple. The sensations he was eliciting were so powerful, I might have come just like this. Without letting up, he ghosted a hand down my ribs and over my hip. Then he pushed my legs farther apart, and finally, blessedly, he ran a finger through my folds.

I hissed out a pleasured breath and shuddered.

"You are so fucking wet," he said, his timbre deep and smooth, and he kissed his way down my stomach. The vibration of his voice sent tingles rushing through me. "I need to taste you."

His breath against the soft skin of my stomach made my core clench as he worked his way past my belly button. His long hair tickled my hips and thighs, teasing me as he lingered just above the place I needed him most. He pressed his lips into my pelvis and then skimmed across to the opposite hip. Desire pounded in my veins, rushing through me.

"I need—" I huffed, unable to form coherent thoughts.

"Tell me what you need." He halted his movement, his breath hot against my outer lips, tormenting me. "Tell me and it's yours."

"Your mouth." I wheezed, shaking my head from side to side. "Your tongue flicking my clit, your lips sucking me. Your—"

He flattened his tongue against me, and a moan worked its way out of my chest and echoed around us.

Despite his command that I tell him what I wanted, he didn't need the instruction. The man was an expert with his tongue. He held me down so that I couldn't move. All I could do was take what he was giving me. With each swipe of his tongue, I rushed closer to the edge, and when he twirled it over my clit and slid one finger inside me, then two, I thought I might die.

I sank my hands into his hair and held him against me. I never wanted him to stop. The throbbing built so deep inside me I was panting and shaking. My legs quivered. His tongue flicked two more times, and I broke. Pleasure rocketed through me so fast it took my breath away. He stayed with me the entire time, lapping up every last drop of pleasure.

After what felt like a gloriously torturous eternity, he stepped away. When he turned back to me, he kicked off his boxer briefs. *Damn.* His cock jutted out, thick and proud. The man was huge everywhere, and my body pulsed, desperate for the feel of him between my thighs.

In his hand, he held a condom wrapper. One he must have retrieved when he stepped away. I snagged it out of his hold and tore it open. Standing tall, chest heaving and eyes burning, he watched as I ran my fingers along his shaft and brushed my thumb across the tip, spreading the pre-cum over his head.

"Fuck." He shuddered. "Do that again."

Obediently, I ran my thumb over him again, but I kept my attention focused on his face. I wanted to see his reaction to my touch. His eyes rolled back in his head, and a moan slipped past his lips, then he went rigid. Without a word, he yanked the condom out of my hand and sheathed himself.

"I need to be inside you." He climbed onto the table and dropped one forearm to the felt beside my head. Lining himself up with his free hand, he looked down at me, his jaw clenched tight.

I grasped his bicep and nodded, a silent plea. With that, he thrust deep inside me, filling me so completely I couldn't help but let out a hiss. He settled on top of me, finally burying himself to the hilt, and we both groaned. The stretch of him felt too good.

"Cortney," I whispered.

"Jesus, you're like a vise around my dick." Grasping one of my legs, he lifted it over his hip and circled his hips, rocking into me, then pumping deep. His skin glimmered with perspiration as his wild blue eyes meet mine. "Fuck."

"Harder," I begged.

Pulling out of me, he hopped off the table and scooped me up. In a heartbeat, he was laying me down again, this time at the end of the table so he could stand. Once I was settled, he grabbed my ass and lifted so that every thrust of his cock hit deep and in the perfect spot.

"Yes," I cried as he pounded into me. "There. Don't stop."

"Never. stopping." He grunted. His pumps got deeper, harder. His grip on my ass tightened. "Gonna." Thrust. "Do this." Thrust. "Forever." Thrust. His pelvis hit my clit each time he plunged into me, driving me higher and sending pleasure skittering through every cell of my body.

"Yes." I moaned and clenched tight around his thick cock as the world around me spun.

"Come on, Dylan. You need to come." Cortney swirled his hips as he drove into me once more, and my body exploded.

"Yes." He growled as his own orgasm ripped through him.

We came down together, eyes locked and panting, until he collapsed on top of me. His heart pounded wildly and his chest heaved like he'd just left practice. The air rushing against my neck had goose bumps popping up along my shoulder and collarbone. I was absolutely boneless, and I couldn't fight my smile as I raked my fingers through his hair.

Finally, he sat up. Sliding his hands under my ass again, he lifted me into his arms.

"Where are we going?"

He chuckled. "My bed. We may only have tonight, but that doesn't mean we can't do this again."

Dylan

7

Liv: Dylan where did you go? Beckett's freaking out about the socks Liam took.

Delia: He's going to have to chill the fuck out. Dylan said she was going bar hopping tonight since Liam is gone.

Shay: She's so damn good at sneaking in and out of places. I swear you float, Dyl.

Liv: She goes out the window. But even if she's bar hopping she should have her phone.

Shay: The window? Seriously?

Delia: Of course she goes out the window. The girl is all bibbidy-bobbidy-fucking-boo.

Delia: GIF of magic dust.

Shay: Her phone is sitting on the bathroom counter.

Liv: Shocking (eye roll emoji)

Shay: I'll put it on your bed, Dylan. Please text us when you get home so we know you're safe.

Delia: 1:30 is awfully late. Someone must be having a good time.

Me: I'm home it's hardly past 3 tell becks I've got the sock thing under control (wink emoji) why are you all still up?

Shay: We binged Yellowstone. I can't believe I've never seen it.

Delia: I'm going to get Dylan hooked on it too.

Me: probably not

Shay: It's the same way I'm going to get her to eat smoothies.

Me: yes it's exactly like that

Cortney
8

"Good morning, Cortney. It's five forty-five on Monday, June nineteenth. Currently, it's sunny and sixty-four degrees. The high for today…"

Startled, I pulled in a sharp breath and cracked one eye open.

Once my brain booted up, I sighed and sat up, brushing my hair off my face. "Off, Bixby," I muttered. "Shades open."

Light filled the room; unsurprisingly, Dylan was nowhere to be found. That didn't mean the sight of her pillow, which didn't even look dented from a good night's sleep, didn't disappoint me. Why the hell was I upset? With baseball season in full swing, I didn't have time to focus on a woman.

In some ways, she seemed like a dream. How easily she could make me laugh, the way she felt in my arms, the moans that echoed in my ear as I sank into her tight pussy… She was almost too good to be true.

I kicked off the sheet and snagged a pair of gym shorts from the dresser, then headed for the living room. The pool cues were back on the wall, the beer bottles were thrown away, and the balls were racked in the center of the table. The only hint that

Dylan had actually been here last night was the note on the finished 3000-piece puzzle.

Puzzles are fun, but not as fun as a game of pool with you. Thanks for an unforgettable night.

♥ *D*

She was gorgeous and funny and only interested in a night. A unicorn of a woman, that was for sure. Right now, though, I didn't have time to muse over her. I picked up the note and stuck it to the fridge using the firefly magnet I didn't hate so much this morning, then got to work packing for the road trip, determined to put thoughts of Dylan out of my mind.

Fate had a different idea, though. When I climbed into the car, ready to head for the airport, the scent of coconut enveloped me, and my little firefly's sunglasses sat in the cupholder as a silent reminder of the woman I already couldn't get out of my head.

Nine days later, my thighs burned as I squatted for another pitch. Only a couple of years ago, I could make it through a doubleheader without muscle fatigue, but here I was, hurting after six innings. It was the bottom of the seventh, and Christian Damiano's game was off. The curveball came in wide, and I had to stretch to keep it from getting past me. With a runner on second, that's all it would have taken for the opposing team to pull ahead. Looked like it was time for a pep talk. Damiano was a hothead who would self-destruct if I didn't intervene.

"Baaall two."

I snapped my mask up and glanced at the umpire. When he caught sight of me, he nodded, giving me the go-ahead. So I jogged out to settle my pitcher the fuck down. Tipping my chin to Tom Wilson, our head coach, I let him know I had this.

"Dragon." I shook my head. "I'm seeing a lot of smoke, but no fire."

He grunted, and temper flashed in his eyes as he glanced at the dugout. Probably to see whether Wilson was on the phone with the bullpen. He wasn't yet, but if Damiano walked this batter, Tom would be at that phone in a heartbeat. He was on a short leash after getting thrown out of three games this season for hitting batters and clearing the team benches with his love of fighting. The last time he'd gotten pulled, he stomped into the dugout and threw a helmet at Wilson. Those temper tantrums cost Damiano tens of thousands in fines. Part of the reason the Revs offered what they did for my trade was because I had a natural ability to settle my guys down. Time to work my magic.

"Dude." I grabbed the brim of his hat, forcing him to look up at me instead of trying to make eye contact with the batter. When I had his attention, I covered my mouth with my glove. "The Yanks' games come with a lot of pressure. I get that. But this guy…" I looked over my shoulder at the young kid smirking at us as he banged the bat against his cleat, sending dirt flying. "He's got nothing. He can't time a fast ball for shit, and a slider has him swinging at air."

"Yeah," Damiano muttered, wiping his hands on his pants.

"I'm serious, Dragon." I squeezed his shoulder and lifted my mitt again. If anyone was watching closely, I didn't want them to decipher my words. "I want to see the heat on the next pitch. Triple digits. I want to feel the breeze when he gets nothing but air."

His jaw clenched, and he dropped his chin.

"No. Focus and channel the frustration into the speed of the pitch. Don't let the pitch control you. You control it."

Finally, a hint of a smirk crossed his face.

"After that, drop in the slider, and the inning will end with him going down swinging."

He nodded. "Got it, Sham."

I turned and headed back to the plate, fighting a wince at the nickname I had acquired since joining the Revs. Yes, I wore socks with shamrocks on them, but I didn't want to be Sham or Shammy, or worse, ShamWow. I wanted to be the guy they could depend on to play the position.

I moved behind the plate and rolled my shoulders out.

"Your boy out there is all talk and no action," the rookie at bat taunted.

"Fucking ironic coming from the asshole wagging his lips." I squatted, pretending I couldn't hear the chuckle coming from the ump.

When I gave Damiano a curt nod, he wound up, this time with a gleam of determination in his eye. Fuck yeah. This one was hitting. The smack of the ball into my padded glove burned just like a fastball should, but the rookie hadn't even attempted to make contact.

"*Strike.*" The umpire's bark echoed behind me. Up in the press box, the announcers were no doubt hollering over the one hundred-plus mile-an-hour pitch. The kid was only twenty-eight and had a lot to learn about patience and perseverance, but he had one hell of a fastball. Though the trade had rocked me and I was still reeling, it was hard not to be excited about working with him for the rest of the season and hopefully next year.

After tossing the ball, I squatted again, and my right knee cracked. Dammit. But I ignored the ache that radiated up my leg. Fuck getting old. I gritted my teeth and sent the sign to Damiano.

Once again, he wound up beautifully. There was nothing in this world like the magic of a ball that dropped just before the plate. I fell to the dirt and caught it with my groin, biting back a groan when the ball made contact. That fucker would bruise just like the one on my left leg. Just like I'd promised Damiano, I was hit with the harsh wind of a big miss.

"*Strike.*" The umpire yanked his hand back.

It took me a second too long to stand up. The days of

popping right back up after every hit seemed more and more distant every game, but I enjoyed the analytics of the game too much to stop playing yet. Once I'd righted myself, I tossed the ball over my shoulder to the ump and caught Damiano on the way into the dugout.

"You really put the *wow* in ShamWow, man." He fluttered the fingers of his right hand as he approached.

With a huff, I shook my head. "You throw 'em, Dragon. All I can do is call 'em." I slapped him on the back and rushed into the dugout to get my gear off. I was batting this inning. The gear-on, gear-off process left no time to dick around.

Three innings, two runs, one win, and seventeen questions from reporters later, I was knocking on the door of one of my best friends. These days, I rarely went out after games—at twenty-five, I'd loved the bar scene, but ten years later, my ideal way to wind down after a game was a night at home.

A zap of excitement hit me along with the memories of my last night at home. I'd never look at that pool table and not see Dylan spread out on it. The woman had haunted my mind since.

"Hey, look. It's ShammyWow." Marc Demoda's teasing brought me back to the moment.

"Don't start with me." Damiano had played into the stupid nickname with the reporters after the game, and now it was trending on social media.

"At least you're almost laughing about it." He chuckled at my glare. "It's good to see ya, man."

"Heck yeah," I said, careful of Marc's wife's no cursing in the house rule. Marc was one of the first pitchers I caught for after I was called up to the Metros. These days, he was the team's pitching coach.

"Come on in." He opened the door wider and stepped back. With a dip of my chin, I stepped inside the massive foyer. His house was enormous, though it had to be to house all the kids running through it. When I met Marc ten years ago, he was the ultimate bachelor. Now, though? He'd morphed into the epitome of a family man and had four kids to prove it. "Way to pull out the win today. I thought for sure Damiano was self-destructing." With a silent shake of my head, I brushed off his comment. He didn't need to know that I'd thought so too. "*Pfft*. When was the last time I let one of my pitchers self-destruct? I'm too good at what I do for that."

"And you're modest too," he deadpanned.

"Mr. Miller." Marc's eight-year-old daughter stomped down the stairs.

"Mandy." Marc's dad voice made me smile. The dude had the role down pat.

Her little hands slammed to her hips. "No, Daddy. He needs to know this."

Marc sighed, but I waved him off. I was used to his daughter's sass.

"What's up, Mandy?"

"I made Mommy buy your shampoo. The one that makes your hair shiny and float in the breeze." Her sweet face morphed into a serious scowl. "But my hair does not float. Or shine."

Well, shit. I'd filmed commercials for three shampoo companies in the last year. God knew which one she was complaining about.

Whereas my hair was mostly straight, the girl's blond hair curled in ringlets, so regardless, we'd have different results. But how could I explain this to a person who'd barely cleared the four-foot mark?

She crossed her arms and *humph*ed. "I want to know your *real* secret."

Normally, I'd squat down to get on her level. At six-six, I had a good two feet on her, but my legs were toast after the game this afternoon, and the motivation just wasn't there. So instead, I beckoned her over and bent close.

"I blow it dry every day."

Her eyes widened and she took a step back. "With a *hair dryer?*"

I nodded solemnly.

"And a *brush?*" she squeaked.

I nodded again.

Dropping her head back, she studied the ceiling before turning her gray-blue eyes on me again. "I'm going to have to think about that. It might not be worth shiny hair."

Marc huffed behind us. "You and brushes. You'd think we were cutting off your fingers."

"They're not my thing now, and they might never be my thing, Daddy." She rolled her eyes and spun, then she stomped right back up the huge staircase.

"Eight going on sixteen." Marc sighed.

I chuckled and shot him a grin. "Better you than me, man."

I had no intention of having kids until later down the road. While I still could, I was focusing all my efforts on baseball. When I retired, then I'd think about dating more seriously.

Red hair, amber eyes, and a heart-stopping smile floated through my mind at just the thought of dating. The woman was stuck in my head. I had jerked off a few too many times to thoughts of her these last nine days.

"Come on." Marc's words pulled me back to the moment. "Corey's out by the pool."

He led me through the house to the back patio. Even in the dark, the home's proximity to the water was obvious. The New Jersey salt air surrounded me, and the second I was through the door, I could hear the crash of the waves just past the dunes that separated the place from the beach.

Savoring the familiarity, I took a big breath. It had only been a month, but I missed this already. The house I still owned was a block down the beach. I could have swung by, hung out there, but it was empty and on the market now that I lived in Boston during the spring, summer, and fall. No one wintered at the New

Jersey shore, so I had no reason to keep the place, even though the thought of selling it still hit like a punch to the gut.

Wintered. Damn. I winced at how easily that verb came to me. I worked hard not to be a rich asshole, but only arrogant tools used words like *wintered.*

"What's up, Masshole? You look a little too comfy hanging out here in Jersey," Corey called from behind me.

Spinning on my heel, I greeted my former teammate with a bro hug.

He slapped my back and pulled away. "I'm surprised you didn't fly out tonight."

You and me both, man. We were home in Boston tomorrow, so I had no reason to stay in New York, yet our flight didn't leave until morning. Must be a Beckett Langfield thing.

"I'm on the Revs' schedule now." I shrugged, taking the beer Marc offered.

"Tillerson doesn't suck, but damn, I miss you." Corey laughed and settled onto a stool in front of Marc's patio bar.

Tillerson was the rookie who'd taken my spot full time.

"Back at ya. Although the talent that Langfield has put together for the Revs should scare the pants off you guys."

Marc snorted. "Trust me, I know. It's like the baseball universe…"

He went on, but with one word, my brain shifted. I'd spent the last week and a half doing everything I could to push thoughts of Dylan out of my mind. I'd failed miserably. Bugs, my ass, the universe, Taylor Swift, my lucky socks, pool, puzzles, beer, cherries, and even my girdle—every damn thing made me think of her.

How was she doing in that crazy house? Was she thinking about me the way I was thinking about her?

"Cort?" Corey called, his mouth drawn down in a frown.

Forcing myself back to the present, I rubbed my forehead. "Huh?"

"How's the head?" Marc asked, his brow furrowed in concern.

"Fine," I snapped. I had no interest in talking about my anxiety. These guys were part of a select few who knew, but regardless, it wasn't my favorite topic.

He sighed. "Look, being traded out of the blue probably has you spiraling and questioning motives, but dude, I swear we weren't actively looking to trade you. The Revs offer, though? The prospects they traded to get you?" Marc shook his head. "We couldn't say no. Take it as a compliment."

The trade was public, so the details weren't a secret. Honestly, it would have been idiotic for the Metros to say no. But still, no one wants to be traded to a shittier team mid-season. They knew that too, so there was no point getting into it now.

Instead, I focused on the only reason that made sense. "The young talent on the pitching roster is second to none. It makes sense that they'd want a veteran to help hone it. And Boston has its perks." My mind tracked back to Dylan.

"Perks?" Corey asked with a smirk. "I know that term. Who is she?"

Shaking my head, I dipped my chin. "You know my rule."

Corey's responding chuckle was a little too loud in the quiet night. "Like my rule about staying away from reporters?" He held up his left hand and wiggled his fingers to show off his wedding band. As if he needed to remind me that he was married to a sports reporter.

"No, it's…" I took him in, then considered Marc. Both men fell for their wives during times they were adamantly against the notion. During what they'd both probably consider their worst moments. But they were happy as shit now, having found their perfect matches.

Musing over that for a moment, I changed directions. "How did you know they were it for you? Did you know as soon as you met them?"

Marc barked out a laugh. "Hell no. If I had known when I met Beth, those six months would have been a heck of a lot easier."

Corey spun his beer. "I didn't know right away either. But from the beginning, things with Taran just hit different."

Marc nodded. "Yeah, that's a good way to put it. And man, from day one, I made up any excuse I could think of to see her." He chuckled, but then his smile fell. "I knew she was different. Special. So if you find that, pull out all the stops. Put yourself in her path. Find any reason to keep seeing her. This kind of love? It's worth fighting for."

Corey lifted his beer. "I second that."

I held mine aloft and tapped it against each of theirs. Maybe they were right. Maybe seeing Dylan again could be a good thing. But she'd been right there with me on the one-night arrangement. So what would she think about that?

Cortney
9

"Auntie Dyl!" Finn screeched.

With a long breath out, I helped Adeline dip her brush in the purple paint. "One sec!" I hollered back, scooting the two-year-old closer to my son. "Watch her for me."

"Sure, why wouldn't I want to watch a toddler with acrylic paint?" Liam sighed and put his own brush down. "Which flower are we painting, Addie?"

"Tis," she said with a toothy grin.

Since it was summer, I had all seven kids home with me. Every day was an adventure.

Quickly, I darted up the stairs. "What's up, Finn?"

"You says I could paint, right?" He glared at his older sister, who was settled at the window next to him.

These two were working in Beckett and Liv's room. When I got them set up, I assumed I could trust the resident artist to watch her brother in here. The big open parlor on the second floor had newly replaced windows, and Delia's head might explode if we painted those. So we were sticking with painting the windows that hadn't been replaced yet.

"Yes," I replied slowly, eyeing Winnie.

"He's making a mess!" the nine-year-old cried.

"No, I not!" Finn stomped his foot, sending his yellow tutu bouncing.

Paint dotted the floor in a few places, but most of it landed on the ugly blue floral sheets I'd spread out like tarps.

"Not on the floor. On the window. We're supposed to be painting a forest, but your trees don't even look like trees." Winnie pointed to the orange blobs in front of Finn. "You're messing up the whole thing."

"You're both doing an incredible job." Flattery normally worked. "Winnie, the scene you taped is gorgeous, and Finn, you're rocking that orange tree. Remember this is a fun project to turn Mom's room into a magical forest!"

"She is going to love it," Finn cheered.

Even Winnie couldn't help but smile at his excitement. At least until he turned back and brought the orange tree down a bit too far.

"At least mine won't be abstract." She shook her head and got back to work.

Finn's tree was oddly bulb-ish at the top now. Oh well.

Once they were settled, I headed back down the stairs. Halfway down, I stopped to take in the parlor and considered having the kids paint the walls in that room. It would become a classroom in the fall. I would continue homeschooling Liam and Kai, and this would give us a dedicated workspace during the day as well as a homework station for the rest of the crew after school. As it was, it was a depressing room, so it would need a lot of love before then. Since the floors were plywood, the ceiling rafters were exposed in half the room, and there were several holes in the plaster walls, this would be a great space to let the kids' inner artists shine. Delia, Shay, and Liv entrusted me to be home with their kids every day, and I took my role as caretaker seriously. It was my goal to encourage all areas of their development. So the next time we were trapped inside due to rain, we would make this room fun.

"You two good?" I called out to Liam as I continued down the steps.

"Yup. What kinds of problems could a teenager and baby get into with permanent paint, Ma?"

Oh, how I loved the sarcasm.

In the dining room, Kai was locked in. He was so focused on painting his hockey stick he didn't notice me peeking in. Shay probably wouldn't love the sports theme here, but the blues would brighten the space. Maybe this would help me get her to loosen up a little and let Kai spread his wings. It was important for kids to have that opportunity in a safe environment like this.

I headed to my room to check in on the twins. The window on the right was separated into eight sections. Seven were already colored with tiny dots, and Collette was adding bright red freckles to the highest space, finishing off the rainbow of color she'd been working on. Her sister was working on the window on the left. Phoebe had four squares done, leaving three completely empty.

"We went with Pointillism," Collette informed me as she finished off her last square.

"Specifically, the Georges Seurat technique. But we went with an abstract scene instead of a picture." Phoebe put her brush down on the windowsill. "I've finished for now."

"Finished?" I asked. The three sections she'd taped off at the bottom of the window were still completely untouched.

"Yes." She nodded. "Since it's your room, the windows represent the male and female auras of the house."

"I'm working on the spaces that characterize each of the girls. I'm just finishing Mom's." Collette added the last few dots of red. She was spot-on with their mother's aura. Damn, their idea was impressive.

I stepped back and surveyed Phoebe's window again. "Beckett, Kai, Liam, and Finn. Who are the other three guys?"

Phoebe rolled her eyes and sighed heavily. "If we knew who they were, we wouldn't have had to leave their areas clear."

"Yeah. We don't know who you, Mom, and Auntie Shay are going to marry yet."

The sound that came out of me was somewhere between a laugh and a scoff. Not only was I never going to get married, but I was pretty sure the other two unfinished spaces would remain clear for a while. Shay's husband had passed away three years ago, but she wasn't ready to move on. And Delia? I blew out a breath and shook my head at just the thought. I didn't think there was a man in existence who could convince her to give him a chance.

Instead of raining on the girls' parade, I went a different way.

"How about filling those spaces with the type of aura you think we should pick?"

The twins considered each other like they were in silent conversation, and after a moment, Phoebe nodded. "Good idea. You need a blue, Auntie Dylan." She picked up a brush.

"Mom needs a yellowy orange." Collette moved over to help.

"Pointillism. Nice." Liam stood at the door holding Addie out in front of him. "Don't do diapers, Ma. Tag, you're it."

Stepping closer, I scrunched my nose at the smell. "Someone had too much kale smoothie this morning." I tickled Adeline's belly, eliciting the sweetest giggle, then scooped her into my arms. Without a word, Liam went back to his window. This was the best idea I'd had all week. Everyone was entertained and, miraculously, on task.

Just after six p.m., my happy bubble burst.

"Dy-*lan*." The tone of Shay's voice lifted on the second syllable of my name, and her call was punctuated by the slamming of a door.

"What?" I called from the kitchen. She wasn't going to insist she help with dinner, was she? I had lasagna in the oven, and it smelled divine, but it was loaded full of gluten and red meat and probably some kind of deadly preservatives Shay would object to.

I had hoped to make a garden-fresh salad to go along with it, figuring Shay would approve of the farm-to-table idea. But between Punxsutawney Phil declaring a long winter and our mama raccoon loving my garden veggies, even the kids and my salutations to the sun couldn't save my little garden. In the end, though, the universe had used me to provide for Junior and her four newborns, so I couldn't be upset.

"Come outside, *now*." She dropped her bag on the counter and pointed at Winnie. "Watch your sister for a minute."

Outside? Was this not about dinner?

Shay gripped me by the wrist and dragged me out the front door to the steps. "Why do we have a dick painted on our window?"

A what?

She flung a hand into the air and waved wildly at Beckett and Liv's window.

Following the gesture, I dropped my head back and scanned the images Winnie and Finn had worked on today. Oh shit. My stomach sank when I took in Finn's orange tree. From this angle, the subject of his masterpiece was undoubtedly phallic. The dread that had hit me quickly morphed into hilarity, and I cupped a hand over my mouth to hold in a laugh.

"Oh my God, Dyl. This is not funny." Shay's lips lifted at the corners as she fought her own smile.

"At least it's on the right window." I couldn't stop the laughter now. "Liv is the only one getting dick regularly."

Shay snickered, but then she sucked in a deep breath, set her shoulders, and forced a more serious face. "What are the neighbors going to say?"

I scanned the numerous chalk drawings covering the steps

and sidewalk and took in the partial skeleton hanging over the railing. At this point, Bobbie was nothing more than a head, a neck, and shoulders. The twins had gotten sidetracked after starting his assembly and hadn't been out in months to complete him. The house was adorned with random holiday decorations, and a litany of Nerf bullets dotted the yard. Not to mention the gutter. One side had been hanging off the roofline since we moved in.

I spun back to Shay and pursed my lips. "When did we decide the neighbors' opinions matter?"

She shrugged. "A moving van was parked in the driveway across the street yesterday. I have a feeling we're scaring people away." She threw an arm out and gestured to the second floor again. "And a dick on the window certainly won't make us friends around here."

"Dick on the window?" Delia's sky-high heels tapped on the concrete as she sidled up next to our friend.

Shay winced and wiped her hands on her fitted yoga pants before turning to Delia.

The brown leather strap of Delia's bag slipped down her arm as she looked up. "Why the *fuck* did we paint the windows?" Her bag *thunk*ed to the ground as she whirled to face me.

"The house's energy needed a change after you fired the latest contractor. The kids and I did a smudging, then gave it some happy vibes." I lifted my chin a little higher and smiled. Dick aside, the windows looked great.

"Does it come off?"

Hmm, how could I tell her no in a way that wouldn't make the vein in her neck throb?

I was saved from answering when the front door opened and Liam stepped out. Brushing his red hair out of his eyes, he trotted down the steps. The Beats around his neck bounced as he came to a stop beside me and turned to see what we were looking at.

"What are we—" He snickered and spun away from the house. "Beckett is going to lose his shit, Ma."

I whacked him in the stomach, because at almost five ten, he was too tall to get on the back of the head anymore. "Don't curse. It's not a good look, and I don't have a bank account to support our curse jar prices."

He smirked. "You've said shit at least twelve times today."

I sighed and bumped his shoulder. "I know, but you don't want to grow up to be me, kid."

Wrapping his freckled arm around my shoulder, he pulled me against his thin frame. "Yeah, I do, Ma. You're great."

Dammit. Compliments always meant he wanted something from me. I gave him the side-eye and waited.

He released my shoulder and took a step back. "I'm going out."

"With friends because it's almost seven and wandering the city alone at night is dangerous?" The concern in Shay's voice was ridiculous.

"No, with Bobbie," Liam deadpanned. "I thought the head and shoulders needed to see the world."

Smart-ass.

"Wandering around carrying bones is a great way to get put on a psych hold. And since our house looks like this"—Delia nodded to the ghosts and the wreath on the front porch—"and we're apparently decorating with penises, child protective services isn't going to be singing our praises."

"Too many moms." He dropped his head back and let out a sigh. "I'm going to the comic store with some friends because a special edition drops tonight at ten." His green eyes cut to me. "I'll be home before midnight. I have Life 360 turned on so you can track me. I promise to only talk to the weird comic book fans, not the weird drug dealers on the street corners." He raised one copper brow. "Cool?"

"Cool." With a nod, I shot him a grin. I worried less than

Shay and Delia. The poor kid needed to get out once in a while. Especially with the way these two smothered him.

With a final chin lift, he turned and took off.

Before he could get far, though, I cleared my throat and called out. "But I want the spray paint."

He froze mid-step.

"Back left pocket, kiddo."

His shoulders drooped and he turned back to me with a frown.

"Art's amazing *when it's legal*," I reminded him, holding back a chuckle at his sullen expression.

He rolled his eyes, but without argument, he pulled the blue spray paint from his pocket and held it out to me.

"Have fun!" I said, plastering on a bright smile.

He grumbled as he walked away.

Delia's lips parted, but before she could speak, I held up a hand.

"I know." I shrugged. "The chance that he'll spend adulthood living out of his van is about as likely as the chance that he'll rule the world."

She shook her head. "There's no doubt about it. Liam's going to rule the world. You're doing an amazing job with him. With all the kids. I hope you know that." Delia wrapped her arm around me and gave me a squeeze.

I loved my dad and my brother, and they'd always been there to help when I needed them, but they'd never accepted me for who I was the way that my besties did. My brother wanted me to do things his way. He was always pushing me to fit into his box. But Delia, Shay, and Liv never made me feel anything but seen and loved.

"I'll ignore the dick masterpiece. Those windows are being replaced anyway," Delia continued. "The downside, though, is that Beckett's going to ruin book club tonight by ranting about it."

"But," I clapped my hands, "who didn't love that book?" I headed back up the stairs with my friends following behind me. "When she puked in the hockey player's shoe, I about died laughing."

"I had tears rolling down my face when he found his stuff in the freezer." Shay chuckled. "I have no idea why I was laughing so hard, but when he came home and found—"

"We aren't talking about it until Liv gets here and we start our session." Delia cut us off. "But I was horrified, once again, to discover that you picked book two in the series. Why didn't you tell me?"

"Oh, live a little, Delia. It's okay to read out of order." I smirked. "Especially when we're fueled by wine and smut."

"Did we get my organic wine this week?" Shay asked as she hit the porch landing.

"Yes." Delia's ponytail whipped over her shoulder as she looked back at Shay. "I know you think lower glycemic whatever is the important part, but I really think it's the alcohol content that matters."

The second we were in the door, the echoes of "Mom!" and "Auntie!" pounded our ears.

"Tag." I tapped them both on the shoulders. "I've got dinner. You're in charge of the offspring."

Thank God dishes didn't fall under my list of duties around here. After the chaos of a meal, sneaking down to my room to escape the madness was pure happiness. Once the meal was finished, I made a stealthy exit and flopped back on my bed, letting out a long sigh. With the thunder of noise above me, I almost missed the small knocks.

I sat up and narrowed my eyes as I scanned my room in search of the cause. Ten seconds later, the *tap, tap, tap* started again. Pulling myself off the bed, I moved to the newly painted window and peeked out.

A tall blond man took up the width of the sidewalk just

outside. A smile almost pulled at my lips before my eyes narrowed. What was he doing here? I snapped the latch and pushed on the pane that opened outward. The window knocked into his hand as he lifted to knock again.

"Fuck. Sorry." He shuffled back to make room for the window to swing open. Without a screen in the frame, nothing but air existed between me and the Thor-like baseball star.

It had been almost two weeks since our night together. In that time, I had watched a few of the Revs games, and every time he appeared on screen, I was instantly taken back to his apartment and the feel of him. I had been too busy to even consider another night with him, but that didn't stop me from thinking about it. Especially when I lay alone in the dark after the house went quiet at night. In those moments, I was plagued by memories.

"Samson, how did you know this was me?"

He cleared his throat and stuffed his hands into his pockets. "You mentioned having a dream catcher in your window."

He seriously remembered that passing comment? "What are you doing here?"

He pulled his hands out of his pockets and clenched them at his sides, as if restraining himself.

Nibbling on my bottom lip, I eyed his fists, then took him in from head to toe. Should I invite him inside? A normal-sized person could easily climb through the window, but he was nowhere near the size of an average man. His long blond hair hung perfectly around his shoulders, shining in the light from the stoop, but it was his blue eyes that called to me. The intelligent, honest eyes I'd spent entirely too much time thinking about.

"I, uh…" He dropped the paper bag he was holding onto the sidewalk and reached for his pocket. "I found these and thought you'd want them back." He thrust his large hand toward me. In the dark, it took me a moment to recognize my sunglasses. Until now, I hadn't even noticed they were missing. Our fingers brushed as I took them, and sparks shot up my arm. Damn, after the multi-orgasm high he'd given me, I was sure at least *some* of the core-clenching yearning would have faded. Usually, the anticipation of what could be was the cause of the kind of desire that coursed through me after that single touch. With Cortney, though, it was as potent now as it had been the night he took me to his place. My heart raced just because he was here.

I cleared my throat. "Thanks." I had about twenty pairs of these things. I picked them up for five bucks from groceries, pharmacies, and dollar stores all over the place. Which was why I hadn't noticed they were missing. Keeping track of my stuff wasn't my thing, so I didn't waste money buying the expensive kind.

"I thought you might need them." The slight flush that crept up his cheeks was subtle in the low light.

It was pretty obvious the sunglasses were junk. The lenses were scratched and the finishing was badly peeling off one arm. This was an excuse. That thought made my heart stutter in a way that had me concerned I was going into Afib.

He kicked at the concrete and peered at me, wearing a bashful smile. "This all sounded a lot less stupid in my head."

I chuckled. I should send him away ASAP. Although the man's kind heart and intelligent blue eyes intrigued me, I wasn't the type to believe in a forever love story for myself.

As his mouth lifted in a shy grin, though, I couldn't stop myself from stepping back. "With the effort and embarrassment you've put into this, the least I can do is invite you in."

He pressed his lips together in concentration as he eyed the two-by-four-foot space. "Through the window?"

"Yes, live a little Samson. It's even cobweb free. You don't have to worry about getting spiders in your magic hair."

He scoffed, but he practically bent his six-and-a-half-foot frame in two so he could fit through the window. "When you told me you used this as an entrance, I thought it'd be bigger."

"It's me-sized." I shrugged, my hair falling over one eye.

"It's good you're here. The house could use a bit of your calm blues. Everyone's tense about Beckett coming home." I grabbed a clip from the nightstand and pulled my hair back. Turning to him again, I found him gaping at something behind me.

"You don't have a wall?" His tone made it seem like a question, but he could see the studs, so it clearly wasn't.

"It makes a great bookshelf, doesn't it?" I surveyed the half of my room missing its sheetrock. I'd gotten tired of looking at the brown boards, so I'd jazzed it up a bit. I painted each stud a color that coincided with a book trope: Blue for sports. Red for forbidden. Pink for accidental pregnancy. And so on. Next to each colored stud was a rainbow of my favorite smutty romances.

"You removed a wall to make bookshelves." Cortney shook his head.

That was a creative idea. But…

"No. Delia would have never let me do that. The leak from the ceiling"—with one hand in the air, I gestured to the hole— "caused some water issues in the walls and floors, so the first contractor took them out. His crew started to drywall the hall, but Delia fired them. The guy was an idiot, so I don't blame her, but that means they never finished my room." I shrugged. "What kind of grown man calls in sick because he's scared of ghost voices?" Every contractor we'd found had either been horrible or sketchy. "But at least we cleared his energy." I scrunched my nose. "That man muddied everything up."

Cortney rubbed his jaw, studying the holes. "Is there mold?"

I sniffed. "I don't smell any."

He pulled in a breath and opened his mouth, but he snapped it shut again. After another moment of assessing my space, he finally turned back to me. "Did you hire a new contractor?"

And full circle back to my morning. "The windows will speed that process up."

With his head tilted to the side, he frowned. "You painted a dick on the window so your roommates would be forced to hire a contractor?"

His confusion was adorable. It lit me up inside just like his awkwardness had that night in his car. "The dick was an accident, and the kids had fun with the painting, but..." I pursed my lips. "It *might* have occurred to me that both Beckett and Delia would be motivated to hire someone if we had stained-glass windows that needed to be replaced."

A chuckle rumbled in his chest. "You're like the happiest evil genius I've ever met."

"Please." I waved him off. Over the years, I'd learned how to make the best of situations. "What was in the bag?"

His attention snapped back to the window, where he'd left the paper sack. "Shit. We're letting in the bugs."

"Eh." I shrugged, watching his ass as he climbed back outside. "The snakes like them."

His blond hair flew around his face, and he smacked his head against the window frame. "The what?" He rubbed his temple as he clambered back inside.

"You okay?"

"Maybe. Depends on how you elaborate on that snake comment." He cocked a brow.

"They're only in the crawl space, but they do eat the bugs. It's also why we don't have mice." With raccoons, snakes, and spiders, we had more than enough critters. Adding mice to the mix would be overkill.

He shut the window. "It takes a special type of person to live here, huh?"

"It's just walls," I said, scanning the room. What was a house but a shelter from mother nature when she was upset?

His blue eyes flicked above my head before coming back to me. "That's true, I guess. When you *have* them."

The smile that flashed across my face was automatic. "Someone's got the jokes tonight."

Stepping into me, he tucked an errant curl behind my ear. His warm hand lingered so close I could feel his heat on my neck. My skin tingled at his proximity, and I couldn't swallow. When he was close like this, he overwhelmed all my senses. His head tipped down just a bit. Just enough that his breath hit my skin and caused me to shiver. My body yearned to move closer in response, like his soul was a whirlpool pulling me in. I almost wanted to forget my rules about not getting attached and give in to the gravity of this man.

But the house vibrated above our heads, and a door slammed, making us both jump. My chest brushed against his ribs before we quickly stepped apart.

"*Dylan!*" The deep voice bounced off the walls.

"Oh, good. Becks is home." I winced. "You should go. I didn't exactly tell him about the other night, and I don't know how he'd feel about me messing around with one of his players."

If I wasn't careful and he found out, he might get ideas about Cortney and me and plans that included more than our one night. Everyone under this roof knew how much Beckett loved to meddle.

Cortney frowned and crossed his hulk-size arms over his massive chest. "If you think I'm going to abandon you when he's screaming like that, then you've got no clue what type of man I am."

The possessiveness in his voice caused a weird ping in my chest, but I pushed it aside, determined to ignore it. There was nothing possessive about our relationship. Hell, there was no relationship. Our one night had happened, and it was done. Time to move on.

"Becks wouldn't hurt a fly. He's all spit and vinegar. Don't worry about me." I pressed my hand into his rock-hard chest, ready to urge him back toward the window, but he didn't budge, even as I planted my feet and pushed. "I promise. I drive Becks insane, but Liv would kill him if he hurt me, and he loves her too much to piss her off."

He narrowed his eyes and stayed right where he was, like the most annoying, most gorgeous marble statue. Beckett shouted my name again, then footsteps thumped on the stairs.

"You don't have to go home, Samson, but you can't stay here." The urgency in my voice finally got him moving.

Dropping his arms to his sides, he let out a sigh. Then he was pulling out his phone. "Give me your number. I've known Beckett my entire life, and you're right—he'd never actually hurt you. But I'm checking on you later anyway."

"Deal." In a rush to get him out, I typed in my number and sent myself a text, all while shooing Cortney back out the window. "Wait," I called, pointing to the bag he'd left on the floor beside the window.

"It's for you." He grinned, making my heart clench, and then he was slipping into the night.

Three hours later, after a ton of ranting and lots of smutty book club laughs, I finally had a moment to peek inside Cortney's bag. I pulled out the box and held it in front of me. My stomach flipped at the image on the front. It was a puzzle. The image was of a woodpile covered in fireflies.

Me: fireworks are illegal in boston???

Delia: No.

Liv: Yes.

Me: which is it because the 4th of july is tomorrow.

Shay: I'm nervous about why you want to know.

Liv: I heard Liam and Finn talking about it. As it applies to anyone in our house YES they are VERY illegal.

Delia: The law requires training and permits for a person to possess or shoot off fireworks.

Me: never mind becks and I have a plan

Liv: GIF of a wide-eyed, panicked-looking dog

Delia: GIF of a man and a woman in jail

Shay: Details please, Dylan.

Shay: Dylan, it's been an hour.

Me: becks said he'd hire someone to shoot them off at the stadium don't worry we are not being a ball of nevers today cause no one's gonna lose a hand

Cortney

11

W hat would the text be today? I was never sure how to start a conversation with her, but after two weeks it was starting to be pathetic that I was still texting her every single day. But I couldn't stop myself. I looked forward to every one of her replies. Even when they were short or worrying.

I stressed a little over a vague statement about working to smuggle fireworks into Boston, but then I got an email from the Revs that put me at ease. It was an invitation for the families of the team. Turned out they were hosting a fireworks show at the stadium while we were playing in Texas. Another day, she sent a photo of a hole in a wall surrounded by an abstract painting. The message mentioned something about painting their classroom. A few days ago, the image that came through included several weird ropes and was accompanied by a message about raccoon booby traps required to protect the strawberries. There was no way to predict what she might be doing on any given day, and, surprisingly, I loved the anticipation and the unknown.

> Me: What was the last movie you watched?

I'd been throwing out hints about wanting to meet up again, but thus far, Dylan hadn't taken the bait. No bubbles appeared in response, and if past patterns held, she wouldn't answer for at least a couple of hours. Just long enough that I'd go insane if I didn't focus on something else.

My phone buzzed, and my heart skipped at the prospect of an immediate response. The damn organ then plummeted to my gut when I caught sight of the real sender.

> Dad: Clint wants to send you some racing footage. We'd love your input on a possible new driver.

I had no input. Didn't matter how many times I watched the footage, I didn't see what Dad and my brother-in-law saw. The ins and outs of stock car racing didn't interest me, regardless of how much Dad hoped it would. No matter how much he wanted me to be involved in his racing teams. I didn't have a plan for when I was too old to play baseball, but whatever it was did not include racing.

The fear of failure was this massive stress in my brain. I had no natural skill that didn't include controlling the game from behind the plate. Or if I did, I hadn't discovered it yet. I'd spent my life solely focused on the game, but in two or three years, I'd have to make a change.

> Me: Send it and I'll watch it after my game.

I dropped my phone into my locker and stood up.

"Hey, Shammy."

I gritted my teeth at that fucking nickname. "What do you want, Emerson?"

"Ping-pong?" The third baseman asked, wearing the smile that was constantly on his face. They all knew I was always up for a game, and I'd yet to lose.

"You really are a glutton for punishment."

He shrugged and bounced a bit on his feet. "Sitting around doing nothing makes my skin crawl, and I hate cards."

At twenty-six, Emerson Knight was the youngest guy on the team. He and Damiano had both been called up from triple-A this off season, and the two couldn't be more different. Damiano currently sat glaring at his phone. After the morning workout, he'd planted himself there, and he wouldn't move again until he went out to the mound. Emerson, though, was like a puppy bouncing off the walls wagging his tail for attention.

Most guys were sitting around reading or BSing or playing cards, killing time for the three hours until the game started. Sitting still left me bored or stressed too. I knew the game plan; I had spent hours focusing on what pitches I would call and studying the other team's strengths and weaknesses. But if I didn't do something to keep myself occupied, I'd end up fixating on the what-ifs. Distraction was my friend.

"Two games," I agreed.

He pounced on me, wrapping his long arms around my torso in a hug. I was a good few inches taller, but he shocked me, so I didn't have time to block him. "Dude, personal space." I brushed him off.

"Aw, come on, man. Show us some love." He laughed.

I shook my head at his energy as he jogged off to the room where the ping-pong table was set up for a game. After I shook out my arms and let out a couple of cleansing breaths, I smacked the ball over the net. But as the ball flew by, he swung at nothing. This dude could snag a line drive out of mid-air. One would think he had crazy good hand-eye coordination, but table tennis clearly wasn't his thing.

"Damn." Emerson laughed at himself. "I keep thinking I'll get better, but I don't."

I served it again, and he threw one long arm out, but he

missed. This time the ball bounced and smacked him in the face. He reared back and hit the table hard with one hip.

"You okay?" I asked, holding back a chuckle.

"Dragon and I set up a ping-pong table in our apartment." Emerson and Damiano shared a place in the city. It would be something to be a fly on the wall in their apartment. Almost like Dopey and Grumpy jumping out of a fairy tale and moving into a high-rise in Boston. "We've been playing a lot."

"Is this you practicing, then?" I served again, and this time when he missed, the ball ricocheted off the wall and rolled under the table. He grinned.

"Yeah, can you imagine how bad I was before." His dark hair disappeared under the table, and after another *thunk*, he popped back up, still smiling.

"Bambi." I shook my head at the young third baseman. "If you get hurt fucking around, Wilson is going to skin you alive."

Peeking over the surface of the table, he tossed the ball at me. "No worries, I'm not going to maim myself playing ping-pong." Then he stood and shrugged. "At least I probably won't."

With a huff, I shook my head. Professional athlete aside, the guy was a walking disaster. I sent another serve over the net. This time I went easy on him, hoping that using a light hand would allow him to actually volley it back.

"You've been quiet. Haven't come out with us much these last few weeks." He shrugged. "You doing okay?"

Baseball teams were gossip hubs, and since I was the new guy, they were all up in my business. Damn. If they were concerned that I wasn't showing up enough, I'd probably have to drag myself out with them. I wasn't up for another trade, so I'd have to make nice.

I shrugged as I whacked the ball and sent it flying by him. He really sucked. "Playing new teams means hours and hours of watching film. I've got a lot of studying to do to keep up."

Switching from the National League to the American League

meant that not only wasn't I familiar with many of our opposing teams, but so many players as well. But failure and I couldn't go hand in hand. I'd own the AL just like I had the NL. In rapid fire, a list of players' names ran through my head. In the National League, I had everyone on lock. Although I kept telling myself I could do it again, nagging doubt hovered in my mind. What if I couldn't? I'd be done, and without baseball, I'd have nothing.

"So it has nothing to do with whoever makes you smile at your phone?" he asked. The twenty-six-year-old smirked and served, sending the ball flying my way.

I missed. I fucking missed. The ball flew past me and tapped slowly on the floor. Had I been that obvious about Dylan's texts?

"It's definitely something," he singsonged, teasing me.

"I don't know what you mean." Crouching over, I snagged the white sphere from the ground and sent it back his way.

"Sure you don't." He smirked as the ball flew past him. "But we don't have to talk about it. How about we talk about me instead? Wilson wants me to stop crowding the plate." His lips turned down in an almost pout.

I laughed. "Typically, I'd agree. But not today. Today, you should crowd the fuck out of it."

The kid stood stock-still and assessed me like he was waiting for an explanation.

"Glendale loves to throw inside. If you crowd the plate, it'll mess with his game."

The right-hander had a nasty curveball, but he couldn't quite hit it right when the batter was too close.

Emerson smiled. "You know, I'm glad you're here." My serve sailed past him again. "Even if you don't lose at ping-pong."

With that, we got serious. He tried his best, but I ended up winning both games before we moved back to the team room.

When Emerson peeled off to chat with a couple of his buddies, I headed for my locker and picked up my phone.

> Firefly: I'm not good at movies

It took me a second to get her meaning, but not as long as it would have even a week ago. I was starting to speak Dylan.

> Me: Sitting still that long too hard?

> Firefly: ha ha yeah and being quiet I have a lot of things to say

> Me: Just not when it comes to texting

Dammit. I winced, and my stomach twisted the second after I hit Send. I couldn't take it back because the second the *delivered* status was displayed, it was replaced by the word *read*.

> Firefly: I don't keep track of my phone well

Was offering to buy an Apple Watch for a one-night stand too much? Most women wouldn't balk at any type of gift, but Dylan wasn't like anyone I'd ever met.

"What's wrong, Shammy?" Bosco asked.

Kyle Bosco was our right fielder, and besides me, he was the oldest guy on the field. He'd been around a while too. Maybe he wouldn't be the worst person to get advice from. But before I could formulate a question, Beckett Langfield sauntered into the team room and pulled up a seat next to me.

All eyes around the room landed on us. "Last time I was traded, I was called up to the office. Wasn't expecting a locker room visit." My tone was all smart-ass, but my heart clenched because, damn, my joke might be too close to home.

"How's Boston?" he muttered.

I leaned back in my chair and stretched my legs out, crossing my ankles. "Humid as fuck."

He scrutinized me with hard eyes and a tight jaw. "I was asking if you were settling in okay."

Beside me, Bosco's brows were in his hairline. Yeah, man, I was thinking the same thing. What the fuck?

"Aw, you worried about me, Langfield?"

He rolled his eyes. "You're not exactly singing our praises in post-game."

I heaved myself upright in my chair, my spine snapping straight. "The fuck I'm not. Every time I'm asked, I go on about how great the team is. I rave about the pitchers and praise the bats."

Since the early days of my career, I'd been a team guy through and through. I never said a negative word about a teammate.

"No." Beckett shook his head. "The city, the front office, the management. You're radio silent. And there are some PR concerns."

Oh. I chuckled and relaxed a bit. "You mean your wifey is giving you shit?"

His tight expression turned almost murderous as his eyes turned to slits. "Don't duck with my wife."

Holding both hands in the air, I huffed a laugh. Now that I knew about the fine for cursing in his house, Beckett's love of the word *duck* made more sense. "Liv's awesome. Everyone knows that. And Boston's all good. I'll praise the front office after the game. No sweat. I didn't realize it was an issue."

My phone vibrated in my lap, and without hesitation, I scooped it up. Fuck yeah. It was another message from my firefly.

"Right, well, if you want to grab dinner or something…"

My attention shot back to him, and I smiled. "At your house?" Fuck. The chance to see Dylan again had my heart skipping a beat.

Beckett frowned at my suggestion. "Duck off. Don't mock

my house. I was trying to be nice. Don't know why Liv won't believe me when I say you're the issue here, not me." He pushed to his feet and stomped out of the room before I could correct his misinterpretation.

Bosco looked from me to Beckett and back again. "Oh," he said. "I forgot your brother and Langfield are friends."

They were, just like our fathers were. My family's world was a small one. Not that I was part of it.

With a shrug, I downplayed the issue between Beckett and me. "Not really. He just wants me to talk him up. I used to sing Philip's praises when I was with the Metros. Looks like that's what he expects of me here."

"Yeah, because he's a dream owner." Bosco shook his head.

"Don't tell anyone I said this," I hedged, leaning closer, "but based on the trades the front of office is making, this is the team everyone will want to play for pretty soon."

"Hell yeah it is." With a fist bump, he headed back to his locker.

Finally alone once again, I unlocked my phone and read Dylan's message.

> Firefly: good luck at the game I'll be watching for my favorite view

I couldn't help my smile, and I didn't give a shit who noticed.

Dylan

12

I held the chain so the rose quartz dangled just above the white plastic stick. I waited, but again, it spun in a tight circle.

The third time's the charm, right? It was true.

I leaned down and stared at the house to-do list. Damn, it was long. And it seemed more important than ever that we get going on it now that the universe had a new plan for me.

Cortney had been consistently texting me for the past two weeks. And even though I dodged his hints as best as I could, it was clear he wanted to see me again. Now, though, there was a good chance he'd change his tune quick.

"Dylan, you okay?" Liv asked, sidling up beside me at the kitchen counter.

"Yeah." I shrugged. "I'm just pregnant."

"You're *what*?" Her voice went up ten octaves, and she snatched the pregnancy test off the counter.

Delia showed up next. "Why are we yelling?"

"Dylan's pregnant."

Delia's eyes went as wide as saucers.

I nodded and pressed my lips together. No use denying what was spelled out so clearly in front of us.

"Wait." Liv slammed the white stick onto the counter. "You didn't take this test."

"Yes, I did."

"What's going on?" Shay asked.

"I think Dylan's pregnant," Delia explained, her voice so quiet it was barely audible.

I nodded.

"We don't know that," Liv snapped.

"Yes, we do." I sighed.

Delia propped a hip against the counter and slapped the green Formica. "Who the fuck is this guy?"

"Hey, quiet. I just got Kai to sleep." Shay shook her head.

"He's the best sleeper of all our kids. He'll be fine," Delia groused. "And, I repeat, who the fuck is this guy?"

It was only ten, and there was a good chance at least a couple of the kids were only pretending to be asleep. Liam definitely wasn't down for the night. Ideally, I'd appreciate it if they'd be sorta quiet. I'd like to be the one to tell him.

He'd probably give me the *I'm disappointed in you* look he'd perfected over the years. We had a weird parenting vs. being parented relationship. I'd tried to get him to watch Gilmore Girls with me a few times so he'd understand the dynamic, but he didn't have patience for television any more than I did.

"You're pregnant?" Shay flicked her hair out of her face.

For what felt like the millionth time, I nodded.

"Have you been to a doctor? Did you start taking vitamins?" She tapped the counter, going straight into stress mode. "We should go back to smoothies…"

I scrunched my nose up and fought a gag at just the thought. That was not happening. I was pregnant, not suddenly immune to things that tasted bad.

"Dylan." Liv shut her eyes and took a deep breath.

I placed my hand over Liv's on the barf green countertop. "I know we weren't expecting this, but it's obvious the universe has a plan."

"I have plans too." Delia pulled my hand away from Liv's and squeezed it. "And mine consist of hiding this asshole's decaying maggot-ridden corpse in the trunk of my car while I help search for his body."

"Well, that ugly minivan is trash, then. You'll never get that smell out." I waved Delia's dramatics away. "He's not a bad guy, so you probably shouldn't kill him. That would be all kinds of bad karma."

"Dylan, who *is* the father?" Shay asked. "I didn't even know you were dating someone."

"I'm not, but it's okay. I'll talk to him." I didn't need Shay to worry, but I didn't know Cortney well enough to know how he'd react. He'd been pissy about Liam's father's lack of interest in his kid, but once the situation was tossed on him, he might feel differently.

"No." Liv grabbed the pregnancy test off the counter. "No. We are not doing this until you actually pee on this stick." She thrust it at me.

Shay cleared her throat and held up a hand. "Wait. You didn't take the test?"

"I did. I asked my rose quartz, and it confirmed it. Three times."

"Ah. I was under the impression we were talking about the pharmaceutical type of test," Shay clarified.

Delia narrowed her eyes on me and dropped her chin. "Pee on the fucking stick."

With a sigh, I gave in to the peer pressure. "Fine."

Not everyone trusted the universe would give them answers the way I did, so I skipped to the bathroom and did as they requested—not that it would change the outcome. Once I finished up, I capped the test and washed my hands. The girls were all sitting around the folding tables in the dining room when I wandered in and dropped the white stick in front of Liv.

Looked like I was going to have a March baby. For fifteen years, I'd figured Liam would be my one and only, but come next spring, I would be a mother of two.

With a sigh, I sank into the seat next to Shay.

"Oh my God, it's positive." Liv dropped her head into her hands.

"What's positive?" Beckett strode into the dining room with a beer in his hand. He stopped behind Liv and dropped a kiss on the top of her head. He froze halfway back to his full height when he caught sight of the pregnancy test. His eyes practically bugged out of his head. He reared back and dropped his beer bottle, causing a volcano of foam to spurt into the air.

Shay hopped up and beelined for the kitchen, hopefully in search of a towel. Good thing the dining room floor hadn't been redone yet. Or the ceilings. Besides replacing a few windows, fixing our broken step—which we'd affectionately named Trippy —and stopping the roof leak, none of the major repairs the house needed had been completed.

Damn. Maybe this wasn't such an ideal place to bring a baby home to. The universe really needed to step up and deliver us a contractor.

"I thought we said…" Beckett swallowed hard and took a deep breath. Then he focused on his wife, and his eyes softened. "Don't worry, Livy. We got this."

"No." She spun in her seat so fast she almost fell to the floor. "*No.*"

"No?" he asked.

"It's not yours." She shook her head.

"What?" Beckett's mouth fell open, and his eyes went wide. "Not *mine?*" He growled. "What the duck does that mean?"

Liv sighed. "This is the whole Joe Arden thing all over again." She chuckled. "Relax, baby. It's not yours because this isn't my test."

He cut a look at Delia. "Duck, Medusa. Please tell me you did not go back to the clinic for more kids."

Delia's glare turned ominous as she held out the half-empty beer she'd scooped up off the floor. "Don't make me dump this on you, asshole."

He held both hands out. "Okay, fair. Your body, your choice."

"You're such a dumb fuck, and yet I can't hate you." Delia shook her head. "It's not my test."

Shay came back in with two towels, and Beckett rounded on her. Of course he wouldn't think it was mine.

"Who's the father?" he asked.

"That's a great question." Crouching low, Shay sopped up the beer on the floor.

Beckett choked on what could only be explained as the air in the room. "What does that mean?" he demanded.

Shay tipped her head back and peered up at him. "I have no idea."

His eyes widened, and he huffed out a hard breath. "I had *plans*."

Shay stood up and crossed her arms.

Liv jumped to her feet. "Baby."

Beckett closed his eyes and pulled in a deep breath. He held it for several seconds before he let it out again. "No, you're right." With a shake of his head, he opened his eyes and trained them on Shay again. "Give me a list. We'll figure this out."

"A list of what?" she asked.

"Possible fathers. However many it is, we'll figure it out," Beckett assured.

"This is why we can't hate the dumbass." Delia crossed her arms. "It's not Shay's test either, you idiot."

"Me?" Shay scoffed. "I'm not pregnant. I'm not even having sex. My orgasms are all self-induced."

Beckett winced and took a step back.

"Mine too," Delia announced.

He cringed. Now they were just messing with him.

"Can we stop torturing my husband and put him out of his misery, please?" Liv asked me.

I sighed and pulled my shoulders back. "It's my test. My orgasms aren't all self-induced."

Beckett huffed and ran a hand through his hair. "You don't even leave the house. I tried—"

"I leave. I just do it at night." Flopping back into my chair, I blew out a breath. Damn, it was like being a teenager again. Beckett had that bossy parent vibe down pat.

"Who have you been sneaking out with?" he demanded. "Dammit, this wasn't part of my plan." He crossed his arms and shot me a glare.

"What plan?" Shay asked.

I waved her off before Beckett could go into it.

Beckett was always working on a half-cocked plan to help one of us with something we didn't know we needed. And he didn't ever seem to mind that, although we loved him, we didn't really want his help.

"Sometimes the universe has its own plan. It's our job to embrace it." Hoping to reassure everyone—including myself—that I had this, I plastered on what I hoped was a chillaxed smile.

"Are you telling me you don't use birth control? You just *leave it up to the universe*?" Beckett's voice cracked.

"Becks." I shook my head and ignored the glare he was shooting my way. "The universe has plans. We don't get to control them. All we can do is embrace them. The universe is blessing me with another child, and we need to welcome that gift."

"Who the duck is the father?" Beckett demanded.

Hmm. Was I ready to let the cat out of the bag? Might as well. I couldn't hide it forever. "Your catcher."

His green eyes widened, and he opened his mouth, but no sound came out.

"Don't worry. I've got it handled."

I totally did. So I didn't get why no one looked convinced.

Cortney

13

Firefly: can I come over tonight?

After two and a half weeks of text conversations initiated by me and me alone, *Dylan* texted *me* first. And it wasn't even a random *hi*. Hell no, she wanted to meet up.

"What has you whistling this early?" Damiano asked as I wandered into the bullpen to warm him up for today's afternoon game.

Shit, I needed to tone it down. Otherwise, by the time we took the field at one, the whole team would be doing the *you got laid last night, didn't you?* thing.

"Nothing in particular." I shrugged. "Life is just good." Sitting, I snagged my leg guards from my bag. The right one was on top, but I pushed it over and picked up the left one so I could clip it on first.

Damiano tossed the ball into the air, watching me. "What would happen if you started with the right guard instead of the left?"

I looked him in the eyes. "The earth would tilt off its axis.

That would lead to climate change, which would melt the polar ice caps. The amount of water in the ocean would rise so high that it would flood most of the coastal areas in the world. Animals and people all over would die and rot in the water, causing diseases to ravage the earth. Crops would wither in the heat, food would become scarce, and the portion of the population that didn't die from flooding and disease would starve."

The ball hit the grass and rolled away as Damiano gaped at me.

I turned back to my left leg and clipped the guard from bottom to top, like I did every time.

"Bro, I thought you were going to say we'd lose."

I chuckled. "You need more creativity than that, man." Then I sighed. I didn't normally hide my issues from my team. Once the right guard was clipped on, I stood. "Honestly? If I put the right on before the left, I'd stress about it being put on wrong. The anxiety would make it hard to focus on the game. I'd end up taking them off and starting again just so I could focus on what I needed to do."

"That's—"

"A little bit obsessive."

"I was thinking stressful."

I nodded and grabbed my chest guard. "I have some obsessive tendencies and anxiety. I manage both. Might make me a bit odd." I shrugged and looked him in the eye. "But it also makes me good at what I do. I focus on the batters' averages and history. I harp on it until I know them inside and out, and it makes calling pitches less of a guessing game. My calls are based on statistics, not hunches."

His only response was a tip of his chin.

"And it will make you great, because I'll teach you." I locked my jaw, waiting for his reaction.

"Respect, man." Damiano raised his fist.

I bumped it, then once I had my face mask on, I moved down the sand to squat at the plate. "You on fire today, or are nerves eating at ya?"

He laughed. "Always nerves, man. I'm waiting for the day I don't burp butterflies during the national anthem."

His throw ripped through the air and smacked into my glove, forcing me to acknowledge the burn.

"Ya never want the game to get old, Dragon." I tossed the ball back.

"Truth."

We had just finished loosening his shoulder when a young brunette in a tight skirt showed up. Damiano whistled under his breath.

"Mr. Miller, Mr. Langfield sent me to get you," she called across the bullpen.

"Langfield's a lucky man." Damiano shook his head.

"He is," I agreed, "but I'd bet money he doesn't even see *that* woman."

Beckett only had eyes for his wife these days. I unsnapped my gear and tossed it back into my bag, focusing on keeping my breaths calm, because I had no fucking idea why I was being called across the street to the owner's office.

"I didn't catch your name," I said as I followed the woman down the tunnel to the side entrance that led to the Langfield Corp office.

"Hannah." Her words were clipped and screamed *not interested.* That was fine. Neither was I.

"Beckett say what he wanted?" Bossman's motive for calling me to his office was my sole focus at the moment.

"*Mr. Langfield.*" She frowned, reminding me that the man wasn't my brother's friend in this scenario but my boss.

I had no reason to apologize, so I kept my mouth shut and held the front door open for her while I waited for her to say more.

"He's tight lipped."

I wiped my sweaty palms on my warm-ups. *Damn it, man. Getting called into the office doesn't have to mean anything.* There hadn't been any buzz about being traded, and I was fitting in well with the team. Almost like I'd always played for the Revs. Not to mention the pitching rotation was on fire. But with the Metros, none of that had mattered. What if he did trade me? I'd have to start over again. What team in their right mind wanted a thirty-five-year-old catcher?

Not to mention it could put me states away from Dylan.

Dylan.

What if this wasn't about baseball at all? Maybe he thought I was bothering her. Except she'd finally asked to hang out, so I hadn't been reading her interest wrong, right? What if she wanted to see me so she could tell me to my face that she wanted me to leave her alone? I hadn't been missing hints in her texts, had I? Would she get Beckett involved? My heart pounded harder at the possibilities. There were too many.

My feet stopped halfway up the stairs, and I swallowed a lump so big I could barely breathe around it.

"Mr. Miller?" Hannah called from a few steps ahead.

Forcing a smile, I pushed myself to follow her the rest of the way up and then down a long hall and through an archway. By the time we made it to Liv's office, I was dripping with sweat and my heart was threatening to burst from my ribcage. As we passed, I searched for her, but the room was empty. I didn't know whether that was good or bad.

Hannah stopped ahead of me and rapped on another door down the hall, then pushed it open. "Mr. Miller for you."

The click of the door behind me was the only noise as Beckett looked up. He pushed to his feet. And glowered. "What the duck is wrong with you?"

"A lot of things, but I need context so I can narrow down

which issue I'll have to explain to you." I smirked. Smart-ass was my armor and I wore it well.

"Sit down, Man Bun." He pointed to a chair.

I sat in the other one, just because I could, still keeping my anxiety under wraps.

"I thought I could trust you." He glared.

Trust me?

"What the hell, Beckett? I've been singing your praises for the last three days. Not just you, but upper management. Have you not seen any of the clips? Every word has been about how the team is the future of baseball. I've done nothing but pimp myself out to Boston. Give me a fucking break." I tossed my hands into the air. "Do you want me to kiss your ass on camera?"

"You're not kissing anyone ever again," he snapped. "Do you not understand what it means to have responsibilities?"

I blinked and sat back in the chair. That was a new one. Never in my life had I been accused of being irresponsible. I was always the one being told to lighten the hell up. And fuck if I knew what that had to do with the team. I'd been on time for every practice, every game, every meeting. I hadn't missed a single one. Hell, I'd been putting in extra hours with analytics and film.

"Ever used a condom before?" He smacked the table with his fist.

What the fuck? I ran my hand over my jaw, at a loss for words. This man had officially lost me. What did condoms have to do with the team?

I pulled myself up a little straighter and cleared my throat. "I don't think it's my place to talk to the media about safe sex."

"No, but you should practice it." Beckett hit me with the Langfield glare again.

I couldn't disagree with him. Everyone should. But I was still scrambling to find the point of his ranting. Because I wasn't one of those guys who was all "baby, we don't need a condom." I used them. Full stop. Every time.

Beckett was getting more heated by the second, but maybe we needed to take a step back. This man was my boss, and he was also something to Dylan. What exactly, I didn't know. There wasn't an easy label, but there was enough of a connection that I didn't want to be on his shit list on that end of things either.

"Let's start over. I'm lost. I was nervous as fuck coming up here, stressed that you were going to tell me you're trading me or that I'd overstepped by texting Dylan." I lifted my hands and shrugged. "And I don't want bad blood on either side of this."

His eyes narrowed. "Dylan's pregnant and she's keeping the baby."

The words echoed around the room so palpably I swore I could see them bouncing off each surface in slow motion. But they didn't make sense. My brain couldn't compute their meaning for several seconds, but when it finally did, shock hit me like an electrical current.

As far as I knew, she didn't even want Beckett to know we'd slept together. Yet she went to him with this news instead of me? My hands fisted at that idea.

"She told you—"

"Not on purpose," he backpedaled. "I saw the test when she was talking to Liv, and she admitted it was yours…"

He kept going, but if she confirmed it, then nothing else mattered. I couldn't stop the million concerns that hit me smack in the chest. All the worries, all the stress, all the ways my life was going to change.

Beckett's lips were moving, but damn, the blood was rushing in my ears so loud I couldn't make out a single word.

I was going to be a father. How the fuck was I going to do that? With my schedule, I spent more time away than I did at home. Even when I was in Boston, my apartment couldn't be considered kid-friendly by any stretch of the imagination. I had a balcony that was forty floors up, for Christ's sake. Were the bars of the railing spread out so far a kid could slip through? Did a contraption exist that would eliminate that risk? I'd heard of *kid-proofing*, but I hadn't done any research on the subject because I hadn't planned on having kids for years still. What should I be concerned about when it came to Dylan's pregnancy? Beyond *don't drink or do drugs*, I knew next to nothing. Wasn't there a thing about cats and cheese? Fuck. I'd have to google it. I'd have to google it all, because right now, I didn't even know *what* I was supposed to worry about, and that freaked me out more than anything.

I was having a baby. How would this work? Because I *would* be involved. A world didn't exist where I wouldn't be *actively in* my kid's life. Whether I was ready for it or not, I *was* having a kid—with Dylan.

As soon as her name hit my brain, the tension coiling my muscles tight released. This meant a permanent connection to a woman who fascinated me. To an intelligent, sexy-as-hell woman I had a shit ton of respect for.

Maybe I didn't know everything about Dylan, but I'd never met a woman I wanted to learn about more than her.

Was the timing ideal? Fuck no. My career would be over before I knew it. I was lost when it came to what I should do with my life after baseball, and in a perfect world, I'd have it all figured out before I thought about kids. But lately, every time I thought about the future, all I saw was red hair and amber eyes. So was it possible the woman was right, even if the timing was off?

Hell yeah.

I took a deep breath and let it out again. I could figure out the rest. Dylan was what mattered right now.

"So you're moving in."

I'd missed every one of Beckett's words except those last four. However, no. That house was a disaster. There was no way it was safe for a baby. Fuck. It wasn't a safe place for the woman carrying my baby either.

"No."

Beckett glowered but didn't speak, like he thought giving me the stink eye would force me to comply.

I scoffed. "That house needs to be condemned."

"Actually, the city says it's habitable." Beckett leaned back in his chair. "They have a CO. It's asbestos and mold free."

Was he kidding? "Beckett, some of the rooms don't have *walls.*"

He waved a hand. "We'll keep the baby out of those."

"One of them is *Dylan's.*"

"It will move up to the top of the to-do list."

"You have rabid animals in the house." And it wasn't just one anymore. Apparently, Junior had given birth to four babies recently.

He raised a finger. "That's a temporary blip. As soon as the babies are old enough, we'll move them out of the house."

"When is that?" I asked.

He winced but didn't answer.

I shook my head at the idiocy. My place might need child-proofing, but that would take a week, not years. "I have plenty of room for both Dylan and Liam at my place."

At the mention of Liam, he cocked a brow.

"Yes, Beckett, I know her son's name." Although that was about the extent of my knowledge base when it came to him. Teenager, red hair. And then nothing. Definitely needed to ask more questions about him. And officially meet him. Shit, how was I going to bond with a teenager?

Pursing his lips, he dropped his elbows to his desk and angled closer. "Dylan's not leaving the other moms."

I supposed her comments about her friends *did* imply that. But that was before she was unexpectedly knocked up. Her situation had changed.

"They have a pact. To live together and raise their kids as a family unit."

That tracked with what Dylan mentioned that night at my apartment. And again, my thoughts spiraled. What if she didn't want my help with our child? What if she didn't think I'd be a good father? What if this baby inherited my anxiety and tendency to overthink? What if my child obsessed like I did?

Sucking in a deep breath, I reined in my whirling thoughts. If any of that was true, there was no person on earth more equipped to help him or her learn how to handle the issues than I was.

"Might be true. I guess we'll see." I shrugged and smirked. But I was already formulating the conversation I wanted to have with her. More than anything, I wanted to be around to help and support her during her pregnancy. I needed to know that she and the baby were okay. Because so many things could go wrong.

My palms were sweaty and my chest squeezed tight at just the thought of what could happen. Again, I took a deep breath to stop my errant thoughts from spinning out.

We could figure something out. My apartment had four bedrooms. It was fairly organized and safe, with plenty of space. Her room didn't even have walls. But if she was set on staying there, then we'd get her room fixed up.

Beckett's eyes narrowed. "If you don't move into that ducking house with us"—he scanned the room and froze when his attention caught on something behind me—"then I'll trade you to the Dodgers."

My stomach tumbled. "Los Angeles?"

He smiled. "Try raising a kid when you live on opposite sides of the ducking county."

"Beckett, you can't—"

The man was controlling, but he wasn't normally a spiteful prick. At the moment, though, I wanted to throw him through the massive windows that overlooked the field behind him.

"The duck I can't." He sat back, the leather cushion beneath him creaking as he did. "Nine months out of the year, you'll be three thousand miles away. They even have spring training out west. So, you'll be in Arizona in March. Probably miss the baby's birth."

Oh no I wouldn't. He wasn't taking away my chance to be involved in my child's life. I'd be there for every important moment. Starting now. If my child and their mother were going to live in that disaster of a house, then I'd be there too, making it as safe as possible. That was my job now. To protect them.

The idea of leaving my future in Beckett's hands suddenly terrified me. I needed to control where I would finish my baseball career. My career was no longer my sole focus. I had one, maybe two more years in me before I retired, then a lifetime with my family.

I cleared my throat as I sat back in my chair, channeling my *I don't give a shit* vibe. "I'll move in on one condition."

He cocked his brow and laced his fingers together in front of him.

"I want my contract with the team rewritten." I crossed my ankle over my knee. "Two years guaranteed money. You pay even if you trade me."

He lifted his chin like he was ready to agree, but I hadn't gotten to the meat of it.

"*And* if I'm traded, I get a fifty-million-dollar bonus paid out over two years *by the Revs*."

"That would kill my salary cap." Beckett frowned.

"So don't trade me." I shrugged, still affecting my best nonchalant demeanor even as my gut churned. The need to be in Boston was as crucial as my need for air. If I was here with Dylan, then I could make sure she was okay.

Beckett ran his tongue over his teeth and fisted a hand on his desk. Finally, he sighed. The sound had my shoulders loosening instantly.

He gave me a clipped nod. "I'll get it drawn up. If you last six weeks in our house, then we'll sign."

My heart rate slowed as I held out my hand to shake his.

With that settled, it was time to talk to Dylan. Because I was going to be a father.

Holy fuck.

Dylan

14

"Y ou can't stay home from work just to keep an eye on me. You'll die of boredom."

Liv and I had just finished morning stretches with Shay before she and Delia headed off to work. Adeline was next to me, using chalk to turn the step blue while Finn and Kai rigged up a rope they were sure would work as a booby trap for anyone who got too close to the house.

My best friend smiled across the stoop at me. "Not every day. Just today." Liv tucked a tendril of dark hair that had fallen from her bun behind her ear. "Hannah's there with Beckett anyway. How much trouble could he get into?"

"It's Becks," I reminded her with a chuckle.

Tilting my way, she squeezed my forearm. "I know, but you need me today."

No I didn't. She was the one who was stressed. I was only placating her. "I'm good. I texted Cortney this morning, and I'm not worried about telling him. No matter what his reaction is, I can handle this. If he decides he doesn't want anything to do with the baby, I can do this by myself."

Her grip on my arm tightened. "You're not by yourself. You have all of us."

That comment made my heart feel a little lighter. "You're right. I've got the best support system. I'm good. I promise."

"I just didn't want it to bring back Brett vibes."

I shuddered. "I'm not twenty anymore. An unexpected pregnancy isn't going to make me dye my hair brown, dress like a senator, and act like a debutant. Trust me. Plus, Cortney's not like that."

She shrugged, and the neckline of her blue scoop neck shirt slipped off one shoulder. "I actually don't know Cortney that well since he's new to the team," she said, tugging her shirt back into place, "but everyone knows the Miller family."

I cocked my head and scrutinized her, my sunglasses slipping down my nose at the movement. "Miller family?"

"Yeah. Like the Miller Foundation, Miller Real Estate, MD Trauma Center, and Miller Racing?" She ticked off the names on her fingers.

I'd heard of all those things. "What does that have to do with Cortney?"

Liv leaned forward and rested her forearms on her thighs. "Cortney *Miller*."

Not willing to give her any reaction while I processed the information, I just shrugged. But internally, every nerve ending in my body went on alert. Liv was right; everyone did know the Miller family. They owned half of New York. Their names were emblazoned on buildings all over the city. Their net worth was probably ten times Brett's family's, and their money was far older.

I hadn't made the connection. Cortney seemed down to earth. He played for a professional baseball team—he didn't own it. He didn't have a driver, just some weird purple car. His hair brushed his shoulders, like he hadn't bothered to have it cut in years. Hell, he wore *Teenage Mutant Ninja Turtle* boxer briefs. He drank beer and joked. From what I'd seen, he was nothing like the prick I dated in college.

"Dylan." Liv put a hand on my knee.

I worked hard not to flinch at the touch. It was one of comfort, but only because she was thinking the same thing I was. That once again, I wouldn't be good enough for my child's grandparents.

"Auntie Dylan." Collette opened the front door and peeked out. "We need your help."

Saved by the child.

The door opened wider, and Phoebe appeared. "The hands are hard."

That was the point. If I didn't want them to be stumped, then I wouldn't have given them a puzzle in bones. But like my dad had when I was a child, I'd given them a challenge to keep them entertained.

"Can you help us? So many look the same." Collette frowned. She disliked being bested by anyone or anything, but she wouldn't be for long. Once I showed them the secrets, helped them discover the slight differences in each bone, they'd figure it out quickly.

"Sure." I hopped up and headed in. The human body consisted of only two hundred and six pieces, but the way they fit together took a special understanding.

"This would be easier if we could use Google," Phoebe complained as she took her seat at one of the two folding tables we had set up in the dining room. She had the left hand, and Collette, who dropped into the folding chair across from her, had the right.

"If you did that, then what would you learn?" I dropped my sunglasses onto the table and pulled Phoebe's tray of bones toward me.

"That AI is the future and we should all embrace it?"

"Why give the robots the power?" I cocked my brow, knowing that would get them.

The twins looked at one another for a long moment, then simultaneously turned back to me.

"Hmm," Phoebe said, her eyes wide and full of awe. Victory. They both leaned in.

"Okay. Teach us. We need the power."

With a smile, I got to work showing them the differences in the bones and how they fit together. We took a lunch break, but otherwise, they were tuned in and working hard, and by three, they had the hands and arms finished.

"Look at you girls. Future doctors?" Delia asked as she came in. With her new job at the prosecutor's office, even Saturdays meant she had to put in a few hours.

"I don't want to be a doctor." Collette's braids fell over her shoulders as she shook her head. "But we will own the robots."

"Yeah, because we have the power." Phoebe picked up her skeleton arm and headed out front to hang it on Bobbie with her twin hot on her heels.

"Should I be concerned about them owning robots and having the power?" Delia asked.

I chuckled. "Are you?"

She pursed her lips for a moment, then shook her head. "No. Mostly, I'm proud."

I stood and gave her shoulder a quick pat. "Exactly. I'm taking Liam out. You've got your two and Kai until Shay gets home." I passed off the kids, then headed to my bathroom for a quick shower.

Although I hadn't mentioned it to anyone else yet, I was working on a plan for the fall. Now, though, things had changed. Could it still fall into place the way I hoped it would?

"It's only one avenue and two blocks, right?" Liam asked, tipping his hair out of his eyes. He needed a trim, but he'd mentioned a while ago that he wanted to let it grow out. If he changed his mind, he'd tell me, so I didn't bother pointing it out.

That meant I was stuck watching him be the clichéd teenager who spent half his day tossing his hair out of his eyes.

At least he didn't have his headphones around his neck today. At home, they were a constant accessory. But the kid knew me well enough to know I expected him to be tuned into our conversation. He and I rarely got time together alone like this.

"Yeah, it's close enough to walk, even in winter."

"That's a plus," he said, getting ahead of me on the sidewalk in front of the row of brownstones.

"Dude, slow down." I had to practically jog to keep up with my son's newly long legs. He heaved a sigh, but he thankfully and quite dramatically slowed his Converse-clad feet to a pace that even Adeline's chubby legs could keep up with. "You seem excited."

He shrugged. "I know it's lame, but I miss working at the preschool."

"Not lame. It was a change of scenery. An aspect to home-schooling you don't get anymore."

He side-eyed me and tipped his head, sending his hair back again. "Ma, our house is a freaking preschool every day."

Who knew where my son got his flair for drama. Wasn't me.

"Think it'll happen by September like you hoped?" he asked.

Of its own volition, my hand floated to my stomach over my white sundress. This pregnancy had the potential to be a bump in the road on our way to opening the first of a grouping of preschools in Boston by September. "We'll see."

Twenty minutes later, it was clear that this was *not* the place.

"No outside space at all." Zoey, my partner in Little Fingers, was connected through video call so she could scout out the site as well. "And the rooms are too small."

"Hell yeah, they are," Liam said beside me.

"Sorry." I shook my head at the real estate agent. "I hate that we wasted your time."

"Not a waste. We'll keep looking," he assured me as he led us out the front door.

"I don't know that we'll get this done by fall, Zoey."

She and I started Little Fingers as one preschool when Liam was four. Now we had multiple satellites, each with a wait list, in Northern Jersey. My income from Little Fingers was what allowed me to stay home with my friends' kids.

"Without the right space, the date doesn't matter." Zoey shrugged. "We'll know when we find it. The schools here are running like well-oiled machines. We're good. It'll be great when we can expand, but we can't force it. It'll happen when the universe wants it to happen."

"That's true. I'll let you know if we find other options."

Once we ended the call, I waved to our agent, then turned to Liam, who was leaning against the building and hunched over his phone. "What's so riveting?"

Liam looked up and shrugged. "Nothing."

"Hmm. There's the lip purse," I teased. "Want to try again?"

"I don't purse my lips when I lie." He pushed off the wall and stood to his full height. "Are we getting dinner? Aunt Shay is making organic tofu and turkey meatballs with lentil pasta, and neither of us is gonna want to eat that." My son had learned his distraction techniques from the best.

"Pub's right there." I tipped my chin toward O'Hannigan's. "Want to get a burger?"

"Or two." With a smile, Liam headed across the street to the bar.

Keeping pace with him, I tried again. "Want to tell me what you were looking at on your phone that had you frowning?"

His entire head rolled along with his eyes. I was so uncool. "It's not a thing. Miller just had a walk off home run to win the game."

"I thought you liked him." I held the door and let Liam go in first.

"Before," he grumbled. "When he was a Metro."

"What if I like him now that he's a Rev?" I asked, brows raised.

I wasn't sure of my feelings for him, honestly, but the Cortney I'd hung out with a few weeks ago had been someone that I could definitely like. The Miller family, though? That notion was intimidating. I hadn't had time to analyze the implications since Liv filled me in.

Liam stopped halfway to the host stand and spun to face me. "Like him *how?*" he asked, flicking his red hair back out of habit.

My noncommittal shrug made him scowl. But then the hostess came to my rescue and guided us to a table. Thankfully, once we were seated and had ordered our burgers, the conversation eased into lighter topics like cars and comics. My son didn't harp on anything long, and although I'd have to tell him about Cortney and his new sibling eventually, I needed to know where things stood first. So until I talked to the man himself, I'd keep the news to myself.

Dylan

15

Liv: Warning - Beckett came home early and is acting weird. I think he's up to something.

Delia: Your husband is always up to something, but if he starts breaking shit in my house again, I will make him hang out with the snakes in the crawl space.

Liv: No I think it's about Dylan and Cortney.

Beckett: You could at least talk about me in a message thread I'm not included in.

Liv: Oops. Ha ha. I meant to.

Me: oh no we wouldn't want to leave you out of our chats becks

Delia: Yeah. Where's the fun in that? This way, we've got someone who's always wrong.

Beckett: GIF of eye roll

Beckett: Not funny.

Beckett: What time is Cortney coming over?

Liv: SEE? I knew you were trying to butt in.

Me: I'm going to cortneys so unless becks follows me like an adorable vampire bat he can't

Beckett: What?

Shay: Vampire bat?

Me: Yes that's how I picture becks following me like a cute little bat

Shay: Bats aren't cute.

Delia: I think you mean all in black and flapping his mouth instead of his wings.

Me: GIF of a cute baby bat

Me: see the resemblance? Its adorable they could be siblings

Delia: I'm not seeing it

Me: black hair and big eyes

Beckett: I don't look like a ducking bat.

Dylan
16

"What are you doing here?" My son's voice echoed through the foyer into the kitchen.

There was a muffled reply, but I couldn't make out the voice over the tap of my sandals on the plywood floor. The sound made my chest tighten just a little. There was not one room in this house that was baby safe. I wasn't usually a worrier, but the safety of the children in my care had always been a top concern, whether at the preschool or at home. Lucky for Adeline, she was almost three. Otherwise this place would be a danger zone for her too.

"She has plans, so you're out of luck."

Before I could get to the foyer, the house vibrated with the force that Liam used to slam the door. He flicked his hair back and glared at me when I stepped up behind him.

"What the hell?" I asked.

"You said you were going out, so am I wrong?" he demanded, but he didn't stop me from opening the door again.

Who was he being so snotty with? Even his own deadbeat father didn't garner this type of attitude from my son.

Throwing the solid oak door open, I scanned the stoop and

turned back to Liam, still waiting for an answer, but then my brain registered who was standing on the porch, and I whirled around again and came face-to-face with Cortney Miller.

"Uh." I hesitated, looking from my scowling son to Cortney and back again. I was headed to Cortney's place tonight. That was the plan. So why was he here? I didn't want to have this conversation on the front porch, so I waved him in. "I thought I was coming by your—"

"I knew this was a thing." My son yanked at the Beats headphones around his neck. "He was staring at you like a dumbass in the locker room last month. Everyone saw him."

Cortney opened his mouth to respond, but I placed my hand on his arm. "Liam, stop." In the end, it didn't matter where we had the conversation, just that we talked. Preferably in private. But before I could say more, Beckett walked in.

He folded his arms over his chest and scowled. "Man Bun."

"Bossman." Cortney cocked a brow.

"Becks, leave." I sighed.

Last night, after a lot of ranting, he had promised to let me handle this, so he needed to make himself scarce.

"Baby, leave them be," a high-pitched Liv-like voice called from the kitchen.

Beckett's head snapped in that direction, then he stomped away.

I slumped in relief. The idiot should know his own wife's voice better than that. I'd been playing with ventriloquism for almost twenty years, and I was good at throwing my voice, but Liv's was really hard to copy. Regardless, I'd take the reprieve now that he was gone.

"When's he going to realize that's not Aunt Liv?" Liam shook his head.

Cortney flashed him a genuine smile. "I wouldn't have known that wasn't Olivia."

"Then you're a moron." Liam huffed.

Cortney, to his credit, kept his face neutral and only let a slight sigh slip.

"Why are you copying my voice?" Liv demanded, coming down the stairs.

Shit. My plan had been to empty the room, not create a bigger audience for this conversation.

Liv crossed her arms over her chest and eyed Cortney. "Oh no, this is not good."

"Nothing like a good old-fashioned welcome home." Cortney shook his head, sending his hair dancing around his shoulders.

If he lived here, this would have been a quiet welcome, but honestly, it was probably worse that this was how we treated our guests. At times like this, it was obvious why the neighbors watched us so warily.

"No." She shook her head, one hand holding the banister in a death grip. "*Beckett.*"

"How are you all over this ducking house?" Beckett stomped back into the foyer.

"Tell me you didn't tell him," she demanded.

"About what?" Liam asked.

Beckett only winced in response.

Liv raced down the stairs and smacked her husband's arm. "You promised to let her break the baby news."

"*Baby?*" My son's eyes were narrowed to slits as he tossed his hair back and looked from me to Cortney.

My heart clenched at his expression. Dammit. His jaw was locked tight and his face had gone red.

"Mom and Beckett are having a baby?" Winnie peeked around the corner from the kitchen so all that was visible was her head.

"*No.*" Liv spun to her daughter for an instant before returning her glare to her husband, who now stood with his arms crossed, wearing a frown directed at Cortney.

Winnie came around the corner and stomped her foot. "Then who's having a baby?"

"What the heck? I thought we weren't telling the kids yet," Shay said, coming from the lower level.

"I can't believe this." Liam hung his head.

"Look what you did!" Liv snapped at her husband, who was focused on his feet now.

Cortney's attention was bouncing from one person to the next, and his eyes were getting wider by the second. None of this was going the right way. I probably should have worried more about telling him about the baby, because when I said *no matter how it goes*, I hadn't taken into consideration the way my family could so easily turn a conversation into a dumpster fire.

Ignoring the chaos, I turned to my son, who was frowning at me.

"Can we talk later?" I mouthed.

He gave me a sullen glare, then he was gone, disappearing down the stairs.

"Samson," I whispered.

Cortney studied me silently, his shoulders relaxing slightly.

"We have a rooftop deck. Let's go up there."

His answering smile was soft. It took quite a person to make it through the kind of chaos only our family could create and still look so chill. In his presence again, it was easy to remember why I liked him.

Together, we made our way up the three flights of stairs, leaving the craziness behind. The rooftop space made the idea of babyproofing the house seem less daunting. This area was in almost perfect condition. The roof deck had already been redone since we'd wanted to enjoy it over the summer, and the railings had all been replaced. If not for the four floors between us and the ground, it would be the safest spot here. But mostly, it showed that when my friends and I had a common goal, we got shit done.

With months before our little one's arrival, we had time to get this house whipped into shape.

"Want me to turn this on?" Cortney pointed to the gas firepit that was built into the center of the table in front of the small sofa.

"Sure."

The view from up here, especially at night, made this my favorite part of the house. Hayden Park was gorgeous in the summer. The park lights cast a glow on the pink and purple gardens in full bloom. The bright city made stars almost nonexistent, but the skyline was its own kind of beauty. And the energy of the space was calm, like a cozy blanket or my go-to sweater.

Cortney sank into the cushion next to me, and the spicy scent of his cologne floated around us. He twisted until he was resting his arm along the back of the sofa just behind my shoulder. A part of me wished I could lean on him, just for a minute. But he and I didn't have that type of relationship.

I had three incredible friends to lean on. Men had never been that kind of support to me.

"That might be my favorite of your smiles so far."

"Hmm?" The fire flickered in front of us. The blue cascaded into oranges, reflecting onto the glass beads around the flames.

"Most of your smiles are high energy and excitement." He brushed a thumb across my temple as he moved my hair back. Then he dropped his hand to the cushion between us. It was so close I swore I could feel his heat, but he wasn't quite touching my leg. "Don't get me wrong. Every one of them is gorgeous. But that last one? It was all peace. Like you finally let out a breath you've been holding for a long time."

He studied my face. His blue eyes dropped momentarily to my lips before lifting again. I'd never had anyone watch me the way he did. So intently. His focus was razor sharp. It made my breath catch.

"I was on cloud nine when you texted me this morning."

Pursing my lips, I raised my brows. "And then Beckett told you why, and it wasn't so great anymore."

He shook his head, his brow furrowing. "I wasn't qualifying that statement, Dylan. Whatever the reason, I've been waiting for the day you'd text me first."

The deep baritone of his voice echoed through me, warming me. He dropped his gaze again, this time to my stomach. I wouldn't show for weeks still, but my hand automatically moved to rest over my lower abdomen.

He cleared his throat and brought his attention back to my face. "When did you find out?"

"Yesterday." With my other hand, I slid the rose quartz along its chain, using the motion to center myself. Although I hadn't allowed the thought of this conversation to stress me out all day, I was on edge now, wondering what he was thinking. "I probably should have realized sooner. I'm just not—"

"Dylan." He rested his big hand on my thigh, sending a zap coursing up my leg. The strong, warm weight of it against me was heaven. I dropped my necklace and swallowed, taking in the contrast of his tan fingers against my pale skin.

"I'm not judging or accusing."

With a deep breath, I forced myself to meet his eye. The fire danced, reflecting in his blue irises. "You're not questioning? You're a famous athlete."

Brett's reaction, the immediate *it's not mine*, weighed heavily on my mind and on my heart. He and I had been dating exclusively for almost eight months when I got pregnant with Liam. Yet he'd made me prove that Liam was his son. From what I knew of Cortney, he was nothing like Brett, but now that I'd put that thought out there, dread blanketed me.

He moved his hand from my leg. The loss of his heat was almost painful. My heart sank. But instead of pulling away like I thought, he wrapped that same hand around the back of my neck and ran his thumb along my cheek.

"Dylan." My name was a whisper. "I trust that you'd tell me if there was a chance it wasn't mine."

His eyes burned into me. The connection between us hadn't lessened. Not after a month; not after unexpected, stressful news.

I swallowed and licked my lips, making sure to keep my focus fixed on his face. "There's not."

His mouth lifted in a not quite smile, then he leaned in and pressed his warm lips to my forehead. He pulled in a long breath through his nose and held me close. For one second, I felt protected, cared for. Although I would have never said I craved those things. But now I wanted to hold on to this feeling, this moment.

All too soon, though, he released me. And the loss of his touch left an ache in my chest.

His blond hair brushed along his shoulders as he sat back. My fingers itched to run through it. It was odd the way my body craved a physical connection to him.

"I want to be as involved as you and my schedule will allow."

With one statement, I was snapped back to the very permanent physical connection I now had to this man. That was why we were here.

"I'll do my best to schedule doctor's appointments around your baseball schedule if you want to come to them."

He frowned. "That's not what I meant." The tip of his pointer finger circled one of my red curls. "Tomorrow at noon, I leave for a five-day road stretch. For the two days after I get back, I'll be at the stadium all day. I have a slow week for all-star break after that, then I head right into the grind." His jaw was tight now, and he was leaning in just a fraction. "Seventy percent of my time between now and October will be consumed by baseball. Another fifteen will be dedicated to sleep. I want to spend the rest of that time with you and our baby."

I tipped my head, inadvertently tugging on the curl he still had wrapped around his finger.

He released my hair and dipped his chin. "Sorry."

I shook my head. "It's fine."

"Give me a chance to be really involved. Not just meet you at the doctor. Please, Dylan."

"You live across town," I argued quietly, focusing on the cushion behind him. "And I'm not leaving—"

"I'm not asking you to move."

Forcing myself to make eye contact, I asked, "What are you saying?" He wasn't just asking me to hang out from time to time. But what did he want?

"Let me move in."

My heart stuttered in my chest, and I jerked back against the sofa. I'd avoided relationships since college. It was no secret that I was a lot to deal with. Although my friends loved and supported me, and my dad and brother had welcomed me back with open arms and would do it again in a heartbeat, Cortney's wealthy family would likely have some choice things to say if he brought someone like me around. I didn't fit into that world, and the last time I tried, I'd found out quickly that I wasn't enough.

"I'm not saying get married, and I'm not asking for a permanent commitment. But we should get to know each other." He rushed the words out. "I'm just asking you to allow me to be here."

Why on earth would he want to move into *this* house? He'd been here three times, and each of his visits had been utter chaos. That was our norm. Plus, the house was falling down around us. Beckett barely put up with it, and he *loved* Liv.

Realization hit me at the reminder of that man. Then, suddenly, the truth of things became clearer. This had Beckett written all over it. "Just because Beckett comes up—"

Cortney pressed a finger to my lips. "Beckett owns the team I play for, and he's a family friend, but he doesn't control me. I make my own decisions. Always have. So, please, will you let me be here? If you say no, I'll accept that. But I want a chance to bond with my child and their *mother*." He cleared the emotion from his throat. "I want to come home and see you before bed. I want to get up in the morning and see you before I go in. Watch our child grow. Feel them kick. Hell"—he tossed an arm in the air—"I want to run out at two a.m. because you need ice cream." He entwined his fingers with mine and studied me with genuine affection. "I want to be a part of this. But in the end, it's your call."

Maybe I shouldn't have believed him, but in the moment, I did.

Cortney

17

She didn't pull her small hand out of mine. That was a good sign. But there was hesitation in her eyes. It made sense. This was a big ask. But didn't she feel the connection between us?

Sparks shot up my arm every time I touched her. That wasn't my norm. She was different. *This* was different. I wanted her to see that.

But maybe it would take her some time. My dad's favorite mantra echoed through my head. *Don't say it, prove it.* Maybe that was what Dylan needed. Showing up here tonight might have been rash, but once I'd walked into my apartment after the game, the need to see her was too much to ignore.

She heaved a sigh. "You swear this suggestion to move in has nothing to do with Beckett?"

Easy. "It's about you." The truth spilled out automatically, but there was more to it than that. "And our future child." Although he or she was still an abstract idea in my brain. I'd need a little time to let the truth of it sink in.

Every fleck of gold in her eyes shone in the firelight as she scrutinized me.

"What will your family say?"

The question surprised me. I wasn't sure why. As a Miller, I should consider the family name in almost every situation. But this one? None of my family would expect me to plan around it.

My partner. My family. That was mine.

I cleared my throat and gave her some honesty. "My mother will be ecstatic about a grandchild. Probably overly so."

She pulled her hand from mine and ran it over her face. "I wish I remembered anything about your family."

Huh. I didn't. I liked that she was unaffected by the name. That the Miller name, brand, and money didn't matter to her. That wasn't usually the case with women.

"I have a brother and a sister. Both older."

She hadn't turned away from me for the last several minutes, but her gaze held an almost shyness that I'd never seen from her and didn't understand. From the moment I first spoke to her, Dylan had been nothing but confident. Now, though, when my family was the topic of discussion, she was almost timid.

"My brother is married, but they decided against having kids." I shook my head. Jamie and Clint had made the call years ago. Parenting wasn't their thing. No matter how much they loved children. I had heard a lot of *make us uncles* jokes over the years. Neither of them would complain about having a niece or nephew. "My sister is married to her job. Not sure whether that'll ever change. But you know moms. They all want grandkids."

Dylan's thin shoulder lifted before it fell. "My dad loves having Liam around so they can tinker with cars together."

"Liam likes cars?" I tried to tamp down on my excitement at the prospect, but I loved a garage. Building cars, fixing problems. I'd grown up turning wrenches, and it had always held my attention.

She dipped her head, averting her gaze. "My dad's a mechanic. He owns his own garage, so they hang out there."

Perfect. That was my way in. Liam hated me now, but we

had a common interest, and I'd use it to help me connect with him. I could see us in my garage space downtown under the hood of my Charger. Or maybe we could pick up something to work on together. He'd be driving in a year or so. The kid would need a car. That might be overstepping, but I really liked the idea of getting to know Liam. Bonding with him.

"My brother was never into cars, so my dad loves having Liam around to get his hands dirty with."

Her voice jarred me back to the conversation. "And your mom?"

"She died. An accident when I was three."

"I'm sorry."

"I don't remember her. Just the stories Dad tells." She turned back to the orange flames as her teeth worried on her lower lip. "So your parents...they'll be excited?"

They'd probably have a lot to say on the matter, especially since neither was ever short of words. They'd be anxious to meet Dylan, but I had no doubt that they would adore their grandchild.

"Yes."

She slid back a little and tilted her face to the night sky. For a moment, I just stared at the smooth skin along her cheek, longing to touch it, touch her. The flames made her glow in the moonlight. Just gorgeous. I glanced up to see what held her attention. It was a clear night, but as usual, the stars weren't visible from the city. I didn't know what she was searching for, but her shoulders suddenly tightened. I still had so much to learn about her. So much to figure out.

"Okay, Samson." She shifted to face me. "Move in."

There was a hint of challenge in her voice. And honestly? I liked it. This would be a challenge for both of us. The immediate future was filled with so many uncertainties. So many things I couldn't control. And Dylan would be the ultimate variable.

We jumped as the door banged open and Liam stomped out. His near constant scowl made it hard to believe that he and

Dylan were related. Even the cool green of his eyes was in complete juxtaposition to his mother's warm golden irises.

"Liam?" She twisted to face her son, her shoulder brushing against my hand where it rested on the seatback behind her.

Liam homed in on the place where Dylan's skin pressed into my arm, and the scowl became a full-on glower. I could have moved, but if I did, it would signal that such an innocent touch was wrong. I didn't want to set that precedent with him. If I had it my way, Liam would eventually see the same touches as my support for his mother.

"Are you okay?" He moved his neck in a weird spasm that caused his red hair to bounce.

Dylan tilted her head. "Why wouldn't I be?"

Crossing his thin arms over his black T-shirt, he cocked a brow at me and jutted his chin. "Because you're up here with him."

She hopped up and wrapped her arms around him. At first, he yanked back, resisting, but Dylan didn't let up. It only took a couple of heartbeats for him to give in to her embrace. She tipped her head up and gave him a soft smile, then murmured something I couldn't make out.

"I don't want him as part of the family unit."

My heart sank. Great. That was just great.

Taking one step back, Dylan whacked him in the stomach. His responding half smile knocked me in the teeth. For the instant it flashed across his face, it was so clear he was her son.

"You used to beg for a brother or sister. The universe finally declared it's time, so get on board and support us."

"Ma, you know I have your back, no matter what." He hit me with another glare, his eyes hardening once more, and raised his voice so he was sure I could hear him. "I will always take care of my mother and my sibling, so consider this your warning: hurt either of them, and I will come after you."

"Liam, you can't address adults that way," Dylan hissed.

Maybe some would consider his warning rude, but not me. In that moment, a deep respect for the kid settled in my stomach. He was protecting his family. He might have beef with me, but beyond that, it seemed that Dylan was raising a boy who was well on his way to becoming a good man. A wave of certainty flooded me. My child couldn't have a better mother, and this kid's loyalty would extend to them too.

Not breaking eye contact, I pushed off the small sofa and held out my hand. "I would never purposely hurt your mother or our child."

He didn't take my hand right away, but I didn't pull it back. Just kept my attention fixed on him until he finally shook it.

"Just remember what I said, Mr. *Miller*." The way my last name spewed from his mouth made it clear he knew of my family and didn't like them. Why, though, were both he and Dylan so apprehensive about them?

Dylan

18

"No, not today, Becks." I rolled my eyes. "You're headed out on the road tomorrow. He'll come after he gets back."

"We're all just supposed to be okay with this?" Delia's wine sloshed over the edge of her glass as she slammed it on the ugly green countertop.

This team meeting was adults only. Cortney had left a few minutes ago, and the kids, apart from Liam, who was downstairs, were all in bed.

"We didn't have much choice but to agree to let Beckett live here since he married Liv. I don't want another man moving in."

"She was asking, not demanding. Chill, Delia." Shay sighed.

"He wants to be involved in my pregnancy. How can I say no to that?" It was true, even if I was super iffy about the whole thing. Living together would create an intimacy I wasn't sure I wanted. Especially because there was one small detail about living here that Cortney and I hadn't discussed. This house was packed, so if my family agreed that he could move in, which they would, he'd be moving into my room.

"At least he's not a rich fucking prick-ass tool like Brett."

Delia crossed herself. "May he rest in peace." Either habit or what could only be called the fear of Delia had Beckett crossing himself too.

I rolled my eyes at their dramatics. "Brett's alive."

"Don't worry, I have plans." Delia smirked.

"Not to kill anyone." Liv took a deep breath. "We don't murder people when we're mad, remember, Del?"

"Exactly." Delia smiled and lifted her wineglass. "We have friends who do it for us."

Beckett choked on his beer, and Shay sprayed wine all over the countertop when she erupted into laughter.

"So we're all good with Cortney moving in on Thursday?" I asked.

Before I could get definitive answers, Shay asked, "What are we telling the kids?"

"I'm pretty sure chatty Cathy over there already told everyone." Delia tipped her glass at Beckett.

"Listen, Medusa, I had one conversation about it."

"And what did that conversation entail?" Liv's sharp voice cut through the air.

"I told ya, Livy. I wanted to help him adjust to the idea."

Liv rolled her eyes at her husband. "Dumbass," she muttered. "I expect better from you."

"I think we tell the kids the same thing we said about Beckett. Cortney needs to be part of our group because he needs us and we need him. The whole idea of the circle of family." It was only as complicated as we made it. The less complicated, the better, in my opinion. Because once the living situation was set, Liam and I needed to have a conversation.

"Exactly, Dippy Do. Kumbaya to the universe and all that duckety duck," Beckett agreed.

Holding back a smirk at his ridiculousness, I shook my head. I should have been upset that he'd broken the news to Cortney without my permission, but judging by Liv's glare, she had mad covered, so I'd let it go. In the end, it had all worked out. Probably just the way it was supposed to.

"All my dealings with Cortney point to him being a great guy." Liv side-eyed her husband.

Beckett blinked at her, his face blank. "What?"

"Cortney's a great guy, right?" The words came through gritted teeth.

"Oh yeah." Beckett took a sip of his beer.

When he didn't elaborate, Liv elbowed him.

"Okay, fine. Yes. I've known him his whole life. Sure, he can be a punk and a ducking headache. But honestly, if I had a sister—"

"You *do* have a sister." Delia huffed.

"Shut up, Medusa. My point is that I wouldn't have an issue with him dating my sister. I think he should move in."

Shay dropped her shoulders and took a deep breath. "If the rest of you are sure, then I agree."

Delia scowled at every one of us in turn. "This is the last time we let a man move in."

"Agreed." Liv nodded.

"Of course," Shay confirmed.

Beckett's response was a silent smirk.

Knowing him, he'd try his best to ruin that plan. But that wasn't my issue, so I just smiled. I had bigger things to deal with than Beckett's agenda.

Now that the biggest issue of the day was settled, I'd leave them to bicker while I searched for Liam. He'd stormed away after threatening Cortney, but I had a pretty good idea of where I could find him.

No one was allowed in Shay's physical therapy room. She did home visits for some of her clients, but since she hadn't found an office space yet, she used the room across from mine as her office. When my son wanted peace, he hid out under her PT table.

"We have rules, dude." I clicked the door shut behind me.

"Pretty sure you break more of them than I do." He didn't even look up from his phone.

"I'm calling a ten-minutes-of-time." Since he was little, we'd done things this way. When important stuff hit the fan, either of us could call ten minutes, and without question, we'd drop everything and work out the issue at hand.

He sighed but put his phone down and pulled the Beats from around his neck. "I thought we already talked."

"I appreciate that you aren't pissed about it."

He frowned but remained silent.

"Aren't you even a little excited that you're going to have a little sister?" I tried again, dropping to the floor beside him.

He tilted his head to the side, surveying me from behind the shaggy hair hanging over his eyes. "You know already?"

I shrugged. "I have a feeling. Very girl vibes. Not like with you."

"Sure, a little sister will be great." He shook his head. "But don't buy shit until you get the tests and stuff, okay?"

I scoffed at my very practical son. "Fine." I nodded. "But can I ask you for a favor?"

As difficult as Liam could be, we'd always had an open, trusting relationship. Although our family unit had expanded exponentially already this year when we added my friends and their kids, Liam and I were still a pair. Soon, though, we'd be adding to our little nucleus. And not only a sibling, but Cortney too.

"What favor?"

"Give Cortney a chance. You used to like him."

He shook his head. "Ma, I liked him as the catcher for the team I root for. In real life? He's a baseball player with more fame and money than any person needs. He gets paid millions to let his hair blow in the breeze." Wearing a stupid smirk, he mimed brushing his hair off his shoulders.

"I'm disappointed." Heaving myself off the floor, I crossed my arms and loomed over him. He was so much taller than me now, so this was the only way I could. I'd given him a lot of space to be himself. Trusted him to forge his own path. But there was one thing I didn't allow. "Haven't I always taught you not to judge a person until you know them? Yet you're boxing Cortney in before you even give him a chance."

"Ma."

"Don't *Ma* me." I shot him my best *you're better than this* frown. "He's a decent person, but you won't get to know that because you've judged him based on his profession and decided you won't like him."

"That's not true."

"Isn't it?" I understood why Liam was slow to warm up to people. I was often hesitant too. But I hated to think that he'd close himself off completely.

He huffed out a breath. "I just don't trust him."

"Or anyone?" I suggested.

"I trust you." He had his head tilted back, and looking up at me like that, he looked so much like the little boy he used to be.

"Good. So trust me when I say you should give Cortney a chance."

"Don't twist things."

I cocked a brow and waited.

"Fine." He narrowed his eyes, and his jaw ticked. "But…"

"But what?"

"I'll give him a chance if *you* promise to be careful."

"Deal." That was easy. I'd already decided that. I might like Cortney, but this time I wasn't naïve enough to believe the fact that we came from two different worlds might not matter.

Cortney
19

"Anyone would be nervous," I said as I took in every aspect of the façade of the house I was moving into. A few days ago, when I'd convinced Dylan to let me move in with her, I was confident about it. However, in the five long days since, I'd worried about every detail. The house was a death trap. The gutter along the roofline was barely hanging on. The skeleton, though, wasn't just a head anymore. I wasn't sure how I'd get along with Beckett in such close proximity. Add in dealing with her friends and their plethora of kids, and that might make this more difficult. And where did Dylan and I stand? We were going to be co-parents, sure, but could we be more? Would she be interested in more? I couldn't even answer *that*.

So to keep my thoughts from getting out of control, I'd tried to focus solely on baseball, and during the games, I was checked in. But every night, when I'd wound down and was alone, the stress and what-ifs would hit me hard. I texted her regularly, and she responded more frequently than she had prior to our big discovery. Especially after I offered to buy her an Apple Watch.

I'd successfully kept myself from spiraling until the plane touched down this afternoon. The moment I'd stepped off, I knew I had to get to Dylan's quick. Dealing with the reality was far easier than letting the endless possibilities float through my head. And as much as I'd tried not to google anything baby related over the last few days, I was stressing about pregnancy, birth defects, baby safety, the house, Dylan, and how much Liam hated me.

My list went on and on.

The wind blew, and dark clouds above me blocked out most of the sunlight. A moment later, thunder rumbled in the distance. Any second, it would pour.

I adjusted my duffel bag and headed up the steps. The front door was cracked open, though there didn't seem to be anyone in the foyer.

"Hello?" I called from the doorway. When I got no response, I pushed the door and stepped inside hesitantly, remembering Dylan's comments about ghosts. A clack sounded above me, making me jump. Then rainbow-colored feathers fluttered from the ceiling, followed by a plastic bucket that knocked me on the crown of my head.

Wincing, I rubbed at my skull.

"Ugh, you wrecked it." The kid who had shot me with a Nerf bullet the first time I was here was standing halfway up the steps and frowning at me. His hair was slightly longer than it was that day, but he was wearing the same tutu.

"Yeah. Uh…sorry." The taller boy with dark hair looked both ways and swallowed so thickly I could hear the gulp from here. "We were trying to get Bossman. He's going to be here any second."

Oh, a prank. And even better? It was meant for Beckett. The right thing to do here would probably be to tell them to forget about the stunt and get the mess cleaned up, but I'd never been one to pass up a prank. And I needed a distraction to calm my nerves.

"You know what you really need?" I tossed my duffel across

the room and snatched the bucket off the floor. I held it on its side against the plywood, and with my free hand, I scooped the feathers into it. "Two buckets."

"That's what I said." Liam leaned against a door nearby. With his arms crossed and clad in a black hoodie, cargo shorts, and a frown, he was as welcoming as always. "Like I told ya, Finn, they don't stick without water."

"Exactly." I smiled at Liam, but he didn't return it. "Finn," I called to the kid I'd had the pleasure of meeting the last time. "And..." I raised a brow at the other boy.

"Kai," he said so quietly I barely caught his name.

"Cool. I'm Cortney. I need one of you to get a second bucket, and I need the other to help me with these feathers." They stuck to everything and were a challenge to pick up quickly, but Kai and I got them back in the bucket just as Finn reappeared with a bright green plastic pail half-full of water.

I rose to my feet and surveyed the door and the space above it.

"You need a step stool?" Kai tipped his head back looking up at me. He wasn't much bigger than Finn, but he spoke more clearly and carried himself with more maturity. Though he was probably older than Finn, he didn't possess the same confidence.

"Man Bun is a giant. He can reach." It wasn't a compliment, but Liam's voice held less disdain than usual.

I cracked the blue door, and the sound of the steady stream of rain that had finally started filled the space. The bucket of rainbow feathers went closer to the hinge. I kept the water closer to the side of the door that opened so it would fall first. Both balanced precariously on the two-inch-wide wood, leaning just a bit against the plaster wall above the door. When it opened, they should both drop.

"Quick, hide! He's pulling up!" Finn cried as he ran from the window and up the steps with Kai hot on his heels.

I stepped into the family room with Liam.

"Beckett's going to be pissed." He shook his head. "They don't usually get him."

"I've been making Beckett nuts since I was younger than you. I'm well aware of how he reacts to this kind of thing."

I swore his lips tipped up a fraction before his eyes went hard and he plastered that scowl I'd become so familiar with back on his face. Like he'd just remembered that he hated everything about me. Apparently, winning this teenager over was going to take some work.

"Why the duck is the door standing open? One of these days Dippy Do is going to lose a kid." The door creaked open, then there was a splash. "Du—" Thunk. "*Dylan.*"

I winced. I hadn't considered that he'd blame her.

Liam waved me off. "She's not here."

"What?" I whispered.

"We got you!" Finn and Kai cheered in unison.

"You did." The teeth clench was clear in Beckett's voice. I didn't need to see him to picture his expression. "Where's Auntie Dylan?"

Liam pushed off the wall and headed out to the foyer. "She's picking the girls up from NASA satellite camp. Man Bun's in charge."

My stomach knotted and my heart lodged in my throat. Well, fuck. I'd walked right into that.

With a shake of my shoulders, I committed myself to owning it and stepped out of the family room. "Welcome home, Bossman."

Beckett's hair was soaked, and a stream of water ran off the section sticking to his forehead. Feathers stuck mostly to his head and shoulders, and a few trailed down the front of his jacket. Just to be a dick, I swiped at a couple of them.

Glowering at me, he batted at my hand. "Clean this up," he gritted out. Then he stomped up the stairs. Halfway up, he paused and rubbed his hand over Finn's buzz cut. "Good prank. Next time, I'll help ya get Man Bun."

"Yes!" Finn laughed and scampered up after Beckett. "I have the best idea. One time I had this glitter…"

Oh boy.

"Want to play *Kirby*?" Liam asked Kai.

Half a second later, I was standing in the middle of the space all alone.

Looked like I was in charge of clean-up. Without knowing where I was headed, I moved toward the back of the house and found myself in the kitchen. For a minute, I stopped and took it all in, because, wow, was it something. Dark wood, olive green counters, missing cabinet faces. Half the floor was covered in yellow tile, and the other half was plywood. I shook my head and swiped the roll of paper towel from the counter, then I peeked under the sink in search of a trash bag.

As I stood, the chalkboard to-do list caught my attention. It was a color-coded chart, and every item was a home repair. The tasks listed in red were listed as urgent. Thank fuck my girl's room was included in that category. It would be a lot of work, but maybe we could get this house safe in the next nine months. Or eight. Was it only seven? Dylan was about to hit eight weeks. I shook my head and moved back to the foyer, surveying the wires that hung where a chandelier should be.

I had just picked up the last of the wet feathers and was still kneeling in the foyer when Beckett stomped down the stairs. He had changed, and his hair was mostly dry, but there were a few feathers stuck to the back.

"Where should I put my stuff?" I tipped my head toward the bag I'd tossed earlier.

Beckett crossed his arms over his black T-shirt. The casual look was throwing me off. He hung out with Jamie occasionally, and they even played hockey together, so I realized he didn't *live* in a suit, but it'd take some time for me to get used to this dressed-down version of the guy.

"You'll be in Dylan's room. I'm assuming, given the fact that you knocked her up, you know where her bed is."

My shoulders tensed and my hands fisted, but I fought against the snappy reply on the tip of my tongue. Instead, I pulled in a deep breath through my nose and let it out slowly, garnering all the chill I had. Pushing up to my full height, I took a step closer to the man who owned the team I played for.

At my proximity, he had no choice but to tip his head so he could look *up* at me. His lips were pinched tight and his nostrils flared. Boy, it burned him that I was almost four inches taller.

"You can give me shit. Trash talk all you want, give me a hard time. I'll swallow it." I clenched my jaw and took another breath through my nose. "But Dylan is off limits. Clear?"

He cocked a brow, and his lips pulled up at one corner.

The door behind us flung open. "Umbrellas down, everyone."

Plastic umbrellas followed by little legs came pouring into the room. Droplets splashed every surface as the rainbow of plastic keeping the brood dry collapsed one color at a time. Finally, Dylan pushed the door shut behind her.

"Hey." The smile she shot me lifted my mood instantly. "I thought we said six. Am I late?"

I shuffled over to her and took the umbrella out of her hand. Once I'd closed it, I tossed the yellow plastic into the cardboard box with the others as a million little bodies moved around us.

"I was early." I brushed her damp curls out of her eyes and soaked in the way her presence alone soothed me. "How you feeling?"

"Good." With a smile, she shrugged. The woman was always good.

I texted her to check in multiple times a day, and she'd yet to whine about being tired or cranky or sick. Her lack of symptoms was starting to stress me out. Could it be a sign that something was wrong?

A throat cleared, and she tipped at the waist to peer around me.

"Becks, did you get into a fight with a bird?" She pranced over and pulled an emerald feather from his hair.

"Ask your boyfriend or baby daddy or whatever you want to call him." He rocked back on his heels. "Hey, Little One," he said, his tone going softer than I'd ever heard it as he scooped the toddler who'd come in with Dylan into his arms.

Dylan scrunched up her nose. "Baby daddy."

Although the term was accurate for our situation, I didn't love it either.

"What's a baby daddy?" one of the girls asked.

There were three girls all about the same age hovering around us. I didn't know any of their names. They were bigger than Kai and way older than Finn. Two of the girls were dressed alike with pigtail braids, and if I wasn't mistaken, the one with darker hair who was talking to Dylan belonged to Liv.

Beckett winced.

"Ask Mom." Dylan smirked at Beckett.

Yup. The dark-haired girl had to be Liv's, and I didn't think Liv would appreciate him teaching her daughter the meaning of that term.

"Dinner?" Beckett asked.

"Brisket's in the crock pot. Potato salad's in the fridge. Everyone should be home by six thirty tonight. Planning to feed everyone food at some point." Dylan patted his shoulder. "Tag, you're it until the moms get home." Then she turned those golden eyes on me. "Grab your bag." She flitted down the hall to the stairway that led to the lower level and disappeared from view.

"You get kid duty too?" I asked Beckett.

Shaking his head, he chuckled. "Oh, Man Bun, you have so

much to learn." He turned to the girls. "Come on, let's check the markets while you tell me all about space camp."

"It's satellite camp, not space camp, Bossman," one of the twins corrected as they headed into the dining room.

"You're going to have to teach me the difference, Phoebe."

Still weirded out by this side of Beckett, I swiped my bag off the ground and headed down the stairs.

"I'm in here," she called as soon as my feet hit the landing.

I followed the sound of her voice and stepped into her bedroom, which was just as unfinished today as it had been a few weeks ago. Sheetrock had been installed in the hallway, but the wall on her side was just studs.

Her room had been marked as urgent on the to-do list. The thought of that sent a wave of relief washing through me. It would be taken care of. Being here with her would ensure I could check up on the status and hurry the process along.

"There are a lot of us, so we don't have extra space." She shrugged and plopped onto the bed, folding her legs under her and looking adorable in leggings and a fitted T-shirt. "We're going to have to be roommates."

Without my permission, my eyes dipped to the half inch of skin between the pink shirt and black leggings. The creamy porcelain called to me. Memories of my hands sliding up her ribs and palming the perfect handful of tits—

"Samson?" Her curls bounced as she tipped her head.

Blinking, I forced myself back to the present.

"I know we're not, like," she waved her hands back and forth, "*together*, but we're both adults. We can manage to just sleep in the same bed." She clutched at the pendant she wore around her neck and slid it back and forth on its chain. "Right?"

Was she kidding? I'd never met a woman who appealed to me more than her. Fuck, my dick was trying to beat its way out of my jeans, and all I'd done was take three steps into her bedroom. And she thought we could "just sleep" together every night?

"Is that okay?" With her teeth pressed into her bottom lip, she watched me.

I cleared my throat and took in the white quilt with purple flowers that covered the small bed. At home, I had a California king—on anything smaller, my legs dangled off—but I wasn't certain this bed could even be considered a queen.

A small crease formed between her eyes when I didn't answer right away. And ridiculously, I just wanted her to be happy.

"Sure, this is great."

My heart lurched when I was blasted with a huge smile.

I was so fucking screwed.

Dylan

20

This was weirder than I wanted it to be. I set out extra celestite and rose quartz on my nightstand to give the room a calm, emotionally stable energy, but even with that, the tension was thick. Maybe this called for incense. I must have the right combination of incense to smudge away awkwardness. I didn't want this vibe to stick in the room for days.

"I made space for you in the closet, and I emptied the top two dresser drawers."

His lips pulled into a tight line. "I don't have much stuff. I'll be fine."

Scooting over to the far side of the bed, I pointed to the corner of the room. "And I set this up for you."

Wearing a hint of a smile—finally—he dropped his bag and moved to crouch in the corner. Today his blond hair was pulled back in a bun, accentuating the hard lines of his jaw. Damn. When did I start considering throats sexy? With his attention fixed on my gift, he swallowed, and the way his Adam's apple bobbed had heat simmering on low in my core.

"You got me a puzzle mat?" he asked, craning his neck to look at me over his shoulder.

I nodded. "And I'm going to do my best not to ruin the puzzles for you."

"What?" He chuckled and shook his head.

With a sigh, I dragged my rose quartz along its chain, stealing some of its energy. "I'm weird about letting puzzles sit. I have this crazy need to finish them. My friends love to make a game out of seeing how fast I can finish them."

Silently, he studied me, his blond brows lifted, but he didn't say anything.

I waved my hand. "But I'm going to control my urge and leave that wood pile for you."

He pushed to his feet and sat beside me. The mattress sank under his weight. "I get being obsessive about things. Trust me. If you want to finish some of them, I don't mind. The idea of watching you puzzle?" He shot me a grin that made me feel like I'd swallowed my tongue. "It's pretty damn cute."

I tipped my shoulder into his. He was so much bigger than me. I had to look up to him. "So you're really okay with this?"

He ran a warm palm up and down my arm. "Firefly." He smiled. "As crazy as it sounds, I'm happy to be here."

Nodding, I climbed off the bed. "Okay. I'll let you get settled. You can snoop all you want, but be warned." I tapped the surface of the nightstand. "Delia and Shay are on a mission to find the perfect vibrator, so I have a drawer full."

His eyes went wide, and he snorted a laugh. "You're gonna keep me on my toes, aren't you?"

I shrugged and headed for the door. "Probably. I'm going to finish getting dinner ready. Let me know if you need anything."

"Where is this guy?" Delia dropped her bag onto the counter and spun in a circle, searching the kitchen.

At the massive old white stove, I was finishing up dinner. I'd volunteered to cook, even though it wasn't my night because I wanted Cortney's first meal with us to be something other than what Shay deemed healthy.

"Cortney's putting his stuff away." I nodded to the pile of cutlery I'd set out on the island. "Go set the table."

"No. I need to warn this man not to duck with you first." Delia frowned.

"He's not really the type of guy you can threaten." Liv shrugged from her stool at the island.

"Why not?" Delia asked.

"I'm curious about that too."

The deep voice had me turning from the stove and holding back a smile.

"Holy heck, you're huge up close." Delia tipped her head back to inspect the man directly to her right.

Standing next to Cortney was an experience.

He chuckled. "I get that a lot."

"How ducking tall are you?" Delia inspected his chest and farther up, up, up to the bun on the top of his head.

"Six-six, two forty," Liv answered, and all eyes swung to her. "What?" She shrugged. "I know most of the team stats."

Cortney chuckled and sauntered over to stand beside me. "These need to go to the table?" He tipped his chin at the cutlery and napkins.

"You don't have to—"

He waved me off and snatched the pile off the counter.

"A Roman god who sets the table." Delia turned and ogled Cortney as he fixed each place setting. "Damn."

"Girls," Shay moaned from the doorway to the kitchen. She shuffled in and flopped her upper body onto the island, her arms spread wide and her cheek pressed to the green Formica. "Today was impossibly long."

"Love the tats."

Shay jerked up at the sound of Cortney's voice, and she slapped her neck, covering the stars for a moment before she dropped her hand to her side. "You moved in today?" Her eyes widened as Cortney meandered back into the room. "Sorry, that was the worst welcome ever."

Cortney rested his palms on the counter next to me. For a second, the urge to lean into his side hit me, but I quickly pushed it away.

"It wasn't the worst welcome I've had thus far."

Liv laughed, and Delia rolled her eyes.

Collette appeared, wearing a thoughtful frown as she eyed the new addition. "Hi. I'm Collette." She stopped in front of Cortney and tipped her head to look up at him. "I won't write C on my forehead, so don't ask me to."

He smiled down at her. "I'm Cortney, and I don't want to do that either, so I don't blame you."

"How tall do you have to be to be considered a giant?" she asked.

Cortney shrugged. "We could google it."

"No." Collette slammed her hands to her hips and cocked her head to the right, exactly like her mother always did. "We can't give robots power."

He dropped a forearm to the island and leaned down closer to her level. "You're right. The robots will take over if we let them."

Collette lit up, her eyes bright and her smile wide. "Exactly. I learned so much about wireless technology today. We definitely need to make sure we own the robots."

"Satellite camp?" Cortney asked.

"I love that you're not as dumb as you look." Collette grabbed Cortney's hand. "Let me give you the tour. I know all the house's good spots."

"Lead the way, Amy Hood."

"Who's she?"

I couldn't make out Cortney's response as he followed Collette out of the room.

"Duck." Delia glared at his retreating form, but then her eyes snapped to me. "He knows who Amy Hood is."

"I don't." I shrugged.

"He's going to have a fan club here," Shay predicted.

Liam snorted from the kitchen doorway.

I narrowed my eyes on my son and pointed. "Remember your promise."

He held both hands up in the air. "I know. I'm giving him a chance to prove he's going to bother to stick around before I'm allowed to hate him."

His attitude made my heart sink. Liv popped up and stood beside me, rubbing my arm. She understood my concern, because when Liam wanted to be, he was all kinds of chaos. And I didn't want him to block the family unit we were trying to establish.

"Don't make your mom's life harder, Liam. If you give Cortney a chance, I promise you'll like him." Liv shot him a warning look. One of the best parts about our living arrangement was the support we gave one another when it came to the kids.

"How about I help with dinner?"

The room went dead silent, and every one of us turned to him, mouths slack and eyes wide.

Delia tilted her head and propped her hands on her hips. "Who are you, and what did you do with Liam?"

She took the words right out of my mouth.

My son huffed and tossed his hair out of his eyes. "Thought I was supposed to make her life easier."

But the smirk that followed the comment made me nervous.

Cortney
21

There were a lot of freaking people here. I stopped at the entrance to the dining room and watched Dylan's friends and their kids settle around two folding tables that had been pushed together. Delia was at the head of one, with the other women around her. The twins and the other kids dropped into seats around the opposite end. Beckett pulled out the chair near the middle.

A throat cleared beside me, and when I peered down, Liv's daughter Winnie was looking up at me and shifting from foot to foot while she fiddled with something pink and blue.

"Oh, sorry." I stepped back to the side of the doorway so she could pass.

"No." She shook her head. "I made this for you to, like, welcome you to our house…" She thrust the thin beaded bracelet at me.

The words *Man Bun* were spelled out in black letters and surrounded by dark blue and pink beads. Crouching so I wasn't towering over her, I smiled. "Whoa, you made this?"

She shrugged. "The Revs are blue so I thought maybe you'd

want blue, and pink is my favorite, but if you think it's ridiculous…" She studied her feet as the words trailed off.

"I love it," I said, slipping it onto my wrist.

She tipped her chin up, and a hint of a smile crossed her face. "You'll wear it?"

"Of course."

She peeked over at Beckett, who was watching us. He smiled at her, then turned his attention to me. His expression was impossible to read. His mouth was set in a straight line, and though he wasn't shooting daggers my way, there wasn't a hint of warmth in his eyes, either. As he continued his assessment of me, he dropped his elbow to the table. The pink and green beads that I hadn't noticed before caught my attention then. I dragged my focus back to his face, and he gave me a quick nod.

Without another word, Winnie skipped over to the table. But she smiled back at me when she sat down. Looked like I had at least one ally besides Dylan in the house. I'd take it as a win.

"You're next to me, Man Bun." Liam came up behind me and thrust a plate full of barbecue brisket and potato salad at me before I'd straightened fully.

I wasn't sure if I just wasn't hungry or if I was too nervous to eat. Because although I was pulling out all the stops to get to know everyone, this was more chaos than I'd expected. Moving into a house with twelve other people was easier in theory than in practice.

Liam sat across from Beckett, almost like the two of them were the wall between the women and the kids.

I wasn't sure what that was about, but I had more important things to worry about now, like keeping track of everyone's names and remembering things like Phoebe was the twin with red twist ties in her braids and Collette had the black ones. Collette had made a comment about not putting the letter *C* on her forehead, but after spending thirty minutes with the twins while they gave me a tour, I understood why she'd said it. They were almost identical.

"I want to sit by Man Bun." The little guy in the tutu pouted next to Beckett as I took the seat between Dylan and Liam.

Beckett cocked a brow at him. "You're always beside me, Huck."

Huck? Before now, I was sure the kid's name was Finn. Shit, was there a second set of twins? And if there was, had we lost the other one? I scanned the table again, but every seat was occupied and there wasn't a second boy wearing a tutu.

"But he has such pretty hair. I want to touch it. Do you think it's soft?"

"He might not want sticky fingers in his hair, Finn," Dylan said.

So he *was* Finn. Beckett was probably just fucking with me.

"Can I rub your hair?" Finn asked.

Every eye in the room was trained on me. What was I supposed to say to that? *Yes, put your sticky fingers in my hair?* or *No, I don't want that?* The kid's eyes were so bright and his smile was so big. Dammit, he looked so hopeful. But he'd also just used his left hand to push a chunk of barbecue sauce–covered brisket onto his fork, and there were still brownish smudges on his fingers. I swallowed past the lump that had formed in my throat. I could wash my hair after dinner. It was that easy, right? And I didn't want to upset the little guy.

"Let's go, Man Bun, let the kid feel your hair." Beckett scowled at me.

Apparently, I hadn't decided fast enough to agree to let his stepson pet me.

I moved around the table and bent to my knee.

"You're still so tall even when you is down low." Finn climbed up to stand on his chair and wobbled a bit. I reached out to steady him, but he bumped into his sister's booster seat, and her cup teetered.

Lightning quick, Beckett snatched the cup and the booster seat before either could tumble. Holy shit, the man moved fast. I was so distracted by the chaos that I hadn't realized Finn had taken the tie out of my hair.

"I wants this hair," he announced, fluffing my hair around my shoulders. Then he turned to his stepdad. "Bossman, can you buy me his hair?"

I jerked back. "*What*?"

Beckett shrugged. "We'll see."

Hell no. No one was buying my hair. I shimmied back a little, ready to make a run for it.

Finn stomped his foot on the seat of his chair, and Beckett steadied him this time. "You cutted my hair off and made everyone upset, so you should get me new ones."

Utterly confused, I looked from Finn and his buzz cut to Dylan and then to Liv.

Liv rubbed her temples. "Let's not talk about that night."

Dylan laughed. "Yeah, Liv's still traumatized." She forked a bite of potato salad and went on eating like there wasn't a debate going on that involved the sale of my hair.

Shay's kind eyes met mine. "Beckett, don't torture him. Tell him you're not going to try to threaten him into selling his hair."

Beckett glanced over his shoulder at me. He smirked, clearly loving how I was buying into this. "I said we'll see."

I was not cutting my hair. It was time to start controlling the narrative here. "Finn, bud." I scooted closer again. "I'll pick up a bottle of purple shampoo for you. It'll help make your hair grow long and shiny like mine."

Finn's eyes widened and a grin split his face.

"And since you don't have boring ole straw-colored hair like mine," I said, laying it on thick, "yours is going to be so much better."

"Yes." He pumped his fist. "I want that."

"Cool. We'll work together to make your hair even better than mine."

I held out my fist, and the little dude bumped my knuckles with his. Relaxing my shoulders, I huffed out a breath, but immediately tensed again when he launched himself at me.

"You almost as good as Bossman," Finn whispered when I caught him. Just as quickly as he'd jumped into my arms, he pulled back.

Taking the hint, I set him back down and bit back a smile. Because I had two allies here now. I glanced around at the chaos, and nerves crept up my throat.

I shook off the anxiety threatening to swamp me. *Control*, I thought as I moved around the table. As long as I had control, I could handle living here.

Liam was watching me as I sat beside him again.

"We good?" I asked, stabbing a piece of brisket with my fork. The way he was focused on me had me on edge.

"Ask me later." Liam's eyes darted to my fork, then back to my face.

Odd. No one else at the table seemed to notice, though. The room was relatively quiet now that everyone had dug in. Even the kids were wolfing down the brisket.

Dude, stop overanalyzing everything.

With a deep breath in and renewed determination, I took my first bite of dinner. The second my fork slipped between my teeth, my tongue started to tingle. In seconds, the tingle morphed into a fierce burn. Then, as if I'd descended into the infernos of hell, fire exploded in my mouth. My eyes started to water.

What the hell was in this? If table manners hadn't been drilled into me from the age of two, I might have spit it out. But instead, I forced the blazing hot food down my throat and snatched my napkin from my lap to wipe at my nose, which had already begun to run.

Water. I needed water. But I hadn't brought a drink to the table.

Blinking rapidly, I willed the tears welling in my eyes to subside even as my tongue continued to scorch. Jeez, that shit was ridiculous. Even my throat was on fire.

"Aw, Samson." Dylan squeezed my thigh. "He was kidding about your hair."

I cocked my head, confused by her words. Normally I liked puzzling out her comments, but I was too distracted by the flames licking up my esophagus and scorching the inside of my mouth.

Dylan dropped her fork and pulled me into a hug. "Becks," she said over my shoulder, her voice more stern than I'd ever heard it, "he's crying. Tell him you didn't really plan to cut his hair."

"What?" I choked, the sound catching on my poor burned vocal cords. Fuck manners. I grabbed Dylan's glass of water and chugged. It relieved the burn a fraction, so I tried again. "It's just the brisket."

Beckett chuckled and leaned back in his seat.

Dylan's forehead creased, then she shrugged. "Oh, I guess it's been known to elicit emotion. My dad's recipe is the best."

The best. I wasn't sure I'd agree with that claim. Although with as blistered as my mouth and throat felt, it might be the only thing I taste this week. Panic hit me then, and I scanned the faces of the kids, sure they'd be in even more pain, but no one else seemed the least bit bothered. How the hell was the *toddler* across the table okay with the spice level? Something was off.

"Is it supposed to be spicy?" I asked Dylan.

She leaned over my plate and sniffed. "No, it's a honey barbecue."

I scrutinized Beckett, then Liam. I couldn't decide which of them was more likely to mess with me, and neither wore even a hint of guilt in their expression. But my stomach dropped as Dylan's fork hovered over my plate.

"No!" Liam and I cried at the same time.

Batting Dylan's fork away, I whipped my head to Liam. For one second, he looked guilty, but then his mask of innocence slid back in place. Dylan watched us both, her face filling with concern. Shit, I didn't want this to be an issue. And two hours ago, I was pranking Beckett with all the boys. I couldn't be mad that I was the victim this time. Or maybe it was a test. Either way, I wouldn't make this into anything.

"It's just me," I breathed out, racking my brain for a reason that would warrant my weird-ass reaction to her dinner. "I've always had trouble with barbecue sauces. They make my eyes water."

"Really?" Delia peered around Dylan and squinted at me. "What kind of wimp can't handle honey barbecue?"

Dylan scrutinized her son, her lips pressed together tightly.

I doubled down. "Yeah," I coughed out. "I've never been able to handle it. My brother has spent his life making fun of me about it." I turned to Beckett. "Right?"

He blinked twice and swallowed audibly, his attention jumping between Liam and me.

Internally, I begged him to agree. To have my back for once in his life. If everyone here made fun of me for the rest of my life because they thought I couldn't handle even the slightest amount of heat, then so be it.

"Yup." He finally nodded. "And I swear we've told you a hundred times. Milk works better than water."

Pushing back from the table, I stood and hurried from the room, taking my plate with me.

"So Liam ducked with your food?" Beckett said from the kitchen doorway.

I shrugged but kept my mouth shut. I needed Liam to be okay with me. Ratting him out wouldn't do me any good.

"He's difficult. He still only puts up with me. You've got your work cut out for you." Beckett patted my back, and for the first time, I felt like maybe *he* didn't hate my presence here.

Four down, eight to go.

Dylan

22

D amn. Tonight's dinner might have been even worse than the food fight that broke out during Beckett's first night here. If I had known about Cortney's aversion to barbecue sauce, I wouldn't have bothered with the brisket, or I could have tried a different kind of seasoning. Although I wasn't convinced that Liam wasn't involved in the chaos that ensued when Cortney took that first bite. Even if both of them claimed he was innocent.

The rest of the evening had been uneventful. Beckett and Cortney handled kitchen clean-up, then the twins talked Cortney into a game of Risk. They were both shocked and elated at his ability to keep up with their evil genius ways. After an intense two-hour game, he could totally claim he was the first resident of our home to best them. All night, I watched him win over the kids one at a time. All except Liam. Though not for lack of trying.

After I'd changed and brushed my teeth, I headed for my room. Normally, I slept in shorts and a crop top. Tonight, though, it felt weird. Cortney sat on the edge of the bed in sweats and a long-sleeve T-shirt. That seemed like overkill, but who was I to judge?

"Do you have a…" He cleared his throat. "A side?"

I hadn't slept in a bed with anyone in fifteen years, so I had no idea. I had never slept well, and when I hooked up, I left once they were down for the count.

"Do you?" I asked.

"You're—" He waved his hand at my stomach. "Growing a person. I need you to be comfortable. Otherwise, I won't sleep."

Pursing my lips, I looked at one lavender pillow, then the other. "Can I try both?"

"Both?" he cocked his head and frowned.

"Like lay down and see which vibe works."

He grinned. "I can never anticipate your answers."

I waved his comment off. "Move over. Let me try the right side."

We lay side by side, but I didn't love being between the wall and the wall of a man. I felt too claustrophobic.

"Nope. Switch." I sat up.

Rather than scooting to the end of the bed and walking around it, I clambered over Cortney. I straddled him, intent on moving to the other side quickly, but before I could break away from him, he settled a hand at my waist. He lay flat on his back, his eyes blazing and his fingers biting into my hips.

"*Fuck.*" Swallowing hard, he squeezed his eyes shut. "Sorry," he said when he opened them again. Releasing me from his grip, he folded his hands over his chest.

I shifted, preparing to dismount, and my ass brushed against his hardening cock. The feel of him made my heart rate pick up and a flame ignite low in my belly.

He cleared his throat and gripped my hips again, but this time he lifted me and scooted closer to the wall, then set me down on the mattress.

"How's this?" he asked.

How was it? Fine. The bed was fine. But my body was still lit up from his touch.

"Great." My voice cracked.

"Glad we're feeling the same way."

Fisting my hands at my sides, I sighed. "Sex complicates things, you know."

He snorted. "Well aware, Firefly. I respect that you want us to be co-parents without complications, but if you talk about sex while you're lying in bed with me…" His eyes tracked over my face and landed on my lips. "I can't promise I won't cross your lines."

"Right." I turned my back to him and settled in.

Behind me, he did the same, shifting until his back pressed against mine. With thick tension blanketing the room, I should have been keyed up. But lying next to him was oddly relaxing. It wasn't until I opened my eyes at the sound of a strange voice and the sensation of a strong arm around my stomach that I realized I had slept straight through the night.

Dylan

23

"Off, Bixby." Cortney's voice was throaty and rough against my neck. The hot vibrations of each syllable rocked down my spine.

At his command, the alarm stopped telling us about the weather, but neither of us moved.

His firm chest was pressed tightly to my back and he kept me tucked in close.

"I don't want to get up," he muttered, his face buried in my hair. "I don't normally have this issue, but damn, Firefly, this feels good."

I was cocooned in his warmth. Though I'd never slept more comfortably, it was almost a little too warm. I couldn't imagine how hot he must be in pants and a long-sleeved shirt.

Shimmying to the side of the bed, I broke free of his hold. He let out a begrudging groan but didn't stop me. I let the sheet fall away and sat on the edge of the mattress, peering over my shoulder. He turned on his back and assessed me. His face was creased with sleep lines, but against the lavender pillow, his eyes were too bright for this early in the morning.

"You feel okay?"

I nodded, arching my shoulders. "Do you realize how often you ask me that?"

The mountains of muscle in his bicep popped against the white cotton of his shirt as he tucked his arm behind his head. *Damn.* That arm had spent the night around me, and yet I'd managed to sleep through it.

"Only about every eighth time I stress about it."

"Jokes this early?" I teased. He couldn't possibly worry about me that much.

His only response was a frown.

"Samson, you've been asking me, like, six times a day."

He chuckled, the sound low and raspy. "Then I'm wrong. I only ask you about once every hundred times I worry about you."

Pulling my knees up, I looped my arms around them and nibbled at my lower lip as I studied him, searching for understanding.

He sighed. "Do you know how many risks come with pregnancy? Miscarriage, ectopic pregnancy, vertigo, preeclampsia, hyperemesis gravidarum, placental abruption, preterm birth, gestational diabetes, still birth, toxemia, birth defects, cephalopelvic disproportion—"

"Stop." I put my palm on his chest and felt his racing heart. I didn't even know what all those words meant. What the heck was *gravidarum*? I shook my head. "I'm fine. Baby is fine."

He shut his eyes and took a deep breath, then another. After a moment, his heart rate slowed under my hand.

I was aware that complications existed, obviously, but looking out for symptoms was about the extent of where I let my concerns led me. Cortney, though, clearly had the *stress about the potential problems* thing going on.

"What do you need me to do?" I asked.

His eyes popped open. "What do you mean?"

"This shouldn't be scary for you. At least not all the time.

You shouldn't have to stress about stuff like that every minute of the day, so what can I do to reduce that worry? I mean it when I say that I'm good. And even if my first doctor appointment isn't until next week, I really feel like she's good too." I moved my hand from his chest to my lower stomach.

His hand jerked up like he wanted to touch my belly, but he pulled it back abruptly before he could make contact.

"You can't feel the baby move yet, and my stomach hasn't changed much." Sighing, I grasped his wrist and placed his huge palm over my abdomen. "But here. I like feeling the connection to her."

He stared at the place where his finger brushed the inch of bare skin between my top and my shorts. My core clenched at the feel of him. Even though I'd done this to give him some peace, I couldn't deny the spike of desire that hit me at his touch.

He swallowed and then rubbed his thumb just under my belly button.

"You think it's a girl?" he asked, looking up into my eyes again.

I shrugged. "Her soul feels very *she*."

He smiled and blew out a breath. "Will you tell me if you don't feel good? Even if you think it's silly or if it's only nausea or morning sickness? I do better with knowledge."

"Deal."

His hand fell away as I hopped off the bed.

"Right now, I feel like I need a cup of decaf coffee before all the moms leave for work."

He sat up. "Do you need help? I could hire someone to watch the kids."

"Oh, Samson." I shook my head. He was so damn cute. "Before I moved in here, I ran a preschool and taught a class of twenty-five three-year-olds. This group of seven has nothing on them."

With a laugh, I skipped out of the room and headed to the

kitchen. I felt good today. More rested than I had in weeks. Bixby said it was going to be beautiful, so while the girls were at satellite camp, I'd take the rest of the kids to the park.

"Liv is going in to work with Beckett, so it's just you, me, and Del for morning stretches." Shay slid a glass across the counter as I walked into the kitchen. "I made smoothies."

The stretches I was game for, but the smoothie? Hard pass.

"Oh, great." I headed straight for the Keurig and popped in a decaf pod. "Cortney worries about health stuff too. I'm sure he'll love the green goop." With a mug in place, I hit brew, then turned back to her. "But baby girl and I are going to pass. I don't want the barfs this morning."

"Be healthy," she said, frowning at my mug.

"Or happy," I added.

Beckett wandered in and shuddered at the smoothie on the counter, then pulled his own mug from the cabinet.

When my coffee was finished brewing, I grabbed my mug and stepped aside.

Cortney walked in next, still dressed in his sweats and long sleeves. Maybe he was chronically cold. He tucked his hands into his pockets as his intense scrutiny shifted around the room. If he worried so much, I was starting to realize this whole moving in thing was probably rough on him. He was in an unfamiliar place with a dozen people he barely knew and a load of routines he was clueless about.

"Shay made you a liquid breakfast." I nodded at the cup on the counter. "She makes them for everyone but Liam, Beckett, and me."

"Why?" he asked.

"Because we're the only ones honest enough to say they're gross."

Beckett coughed to cover up a laugh. The click of heels had him straightening up and ogling his wife's legs as she walked in wearing a fitted black skirt. It was swoony the way Beckett's attention shifted to her the second she was around. Liv was a lucky woman.

"Oh, it's a smoothie morning." Liv took the cup Shay held out to her. "Yum." She worked hard to hide her grimace as she swallowed.

Hesitantly, Cortney picked up his glass and sniffed, then he took a sip. He eyed the glass as he swallowed. "It's just, what? Protein powder, kale, pineapple, and honey?"

"I add in a little Greek yogurt and natural peanut butter." Shay turned back to me. "Try some, please."

I shook my head. "*Oh,* no." My eyes shot to Cortney. "That idea causes the morning sickness we're trying to avoid." I lifted my hands to my lips.

"Fine. But have something besides coffee for me, please." He took another big swig of smoothie. He was a better human than me, that was for sure.

"Better get dressed, Man Bun. Car will be here in ten minutes." Beckett tapped his watch. He had every moment of his life scheduled down to the minute. Except when he was inside this madhouse, of course. When the team had a night game, his car came at eight on the dot. And may the universe help us if Liv wasn't ready as soon as the car pulled up.

"What?" Cortney asked.

"The car will be here in ten minutes," Beckett repeated, louder this time.

"I'm not deaf." Cortney shook his head. "I just don't get why I need your car. Mine's parked in the garage around the corner. I rented a spot."

He'd already finished his smoothie, and Shay was looking quite pleased about it. This better not lead to her thinking I'd be open to eating the gross stuff.

Beckett scowled. "The stadium and my office are next door to each other. Taking two cars would be a waste. Are you too good to ride with Livy and me? It's not like she smells bad or anything."

"Why would *I* be the one to smell bad?" Liv put her half-empty glass on the counter. That was probably all she'd drink.

Beckett handed her his coffee mug, and she took a big sip. "You smell perfect." Wrapping his arm around her waist, he pulled her close and nuzzled her neck just above the collar of her white blouse.

She smiled against the mug. They were so freaking cute.

"We're all going to the same place, and I don't see why we need to waste all the world's resources—"

"Since when do you care about that?" Shay asked. "I keep telling you we need to shrink our household energy footprint, and you keep ignoring me."

"Now you're complaining that I'm actually listening to you?" Beckett lifted his head from Liv's neck and shot Shay his signature scowl.

With his glass in hand, Cortney shuffled to the sink. "Not causing waves, Bossman," he said, turning on the water and rinsing the glass. "I'll be ready to ride with you."

"Good."

"There's no control freak like a Beckett control freak." I snickered to myself as I added creamer to my mug.

"Are you talking to yourself, Dippy Do?"

"Sometimes I do." I spun back to him. "And then we both laugh and laugh."

Beckett stared blankly, unamused.

Across the kitchen, Cortney chuckled. The small smile that played on his lips flipped my stomach. He pointed to the bowl of fruit with a raised brow. Damn the man for always getting my humor, worrying about me, and fitting into this chaos. Because he was making himself very hard to resist.

Cortney
24

"Look at these." Beckett thrust a folder at me. "Which one would you pull up?"

The leather seat creaked under me as I shifted to take the papers from him. We'd been carpooling to and from the stadium for a few days, and every ride thus far had been filled with nothing but Revs talk. I didn't understand why he kept asking for my opinion, especially since he had a full staff to deal with these questions.

I flipped through the pages full of information about minor leaguers. "This for Berry?" The fourth guy in our pitching rotation was listed as questionable.

He inclined his head. "Seems the week of rest won't be enough for his elbow. They want to pull him from the rotation for two cycles."

"You want the same guy for both games?" None of these three guys would fit the bill perfectly since the Revs had a couple of big games coming up.

"I'm not set on anything."

"Don't you have a general manager for this shit? Why are you always making these calls?"

He scowled, but I raised a hand and waved off his answer. "Sorry, none of my business." I shut the folder. "If it were me, I'd pull the lefty for the Sox game. Both their heavy hitters are shit against left-handers. I'd bring the young one, John whatever, on for the Rockies. Even though his speed isn't as great as some of the others, he has damn good control. But Denizit is the best in the league against left-handers, so you can't use the lefty for that game."

Beckett nodded, then pulled out his phone and shot off a slew of rapid-fire texts.

My phone buzzed in my pocket, and my heart lurched. I yanked it out, instantly worried that something was wrong with Dylan. I was actively working to tamp down my natural tendency to panic. She promised that bad news would never come through text, but that didn't stop me from worrying about her.

Dad: Did you look over the stuff we sent?

Me: Yeah, it's fine. Have your assistant electronically sign it for me.

He still didn't understand how little I was interested in being involved with any of the company's real estate dealings. My dad was set on bringing me into the family business after I retired from baseball, so he kept me on the board of Miller Real Estate, regardless of my lack of desire to be included there. I'd never be a good fit for that. Sure, I enjoyed the data analysis involved, but the housing market relied too heavily on luck, and that just stressed me out. I didn't want to make those calls. The way my brother, Jamie, could buy a building and evict all its tenants without losing sleep was unfathomable to me. Just the idea left my hands sweating.

Plus, Dylan and our child were in Boston, so that meant I was staying put. Eventually, I'd have to share that news, but my family would have a lot of questions, and right now, I wasn't equipped to answer most of them. I couldn't even explain our relationship. Her ass cradled my dick every night in bed, but otherwise, we were…friends?

Prior to the pregnancy news, I'd hoped to talk her into a casual dating situation until the season was over. I envisioned us hanging out, having a good time, spending some quality time between the sheets. Then we'd go from there. But casual and co-parenting didn't go together. As much as I wanted her, I had to be sure I was ready for the real thing before I crossed any lines.

And even if I was, Dylan didn't seem remotely interested in anything serious.

Over the last three days, we'd fallen into this co-existence that wasn't necessarily horrible, but it left a lot to be desired. If I had to keep sleeping in full clothes, I might sweat off ten pounds. But with her in nothing more than a few scraps of material every night, I needed some kind of armor against bad decisions.

Dad: Mom said you canceled the visit you had scheduled for this week. Why?

Me: Just need to stay in Boston. I'll call you and Mom in the next couple of days.

"Everything okay?" Liv asked.

My head snapped up and my stomach dropped.

"Just finalizing the details. Gonna pull Aaron up, then drop him back for Toker," Beckett mumbled, giving her leg a quick squeeze.

"I was talking to Cortney," Liv said.

My mind swam as I took Beckett in. "You took my advice without a second opinion?"

He shocked the shit out of me sometimes. I made that call based solely on the information in the folder he'd shown me. It was just my gut reaction. If I'd known he was going to take my advice without question, I would have looked at a lot more data before giving him an answer.

He didn't lift his head, but he eyed me over his phone. "You know the league stats better than I do. Why wouldn't I listen?"

He and I were very different people.

The limo came to a stop in front of the brownstone, and Charlie, Beckett's driver, opened the door. Beckett climbed out first, then turned back to give Liv a hand.

And that was that.

Looked like I'd spend the night watching tape. I needed a game plan for Aaron since he'd be playing in the first game after the break.

I quickly grabbed my computer and checked on Dylan, who was in the parlor with Adeline and Finn. But as I made my way to the steps, I ran into Delia. She narrowed her eyes, looking about as welcoming as Liam usually did. She didn't speak to me, just headed toward her room at the back of the house. I'd been wanting to get her alone, so I followed her.

"Delia?" I called.

Halfway down the hall, she turned and raised one perfectly sculpted brow in my direction. She tapped the toe of her stiletto on the hardwood floor and glowered. Damn, she was a lot like my sister. Almost a foot shorter than me, probably half my weight, and yet totally terrifying.

I cleared my throat. "Listen, I know you're not thrilled that I'm here…"

She tipped her head, and the end of her blond ponytail fell over one shoulder.

"But you've given me a chance regardless," I hurried on, "so I wanted to do something for you…" I reached into my back pocket and pulled out a card.

"If you've hired a contractor to touch my house, I will slit your throat." She fisted her hands on her hips.

My stomach dropped, but I cleared my throat and went on.

"No. I know you've got plans for restoration. I wouldn't want to get in the way of that." I shook my head. "But I noticed that you don't have a dining table. My mom has a guy who does custom furniture. He specializes in period pieces, the kind that would fit perfectly in a 1920s brownstone."

Slowly she let her hands fall to her sides, and her face relaxed, so I kept going.

"I wanted to say thank you. So I reached out and asked if he could do a custom piece for the dining room." I held the card out to her. "I told him to bill me for whatever you choose. He can't start right away, but he said he can have it ready before Thanksgiving."

After a brief hesitation, she took the card, studied it, and blinked twice before meeting my eyes. "You hired someone to make me a dining room table so we have one for the holidays?"

"Uh." I cleared my throat and rocked back on my heels. "Maybe it's dumb." I shrugged. "But by letting me be here, you're giving me a chance to be present for Dylan and our baby, and that's…" I didn't have the words to explain how much it meant to me, so I just shrugged again. "Anyway, no one will let me pay rent, and I didn't know what else I could do."

Delia shut her eyes and shook her head. "Thank you." Reaching out, she squeezed my hand, then opened her eyes and focused them on me again. "And as long as you're taking care of my best friend, you're welcome here. But…" Her jaw locked and her voice went flat. "Hurt her, and I end you."

I put both hands in the air. "Understood."

Without another word, she turned toward her room, but not before a hint of a smile played at her lips.

The vise gripping my chest loosened a little. That interaction couldn't have gone any better. I headed down into the family room next, feeling lighter than I had all day. There, I found Liam sitting on the sofa with a comic book.

"Hey. Whatcha reading?" I asked, dropping onto the

sectional across from him. I inspected the fireplace grate, but the raccoon didn't appear to be home, or there or whatever.

He snapped the comic shut, revealing a big guy with a hammer on the cover and frowned. "What do you want?"

I'd just dealt with Delia, so a conversation with this teenager should be a piece of cake, yet it was far from it. My shoulders tightened, and I forced myself to keep trying.

"I was going to cast some film onto the TV and watch a few old games. Your mom said you were a baseball fan, so I thought maybe you'd want to watch with me...see what I do?" This was a stretch; watching the same guy pitch over and over wasn't exactly exciting.

Liam heaved himself up. "Nope, I'm going out."

"Where?" I asked.

"I'm not your business. Worry about my mom and your kid, and we're good enough, Mr. Miller." The kid strode out of the room without a glance back.

I ran my hands through my hair and slumped against the cushions. I wanted more than *good enough* with Liam, but maybe that was wishful thinking. Everyone else here was slowly coming around, maybe even Delia. I should have probably been happy he hadn't messed with my food again.

"Give him some time." The unexpected voice behind me had me shooting up to my feet and whirling around.

Shay smiled at me. "Sorry, I didn't mean to eavesdrop."

"It's your house." I dipped my chin and sat down again.

She surprised me by rounding the couch and sitting two cushions away. Her sympathetic expression made me feel stupidly unprepared to deal with teenagers.

"I hoped Liam and I could get along, but I guess I shouldn't push it. He's not as easy-going as his mom. That much is clear."

"Liam's very protective." Shay tucked the longer side of her black hair behind her ear. "Do you know Brett Channing?"

Channing. I knew the name. My mom was on a couple of

charity boards with at least one of them. I'd likely met them at fundraisers or events over the years. Since I mostly stayed out of that world, though, I didn't know much about them. The name Brett tickled something in my brain, but I couldn't place it.

"My parents or siblings might, but I spend more time on baseball than fundraisers and galas."

Shay cleared her throat and focused her dark eyes on me for a full minute before she spoke. "Brett is Liam's biological father."

Oh.

Dylan had mentioned Liam's father's name in passing, but what I'd focused on during that conversation was that the guy was a flake. By the way Dylan described the man, I'd pictured an artist or a world traveler. An eccentric guy who wasn't in Boston often. But if he was a Channing, then a lack of funds wasn't what kept him from being involved with his son, and it wasn't distance either. The guy was just an ass.

I blinked, searching for a response that was a little more gracious than my thoughts, but Shay went on.

"He's made it pretty clear over the years that Dylan and Liam don't belong in his world." A timer beeped in the kitchen, and Shay stood. "Give him time to see that you're different." She gave my shoulder a squeeze, then headed out of the room.

White-hot rage rushed through me at the idea that anyone would make Dylan or her son feel like they were less than. It was one of the things I liked least about the rich pricks I had spent so much of my childhood with. My parents and siblings weren't entitled assholes, but their circles were full of them. Dylan's hesitation about my family and her son's aloofness made so much more sense now. But how did I fix that?

"I know it's your night, Shay, but I'm not sure the baby is on board with tofu. From what I can tell, she's a vicious carnivore."

Dylan's voice pulled me from my thoughts. From the sound of things, I'd eat most of her dinner and then sneak out the window to pick up a burger for her again tonight. At least I was the one wandering the streets of Boston after dark rather than her. Although she was capable as hell, the image of her tucked into the window seat with a book was much more soothing than the one of her wandering out for food at ten p.m.

"What's got your aura tinged such a violent red?" Dylan dropped onto the sofa beside me and brushed her chaotic auburn curls away from her face.

I let out a sigh. I wasn't ready to talk about Brett yet. Not until I'd had more time to consider the situation and how to broach it with her.

Something clinked against her teeth. Probably a cherry Jolly Rancher. For the last three days, she'd been constantly snacking on them. Food was definitely a thing for her. She ate what she wanted, and the other women, especially Shay, constantly urged her to put more thought into healthy choices. It made me wonder if she'd eat at all if I wasn't bringing food to her.

"Do you think DoorDash will deliver to a window?"

"I'll work it out so I cook on the nights you're on the road. Don't stress." She was so tuned into my thoughts that sometimes it felt like she read my mind. If only I possessed the same skill with her.

She settled back into the sofa cushion and I got smacked with my new favorite scent. Coconut with just a hint of a sweet cherry candy.

"Is it going to bug you if I read while you do whatever this spreadsheet stuff is?" She waved her paperback at my computer, where I had my Revs analytics sheets pulled up.

"Not at all." I settled back with my laptop on my thighs, and she tucked her legs under herself and snuggled against my arm. I tried not to smile, but damn, it was tough, because in the moment, life was good. The stress eating at me melted away. Thoughts of Liam and his disdain for me faded, along with the anxiety that churned in my gut at the idea that he and Dylan were apprehensive. For a little while, when I was this close to her, life felt easy. Tomorrow, I'd work out how to fix the issues that hovered between us.

Starting with proving to Dylan and Liam that I wasn't what they were used to.

Dylan

25

"I just don't feel like this works effectively," Liv complained.

"The book's plot?" Shay asked, pouring herself a glass of wine.

I mentally sighed at my ice water. The joy of pregnancy meant that my book club experience was now fueled by water and smut. I could really go for a cherry Slurpee. If I thought Shay would let me get away with skipping the glass of water for the icy goodness, I'd have one.

"No, the book was cute." Liv tipped forward and pushed the bright orange paperback to the middle of the table. "I loved Blue."

"But?" Delia asked.

Liv glared at me. "When Dylan chose a fake dating trope, my relationship with Beckett totally changed. This time, we pick a one-bed trope, yet she and Cort are just as platonic as they were last week."

With a chuckle, I shrugged. "You and Becks were written in the stars long before I picked the book. You just needed a shove to get the universe's plan rolling."

Cortney and I were different.

"I'm not saying you're wrong, Man Bun," Beckett called over his shoulder as he rushed through the kitchen, "but I want to see the stats to back that up. It's too far-fetched." He pulled two Knocked Outs from the fridge and headed back into the family room.

For the last few nights, Cortney had been watching tape of players from a different team or something. Then he and Beckett would spend hours debating, discussing, fighting, whatever. If not for Liv, I'd wonder if he and Cortney were the two written in the stars. When they were together, they had this energy. They not only meshed, but they fed off each other. They were like an old married couple. I chuckled at the back and forth. Clearly, Cortney and his stats were winning the battle.

"Dylan?"

"Did you just not like *Natural Born Charmer*?" Delia asked.

I waved her off. "No, I loved it. The wall of pillows and the Speed Racer oops had me laughing."

Cortney's voice was low, but I could just make out his words. "In the end, it's your team. I don't know why *I'm* even debating the merits of a new center fielder for next year. You have staff for this."

He was right. It wasn't his job, but I understood Beckett's interest. Cortney could spend hours watching baseball. He'd even gotten the twins into helping him with stats. The sight of the big man with two little girls on his lap was adorable. The way he interacted with all the kids made it obvious that he'd be a great father.

"She's distracted by the Roman warrior in our living room." Delia laughed.

"What?" I asked.

Shay cleared her throat. "I think Liv is wrong." She nibbled on her nail as she assessed me. She had an oral fixation, which was half the issue with her hidden vice. I hadn't caught her smoking lately, thank God, because if Cortney found her, he'd probably stress about secondhand smoke. "Are you, in fact, smitten with your new bed mate?"

"He's as hot as he's always been, and you know how I love the baseball boys," I joked.

"I like him." Shay tucked the longer side of her hair behind her ear.

"What?" Liv's eyes widened and bounced between the two of us.

"She doesn't mean like that." Their energy didn't mesh that way. There was no orange-y heat between Shay and Cortney.

"I was nervous about letting him move in," Shay said, resting her chin on her hand and turning to Liv. "Beckett was different. We'd all known him for years before you accidentally married him in Vegas."

Delia snickered. "There was no way that was an accident."

"Shut up." Liv brought her wineglass to her mouth to hide her smile, but the damn grin was so big it did her no good.

"Anyway. I was nervous about bringing a random man into the house, but Cortney's"—she scoffed—"incredibly polite, super easy-going, wonderful with the kids, and easy on the eyes. And he's working so hard to win Liam over. He's a dream of a man."

"You know what he did the other day?" Delia's eyes cut to the family room and then back to us before she leaned in. "He thanked me for letting him stay here by ordering a custom table so we'd have it for the holidays."

"He picked out a piece of furniture for the house without asking you?" Liv gaped. "How is he still alive?"

Cortney was walking around without a limp or a black eye, so there was no way Delia's claim could be true.

"He paid for the table and arranged for me to work with the guy on a custom piece. He didn't pick anything." Delia smiled.

He was winning everybody over—all but one person.

"He is kinda great, Dyl," Shay said, proving me right.

All eyes were zeroed in on me. All I could do was shrug. They weren't wrong. Hopefully Liam would eventually give him a chance. Because although he wasn't openly hostile in front of me, my son pretty much ignored Cortney. And our family unit couldn't work like that forever.

"It's almost like the universe had a plan," I said, ready to move on. "Can we go back to the book now?"

They groaned, but we dove into a discussion about *Natural Born Charmer*. After a way too intense conversation about the waterfall role play scene, I headed downstairs.

Cortney was sprawled out on our bed with his laptop resting on his stomach, wearing an intense expression.

He was too big for the bed. His feet hung almost a foot off the end, but he'd yet to complain. He had one arm tucked behind his head, and his finger moved along his bun, carelessly playing with the blond strands. Normally at this time of night, he'd be working on his puzzle. He'd only been here for a few days, but he'd already finished one and moved on to a second.

He pulled in a breath, and his blue eyes snapped to me. "Is it a burger or ice cream or cherry Slurpee kind of night?"

At this moment, none of those options were appealing. I was keyed up. That's what I was. Book club was usually a highlight of my week. But tonight it had been a distraction. Or maybe Cortney was the distraction. His laugh had broken through every conversation. His voice had pulled me into his discussion with Beckett, and I hardly listened to my friends chat.

"Just bed." I headed for the dresser to pick out a set of clothes to sleep in.

Two minutes later, I was back, and Cortney had already put his laptop away. We had already developed a routine. As soon as we'd both changed and were in the room, it was time for lights-out. So I turned off the switch and shut the door.

Normally, this part of the night was relaxing, but tonight the dark felt more intense than his stare.

"You okay?" he asked.

"Yeah." I crawled under the sheet and stared up at the ceiling. I was antsy.

"Book club is much more detailed than I expected." His chuckle floated in the air.

"Everyone else is probably having an orgasm right now." Might as well throw it out there so this wasn't awkward.

His breathing hitched, and he swallowed audibly. "Uh. Do you need me to leave so you can take care of that?"

If I planned to take care of that, then the last thing I'd want would be for him to leave. Memories of his hands slowly running up my legs and separating them hit me suddenly. The feel of his hot breath between my thighs... My heart sped up when I imagined his lips pressing into me. His tongue lapping against my clit. Once. Then again and again.

My breath sped up and heat unfurled low in my belly.

"Dylan?"

My heart lurched at the interruption, and I snapped out of my memory.

He propped himself up on an elbow and looked down at me.

What the hell was I doing?

"Sorry."

He cocked a brow. "You okay?"

"Yup." I turned away from him. I was perfectly fine. Just frustrated.

Cortney
26

If I'd never seen Dylan come, if we'd never slept together, I wouldn't know what that hitch in her breathing meant. I wouldn't know that her cheeks flushed a rosy pink and she nibbled on her lower lip when she was turned on. I wouldn't burn with the knowledge.

But I had watched her come, with my face between her thighs, with my cock buried deep. Several times. So I knew. And I craved her.

She turned her back on me, but that did nothing to help my problem.

I flopped down onto the pillows and stared at the ceiling. Every time she sucked air into her lungs, my dick throbbed. She was so close. My hands itched to reach out and touch her.

She'd walked into the room tonight, all gorgeous crazy curls and bright gold eyes, and my cock surged. Every day, it got harder to resist dropping a kiss to her pink lips. Every night, it got harder to sleep next to her knowing she wasn't really mine.

Then the fucking book club and the conversation about the police officer role-play sex scenes. Jesus. Even from the family room, Beckett and I could hear every word they said. What had I done in a past life to deserve this particular type of torture?

We were two consenting adults lying in a bed together, so turned on it was painful. If I slid my hand along her smooth skin and slipped it under her shorts, I'd find her wet and ready. I had no doubt.

A part of me longed to say *fuck it* and do just that.

But I couldn't. As much as I wanted Dylan's body, I wanted it to be more than a simple release. And we weren't there yet.

So I locked my jaw and silently recited batting averages for the American league, pretending not to notice the heat wafting off the woman next to me. Ignoring the coconut scent in the air. Denying the way her soul called to mine.

"Maybe I do need ice cream."

Thank fuck. I tossed the covers off and practically jumped out of bed. I didn't need to get dressed. I slept in so many layers it was laughable. Tonight, I was wearing two pairs of boxers under my sweats just to be safe. I was losing my fucking mind.

"Very cherry blizzard?" I crammed my feet into slides and headed for the window.

"Please."

I slipped out. The night was warm and humid. Though the sun had set, it hadn't taken the thick layers of heat with it. Two avenues and a block to ice cream. Two avenues and a block back. The walk did me good. It cleared my lust-addled brain so that when I slipped back through the window, I had some semblance of control over my thoughts and reactions.

Dylan was sitting at my puzzle mat, working. I'd put maybe two hundred pieces together so far, but while I was gone, she had more than doubled that.

She tipped her chin up and winced, dropping a piece back into the pile. "Sorry."

I dropped to the floor next to her, ignoring the way my knees popped, set the blizzard down, and picked up the piece she'd been holding. "Don't be sorry." I held the piece for her. "You know I think it's cute when you puzzle."

"It's just"—she spun the piece between her fingers before popping it into place—"this is your stress relief. I don't want to take that away."

"It could be *our* stress relief," I offered.

Silently, she assessed me. Dylan usually took everything in stride. She rarely seemed concerned about anything, but tonight, there was a storm raging in her eyes. Giving her a small smile, I grasped her hand. Her touch was as electric as ever, and from the way goose bumps rippled up her arm, I'd say she felt it too. No matter how hard she fought to keep us in this friends limbo, we had a connection. So I'd keep fostering it. "I'd like to have things that are ours."

She sucked in a breath and smiled. "Yeah, I think I would too."

Her words had my heart practically floating in my chest. I couldn't help but pull her in for a celebratory hug. Because damn if her admission wasn't a huge win for me.

She melted against me. "You're a good hugger." Pulling back, she shot me a smirk and picked up her ice cream.

"Anytime you need a hug, my arms are available, Firefly." I swiped the puzzle piece from in front of her. "Now tell me where this one goes, because you're a helluva lot better at this than I am."

With a laugh, she scooped ice cream into her mouth, then she spent the next fifteen minutes teaching me her tricks.

When she'd yawned for the third time in as many minutes, I convinced her to climb into bed. Normally I wouldn't wrap an arm around her until she was asleep, but tonight, I didn't want to wait. So I draped my arm over her midsection and pulled her into my chest. It was a gamble. I half expected her to pull away and keep her distance, but she snuggled right into me. My big spoon to her little. I didn't have it all yet. But at least I had this.

Cortney
27

The loud banging shook the door and the frame.

"There's a line, you know." Liam was in a great mood again today. Fantastic.

"Two minutes." I glared at the door like it was the reason I was pissed off this morning.

"Forget it. I'll go upstairs."

For the most part, I'd been showering in the locker room. Not only was this bathroom the size of a tin can—the water hit mid-chest and I had to twist into a pretzel to wet my hair—but there was always a line and not much hot water.

But after waking up surrounded by soft skin and with Dylan's silky hair brushing against my chest, I needed to take the edge off. And that wasn't happening in the locker room. Since I'd already taken care of that, I'd definitely broken the six-minute shower rule that Delia harped on constantly.

I dipped my head to what felt like my belly button and rinsed the conditioner out of my hair, then I snagged my bottle of body wash. Squirting the liquid into my hand, I sniffed. The scent was different from the body wash I kept at the stadium. I wouldn't be buying this one again, especially since it made my skin tingle when I scrubbed. After a quick rinse, I grabbed a towel and tucked it around my waist.

I opened the door to the hall just in time to catch the flash of Liam as he disappeared into Shay's office. The kid wasn't supposed to be in there, but he shared a room with Kai, so I couldn't fault him for needing some alone time.

Rubbing at my hair with a hand towel, I stepped into my room and startled when Dylan popped up from beside our bed.

"Sorry, I was just grabbing my phone." She held up the device and wiggled it. "Who knows why it was under the bed."

I needed to get the woman an Apple Watch. She was always misplacing her phone. And in two days, the all-star break would be over and I'd be traveling again. The idea that I wouldn't be able to check in on her or just chat had already activated my anxiety.

She rounded the bed, her head tilted and her lips pursed. "What...?" She scanned me from head to toe. If the look on her face wasn't somewhere between confused as hell and worried, I might like that she was checking me out. "What's wrong with your hair?"

My hair?

My hands automatically shot to my head. The jerky movement loosened the towel at my waist, and before I could grasp the terry cloth, it fell to my feet.

Dylan's eyes widened. "Holy shit."

She was staring at me again. Still in horror rather than in awe.

Dipping my chin, I looked at my body, searching for the reason for her concern.

The issue was instantly obvious. My hair.

Not on my head, thank fuck. But every other part of my body was almost or completely hairless. I swiped for the towel and covered my dick and my very hairless balls. My face heated and my stomach sank. Why the hell was all the hair on my body falling out?

She stepped close and ran a finger over my arm. A few of the strands loosened and stuck to her finger as she did. "Did you use Delia's Nair?"

That was why my body wash smelled weird. My chest tightened, constricting my lungs, and I clenched my jaw to hold back a curse. First shower at home and *someone* put Nair in my body wash. Thank God I hadn't used it to wash my face, or I'd be browless.

"I...uh." There hadn't been an incident since the brisket, but only because I hadn't used my body wash yet. As badly as I wanted to tell on Liam, I wouldn't. "Yeah, I Nair sometimes." That was a total lie. On occasion, I'd been asked to for photo shoots. "You know." I swallowed. "Less hair, less wind resistance."

The little line between her brows appeared. "I thought that was just swimming." She eyed me again and laughed. "But damn that's dedication. Full-body dedication." She shook her head and left the room.

Sighing, I rubbed myself down, saying goodbye to the last of my body hair. Damn kid. I tossed on a pair of shorts and a T-shirt, then dug my hair dryer out of my duffel. Before I could plug it in, the lights flickered and went out.

A power outage? It wasn't even raining. Could have been a brown out. With temperatures in the nineties, it was hot in the house. Although it had central air, it worked about as well as most things did around here.

Just as I came out of my room, Liam appeared in the hall, glancing around with a lip pulled between his teeth and a furrowed brow. He scuffed one black Converse on the rug. "I wasn't in there."

The lie was almost a whisper as footsteps echoed on the stairs.

"Demon Spawn, Man Bun. Who blew the fuse?" Beckett stopped on the landing and scowled at the hair dryer in my hand. "Did you really try to blow dry your hair?"

I was standing in the hall with water dripping from my hair onto my T-shirt and the thing in my hand, though I hadn't gotten it plugged in yet. "Is that not allowed?"

The rules in this house were fucking weird.

"The ducking idiot who wired this place put the kitchen and these two rooms on the same fuse." Beckett waved from Shay's office to Dylan's room behind me. "If the microwave is going and you turn on the window unit in the office or the vacuum"— he glowered at the black hair dryer again—"or dry your ducking hair? Pop." He threw his hands up.

Liam hit me with a pleading look, and I got the silent message. He had turned on the AC unit, probably to cool Shay's office down. The office he'd been told to stay out of at least ten times since I'd been here. The last threat I'd heard tossed his way was that he'd lose the Beats that pretty much lived on his ears or around his neck if they found him in there again.

He had stolen my lucky socks, put hot sauce in my food, and now he'd put Nair in my soap. I had a split second to decide between being the adult in this situation or the friend. In the end, I still wanted to build a bridge between us.

"Sorry, Bossman. No one told me." I shrugged.

Beside me, Liam's entire body relaxed.

Beckett shook his head. "Of course you use a blow-dryer. Go flip the breaker. If you're gonna trip the breaker every time you need pretty hair, then you can be the one to fix it."

Liam fought his smile. *Nice, kid. I just saved your ass, and you're mocking me?* Maybe it was hopeless. Maybe it was time to give up on him.

I sighed. "Fine, where is it?"

Beckett pointed down the hall to the back of the house. "In the crawl space."

Of course it'd be in the only place smaller than the tin can of a shower. I moved in the general direction before the other conversation about this crawl space hit me.

Wait.

I spun back to Beckett. "The one with the snakes?"

He pursed his lips. "Eh. I've seen a couple, but they usually just move away as I crawl past."

I shot a look at Liam, who shrugged.

"Got a thing about snakes, Man Bun?" Beckett rocked on his heels, wearing a smirk.

The skinny slithering demons with unblinking eyes and rapidly flicking tongues whose mouths opened to four times the width of their bodies? The darty creatures that ate their live prey whole and let the massive bumps of the corpses rot in their stomachs for days? The gross reptiles that shed their skin, leaving skeleton-like husks in their wake each time they grew?

Hell yes, I had a thing about snakes.

"We could get Mom to do it," Liam offered.

Make the pregnant woman I was trying my damnedest to impress every day crawl into a dirty snake-filled hole? Might as well turn over my balls. I was pretty sure they would wither away if I did that.

"Nope, I'm good." Blinking back the panic threatening to bubble to the surface, I turned and shuffled toward the crawl space. The chance of there really being a snake inside a house were low, right? They were just messing with me, weren't they? Probably. But in *this* house? Anything was possible.

"Go down those three steps and through the half door. You'll see it. It's straight ahead," Beckett called after me.

The term *half door* was generous in this case. It didn't even come up to my waist. That wasn't the best sign. If I opened the door and a snake was sitting right there, I'd close it again. That was all. No sweat.

Slowly, I cracked it open and was hit hard by the smell of old dust. I braced myself. For nothing. Just darkness and a step. I pulled out my phone and turned on the flashlight. In the beam of light, I could make out a floor that may have been dirt or may have been concrete coated in years of dust. There were five support posts and beams running along the ceiling, but the place was mostly cobwebs and dust. Hundreds of cobwebs. About eight feet straight ahead was the fuse box. The path to it was mostly clear. Only there was no way I could stand up straight. I shuddered at the thought of crawling, so crouch-walking it was.

I did one more scan with my phone's flashlight. The floor was even, so it likely was a slab of concrete under the dirt. With my phone between my teeth so the light pointed toward the floor, I crouched and took two steps toward my goal. I had this. Two more steps. Another step in, and a crunch sounded behind me. Fuck.

I spun and let out a high-pitched and embarrassingly loud sound. Then I teetered. Dammit. I heaved my body the other way and almost caught myself, but I'd overcorrected, and before I could stop, I tipped too far forward. As I tried once again to gain my balance, I wobbled face-first into a layer of sticky webs. I yelped again and fell straight down into the dirt.

"Uck." I beat at the clinging strings.

A throat cleared above me as a light shined down at me.

"You okay?" Liam asked. He was nothing more than a silhouette behind the piercing light.

I was lying in dirt, possibly next to a snake or two. I had cobwebs in my hair, and it smelled like something had died down here. I was not okay.

"N—" I stopped myself and tried again, two octaves lower. "I'm good."

"Need help?"

Brushing another web off my face, I willed my heart to beat normally and fought back the panic that was seconds away from taking over. All I had to do was reset the damn breaker and get out. Where was my phone? I couldn't see a damn thing now that Liam had dimmed his flashlight. I wasn't sure I could trust his help, but I wouldn't mind a little light down here.

"Could you hold the light and keep an eye out for snakes?"

"Sure." The space was illuminated again as he scanned it. I found my phone first. It was face down in the dirt so the light had been covered. I dusted it off, turned the light off, and dropped it back into my pocket. Even though I'd have to take another shower once I got out of here, no part of me wanted to crawl on my hands and knees to the fuse box. So I got back in a crouch and quickly made my way across to the box, then high-tailed it back to Liam.

He backed up as I got close, and once I'd cleared the opening, we slammed the door shut.

Liam's mouth lifted in the corner as he took me in, but in an instant, his eyes widened and he almost fell on his ass as he backed away from me.

"Oh—oh shit." He crashed into the wall behind him.

Why was he freaking out? I peered over my shoulder, but the door was firmly shut, and it didn't appear as though any critters had escaped.

He pointed at me. "Y-your hair."

Oh, the cobwebs. I lifted my hand to wipe them away, but as I did, something moved against my scalp. My heart clenched.

"What the fuck is it?" I brought my hand closer, then froze. Did I want to touch whatever it was? Hell no. I dropped my hand again. But I didn't want it on me. I brought it up again, and the creature moved. And it *hissed.* It fucking hissed. Nope, not touching it. "What *is* it?"

Liam swallowed. "The biggest spider I've ever seen, and it's coming for your face."

"Get it off. Get it *off.*" I flapped my arms and shouted, not caring that my voice had gone so high I sounded like a five-year-old. "Get. It. Fucking. Off."

Liam shook his head so violently his Beats swayed around his neck and his hair whipped his face. "I'm not touching it."

"Get something."

He pushed off the wall and ran to the closet by the stairs.

The hiss grew louder as the spider crawled over my ear. In a panic, I batted at my hair as hard as I could. There was a tiny thump against the wall, then the spider that had to be three inches long slid down to the carpet.

Liam came back with two brooms in hand. He narrowed his eyes at the awful thing. "Wanna just leave it?"

"Hell no. I don't want that thing to end up in my bed tonight."

His brows were practically in his hairline now. "You're going to stay?"

Between the shock on his face and the incredulous tone, I finally got the reason for all of this. He figured if he tortured me enough, I'd leave. This kid had a lot to learn about me.

Squaring up to him, I looked him straight in the eye. "Unless your mom kicks me out, I'm not going anywhere. So let's kill this thing so it doesn't crawl on our faces tonight."

He shuddered. "Yeah. I don't want that."

Taking a broom from him, I tipped my head. "You go on that side. I'll stay here. We'll just have to beat it with the brooms until it's dead."

"Good plan." He nodded solemnly as he moved into position.

We both lifted our brooms—

"What the heck are you two screaming about?"

Startled, I glanced up. Dylan stood at the bottom of the stairs, brows pinched and lips parted in confusion. One step up, Delia's head was cocked to the side and her hands were on her hips. Her mini-mes affected the same stance behind her.

Okay, fine, we looked ridiculous.

"Ma, it's the biggest, grossest spider I've ever seen."

Dylan rolled her eyes and strode past us. Before I could

protest or pull her away from the beast, she scooped it into her hand and headed for her window.

I wasn't sure if I was embarrassed, impressed, or grateful that I didn't have to touch the thing.

"Fish spiders are harmless," she called from her room.

"Harmless, my ass," I muttered.

I looked to Liam for backup to that statement, and for the first time ever, he smiled at me. My phone buzzed in my pocket. I pulled it out, finding a notification for an invoice from Momcom. The bill was four thousand dollars, and the description read *bad word fee*.

I glanced from my phone back to Liam, who was still smiling.

Worth it.

Cortney

28

"Will we all fit on the way home?" I asked, bringing my glass to my lips. Everyone complained about Shay's smoothies, quietly calling them swamp sludge, but as far as protein drinks went, they weren't bad. And she used a variety of recipes, so we wouldn't get sick of one particular flavor.

"Define all, because I'm sure as duck not bringing the entire team here," Beckett snapped.

Dylan giggled. "What if he wanted to invite his friends over?"

Delia tipped her head to the right and batted her long lashes at Beckett. "Yeah, like for a play date."

Liv smacked the counter. "You two egg him on and then act shocked when he gets mad."

"Neither of them is shocked when that happens. It's their end game," I assured her.

Dylan loved to stir shit up, then stand back and watch the fall-out. Normally I'd play into it, but this conversation with Beckett mattered. If Dylan and Liam wouldn't fit, then I'd take my own car this morning. They trumped Beckett's weird need to carpool.

"All of us means you, me, and Liv, plus Liam and Dylan. They're coming to the stadium today."

Beckett paused with his mug halfway to his lips. "Why are you just telling me this now? I would have planned some—oof." He stumbled forward and almost dropped his coffee. "Livy, what the duck?"

"Is it not okay?" Dylan looked from me to Liv, who was at the table.

"It's perfect. Cortney cleared it with us." She smiled at her friend.

"I asked Liv," I said when Beckett grumbled.

"Because Beckett would say no." Dylan laughed.

No. Beckett would have been happy to have them there, but he also would have taken over. He'd bring Liam to his office, introduce him to the staff, probably get him into more places than I could. But I'd finally cracked Liam's armor yesterday, and I needed to win a few more points to keep my momentum going so we could move past the lashing-out stage. Maybe eventually we could even become friendly.

Liv canted to the side and whispered in her husband's ear.

"All good, Dippy Do, you and Demon Spawn can come to the stadium anytime you want. I'll make sure Charlie brings the Escalade for the ride home. You don't need to take your car this morning."

Why the hell was Beckett so adamant about me riding with them? At first, I went with it, figuring he and Liv were feeling me out. Now, though? On day six? It was just weird. He spent far more time asking me about baseball than anything to do with Dylan.

Typically I spent the all-star break with the guys who were playing the game. This was the first year in a long time that I hadn't gone as the starting National League catcher. Insecurity said I was losing my ability to play already. Rationally I knew that the Metros young guy was now filling the spot the fans had elected me to.

Having extra time at home with Dylan was one of those blessings in disguise. Or as Dylan said, the universe must have had a plan. It relaxed me, thinking about life the way Dylan did. Like the pressure to make sure every aspect of my life worked out wasn't on me.

Blessing or not, though, sitting around the stadium all week left me too much time to think. I worked out and went to practice sessions, but if not for the reports Beckett kept throwing at me and the lists of players he wanted me to check out, I'd be going stir crazy. That nagging fear surrounding what I'd do after I retired kept nudging its way back into my brain. Especially when Beckett insisted that I help him find my replacement.

"It has nothing to do with not wanting to retire." The leather of the guest chair cracked as I scanned the spec sheet he pushed across his huge desk. My hair, still damp from my post-workout shower, fell against my cheeks.

"I didn't call you up here to say no," he growled.

"You called me up here to say what?" I sat straighter and pulled my hair into a bun, securing it with the elastic I wore around my wrist. "I get that I'll have to start working with my replacement next season. Makes sense; I'm thirty-fucking-five. I've got one, maybe two more seasons in me."

"What's the issue, then?" Beckett cocked a challenging brow.

"Lewis is not the right fit. You have three pitchers on the roster that need to be calmed down just about every time they're on the mound." The team Beckett was putting together would be leading the American league in a few years. The guy was smart, but sometimes he missed the subtleties of the interaction between players. "Some of your pitchers have a short fuse. Others have crazy nerves. You pick the hottest head in the game to be the person to talk them down? How the hell do you see that playing out?"

"He's leading the league in home runs. I see that as scoring more and winning more." Beckett tapped hard on the paper he wanted me to read.

Ignoring his urging, I slumped back in the chair. I knew Lewis's stats. "I get the appeal of a lefty catcher whose bat is on fire." That used to be me. At twenty-five, I led the Metros in batting average and RBIs. "But in two years, when his age catches up to him and he's feeling the wear and tear of the game, he won't be your heavy hitter anymore. Then you're just stuck with a hothead who doesn't know how to call pitches. You want to hold your catcher's hand like you do your management team?" I crossed my arms over my chest. "You need to have someone controlling the game from behind the plate. Someone smart, not someone who is controlled by the guy in the front office."

Beckett pursed his lips and squinted at me, then at the paper on the desk.

A knock sounded on the door behind us, and Liv peeked in. "I didn't realize you were up here. I just dropped Dylan and Liam off in the locker room. They're looking for you."

Shit. I wanted to be down there to greet them.

"Good luck." I stood and headed out the door.

Dylan
29

"This is way bigger than I thought it'd be." Liam took in the locker room, scrutinizing the few players scattered on the sofas in the center of the space. "Each person has their own area, not just a locker."

The day Beckett had brought us all to a game, we'd hung out in the team room with other families, but because the guys had been showering and dressing and talking to reporters, we hadn't come in here.

Liam was right; it was much bigger than I expected and so much cleaner. No garbage or dirty clothes like the locker room of my high school days. Every locker housed a few neatly hung uniforms and gear. The one with the most stuff was labeled *Miller*, but even with all the protective gear, Cortney's was organized. A white folding chair with the Revs' logo sat in front of each locker. The light wood lockers were polished to a shine, and the room smelled clean.

"Wait." I spun on the navy carpet. "Didn't you come in here after the game a couple of months ago?"

"No." Liam frowned at me. "Remember? Beckett made us leave after Adeline threw up."

That was true, but... "How did you get Cortney's socks if you weren't in here?"

His brows lifted practically to his hairline. "What the hell are you talking about?"

There was no twinkle in his eyes, no hint of a smirk, no purse in his lips. Weird. It was almost like he was truly confused.

"Well, this is different." One of the guys stood from the brown leather couch and headed our way.

My son would probably know his name, but I didn't pay enough attention to the games to recognize him. He had perfectly placed blond streaks in his light brown hair. I couldn't tell whether they were natural or if I should ask for his hairdresser's number.

He stopped in front of us and grinned. "A gorgeous woman and a Metros fan."

"Hi." I smiled.

Beside me, Liam scowled. "We don't need you."

"Liam." I whacked his arm. My stomach knotted. Just what I needed. For my kid to piss off another Revs player.

The man only laughed in response. He was good-looking, with a straight nose, white teeth, and dimples. Not in that stomach-twisting, steal-my-breath way that Cortney was, but hot all the same.

"You're friends with Mr. Langfield, right?" His brown eyes bounced to my son and back to me.

"Yeah. His wife, Liv, is my bestie." I held my hand out. "I'm Dylan, and this is my son Liam."

"Kyle." He grinned.

Liam sighed.

"You know what you need?" Kyle spun and sauntered across the room.

"I bet you're going to tell us," Liam mumbled as Kyle stopped at the corner locker.

"Be nice," I hissed.

I'd let it go if Liam's attitude would only make Beckett and me look bad. Beckett didn't really give a shit anyway. But if Liam was a jerk today, it would stress Cortney out. And where was Cortney? He said he'd meet us here, but he hadn't replied to my text when we arrived. Liv had been certain he was in the locker room when she dropped us off down here.

"I'm not wearing that guy's jersey, Ma." My son glanced down at his green Metros T-shirt, then back at Kyle as he returned holding out a jersey emblazoned with a big number 29. "I'm not a Revs fan."

No, he was not. However, the Metros shirt he wore did bear Cortney's name and number. Liam had slowly been warming up to him. Seeing him in it would probably make Cortney's day.

"Give this a try?" Kyle held up his white jersey with navy pinstripes. Liam folded his arms over his chest, but before he flat-out refused, I jumped in.

"Can I try it?"

Cocking a brow, Kyle held it out for me. I spun and slipped my arms into the large sleeves. He was nowhere near as big as Cortney, but it still hung on me like a tent, so I quickly tied the ends together over my navy sundress.

Kyle smirked and gave me a once-over. "Looks great—" As his attention drifted back up to my face, his eyes darted to one side like he was looking over my shoulder. "Hey, Shammy. You okay?"

I turned and smiled as Cortney came up and towered over us all. The smell of his cedar cologne blanketed the air instantly. I never would have said cedar was my favorite scent, but the more time I spent with Cortney, the more I appreciated the spicy, woodsy aroma.

He lifted his arm for an instant, then dropped it to his side and squeezed his fingers into a fist. His normally cool blue aura was muddled with dark colors like he was being pummeled by a storm of emotions. He took in my shirt and took a quick breath in through his nose. In an action that seemed forced, he smiled at us.

"Sorry. Beckett had me upstairs."

I waved him off. He was busy; we understood that. There was no reason he should stress about us.

"Do you guys know Shammy?" Kyle asked.

"*He's* who we're here to see." Liam flicked the hair out of his eyes.

"Oh." Kyle scanned the three of us. He opened his mouth but snapped it shut again and took a step back toward the center of the room, where the big Revs logo was affixed to the carpet. "Well, have fun."

"Thanks for greeting them, Streaks." Cortney gave me another quick look and frowned.

"You okay?" I tipped my head back to meet a pair of blue eyes I'd never seen look so harsh. He was irritated. Hopefully he hadn't had a fight with Beckett.

"I'm fine." He dipped his chin and turned to Liam. "I thought you might want to see the field and the bullpen."

We followed him through the tunnels and ended up in the bullpen. Cortney started explaining warming up pitchers and practice time. He squatted to let Liam throw a couple of pitches, then he opened the door that led to the field of green.

Wow. I'd never seen the field from this angle. I'd only been near the dugout. The grass was almost impossibly green, and the white lines in the sand were perfectly straight. We were surrounded by what seemed like endless stands and a clear blue sky.

"So cool." Liam flicked his head, sending his red hair flipping back. "Can we go out there?"

"Sure." Cortney tipped his chin.

Liam took off for the grass, and for the first time since we'd arrived, Cortney's face lifted in a real smile.

"He might be in Metros green, but he's got your number on."

The grass tickled my feet around my sandals as we strolled into the outfield and headed for the dugout where Liam had gone.

"I see." His frustration had mostly melted away as he yanked his phone from his pocket and fired off a message. "So, you a Bosco fan?"

Bosco?

"Uh." I fingered my rose quartz and pulled it along its chain. "I'm not sure I know what a Bosco is. Is it a game or a baseball thing, or is it food?" Just the thought made me hungry, so I dug a cherry Jolly Rancher out of my dress pocket and popped it into my mouth.

He threw his head back and laughed. "Where did you get the shirt, Firefly?"

"Oh." I stopped in my tracks and spun, trying to see the name on my back. But I couldn't. "Your friend tried to give it to Liam, but he was refusing to put it on, so I did it to appease the guy."

Cortney nodded. "Can I have it?"

"Sure." I unknotted the ends and, with his help, shrugged out of it. "Did I mess it up by tying it? He didn't say anything."

Balling up the shirt, he trotted over to the dugout and tossed the jersey onto the ground in a heap.

"Samson, they're going to have to clean that now."

He shrugged and strode back to me. "They can burn it for all I care."

For a second, I panicked. Had I done something to ruin the shirt? But then a realization hit me.

"Are you jealous?" I asked, batting my lashes at him.

He wrapped his arm around my shoulders. "Would you like that?"

I smiled up at him. Because I very much liked the idea that he might want me wearing his jersey.

Dylan

30

I blew across the surface of my coffee, then took a small sip. My attention wasn't on my favorite morning drink, though. No, it was locked on Cortney's wide shoulders and the way they strained the fabric of his button-down as he worked at the counter.

His hips moved slightly to music I couldn't hear. But I was pretty certain I knew what he was listening to. He mouthed the words to the song he said was ours. Although I had no idea why he picked that one for us, I loved watching his ass shake to the beat.

The man was gorgeous, and it was getting harder to ignore that fact every day. My traitorous body reacted every time he was around. At night, we talked before falling asleep. Every morning, I woke up wrapped in his arms like our energies couldn't resist the connection while we slept.

"You're drooling." Delia rested her elbows on the counter next to mine and bumped me with her shoulder.

"A million percent accurate. That man wears a button-down and pants like no one else." And being so close to something I couldn't have made me want it more.

"Is he singing a Taylor Swift song?" She chuckled. "Is it 'ME!'?"

With my attention still firmly locked on Cortney's ass, I nodded.

"Regardless of the song, ogling those perfect shoulders and one of the best asses I've ever seen is the most fun I've had in far too long." She leaned closer. "Please tell me you aren't still being ridiculous. You're taking advantage of that man at night, right?"

Eyes wide, I spun to face her.

She tilted her head, and her long blond ponytail fell over her shoulder. "You're the one who's always saying a man is better than a vibrator. Why do you look so shocked by the question?"

"Because you're the one who's gifted me fifteen vibrators to prove I don't need a man."

She slapped the countertop and cackled.

Cortney turned to look at me with one brow raised.

"Just admiring the view, Samson," I called across the room.

He rolled his eyes and went back to the eggs he was scrambling. Although breakfast mostly fell on Shay's job list, she had an early appointment today, and Cortney had volunteered to take over. The universe was on my side today. This meant his delicious eggs instead of whichever disgusting concoction she decided to whip up.

Beckett snorted behind us. He had his laptop set up at the table. The man worked a good twenty hours a day. "Don't make him a piece of meat, ladies. Athletes have been up in arms about that recently."

Cortney scooped up three plates and dropped one off for Beckett. "Does that mean you get offended when your wife checks out your ass, Bossman?"

Beckett huffed. "Of course not."

"Then let Dylan be Dylan." Cortney set a plate in front of Delia and one in front of me. Along with eggs, my breakfast consisted of toast, pitted cherries, and yogurt. He squeezed my shoulder and hovered close. "I'll see you at the game tonight, right?"

The all-star break had ended, and he was heading in to work with a new pitcher, but he had gotten tickets for Liam and me.

"Of course."

His responding smile made my stomach flip. And when he moved in even closer and his breath skated across my face, goose bumps erupted along my neck and arms. His warm lips pressed against my forehead, and my heart skipped. "I left something on the bed for you."

I wanted to ask him exactly what he meant, but his eyes shifted to the door as Liv came in. "Eggs on the stove, toast on the plate, fruit is cut in the bowl."

"Thanks, Cort. Good luck at the game." She moved to make her kids' plates.

"Are you not coming?" he asked.

"No, I'm staying with the kids so Dylan can go, but Hannah will be there." Liv turned back to the breakfast plates.

"Get Aaron ready to play. I'm counting on you, Man Bun." Beckett tipped his chin before turning back to his laptop and breakfast.

Cortney's hair brushed his shoulders as he shook his head. "Aye, aye, Bossman." He gave my shoulder one more squeeze, then headed out of the room.

My eyes tracked him the whole way.

"I know I'm always saying you don't need a man. But one who's willing to bend into a pretzel to make your kid happy, who deals with your best friends every day, cooks for you, and smiles at you like you're his world?" Delia stabbed her scrambled eggs and brought her fork to her mouth. "Maybe one like that wouldn't be such a bad addition to your life."

"Cordelia Masters, has Cortney worn you down?" I popped a cherry into my mouth.

"I was about to ask you the same thing, Dyl." She tipped her head.

I didn't know how to answer her. Cortney and I weren't together—not like that. Part of me wished we could have more. But with him being a Miller, that would probably never be the case. Rubbing my stomach, I fought back the pit of dread that formed every time I thought about whatever this was with Cortney coming to an end.

After I finished breakfast, I went down to see what he'd left me. The bed was made, and three bags sat in the center of it. I set aside the one with Liam's name scrawled across it. In the first bag I opened, I found a navy jersey with a big 8 on the back.

Just like yesterday, my heart skipped. He wanted me in his jersey. The next bag was much smaller. Under the tissue paper was a small piece of pink fabric. I sucked in a hard breath as I realized what it was. It was so tiny. It was hard to believe that our little girl would ever be that small. But I unfolded the pink pinstriped number 8 and swallowed hard. Then I unfolded his note.

I won't be able to focus if anyone else's name is on your back.
♥ Cortney
PS I broke Liam's rule, but I have faith in you.

Cortney
31

Absentmindedly, I clipped into my gear. Shit, I couldn't get the smile off my face. Thousands of people wore my jersey to every game. For ten years the Metros had been making hundreds of thousands of dollars a year off my number. Now the Revs were doing the same. But seeing Dylan and Liam sitting to the right of the dugout with my name on their backs? It was fucking priceless.

My parents and siblings had come to games more times than I could count. They had a box at City Field where the Metros played.

But having Dylan here bolstered my spirits and had me flying high.

Kyle Bosco scooted down the bench until he was next to me. "So you and Dylan?"

"That's my goal." The answer was both that simple and way too hard to explain. But after almost losing my mind yesterday when I saw Dylan in this guy's jersey, I was making it simple for him. "So for you, as my friend, Dylan and I are a thing."

Seeing as I was not a caveman, I understood that I couldn't toss her over my shoulder and claim her. She had free will, but

I'd be damn sure I did everything in my power to convince her to choose *me*.

Kyle got a lot of attention from women. He was a good-looking guy, and the ladies all loved the 'streaks' in his hair. I had never paid attention to that shit, but I didn't want this guy smiling at Dylan.

He ran his hand through his hair. "If ya had mentioned it, I wouldn't have—"

"Streaks," I said, "we're good."

I hadn't told anyone about the baby yet. It had only been two weeks, and I wanted time to see where Dylan and I were headed. I knew what I wanted, but I wasn't sure where she stood. I hauled myself up and snapped my chest guard on. The teenager singing the national anthem was headed out to the center of the field with the color guard, and we both needed to be in the grass before it started.

"Let's just focus on the game," I said, holding out my fist for a bump.

He tapped his knuckles against mine, then we took off to line up with the rest of the team. "I'm surprised the white clip isn't making you insane."

"What?" I craned my neck to take in the bottom clip on my left leg. The one that had broken during warm-ups had been replaced by someone on staff. But the clip used to tighten the strap was white instead of black, making it pop against my navy socks.

I was busy talking to Bosco when I was putting the gear on, so I hadn't noticed, but now as the young girl sang the Star-Spangled Banner my brain fixated on it. I never wore white gear. Black, it was always black. Never white, because change threw off my game. If I couldn't focus, I wouldn't be able to help Aaron through the innings, and this was the kid's first major league start. He needed me tuned into him at all times, not stressing about a stupid detail like the color of one lousy clip. I had to get it off. That meant I'd have to take the pads off, then put them on again left to right.

My heart took off at a gallop behind my ribs. I wouldn't have time to change pads after the anthem. I barely had time to grab my mask and get back to the plate. If I caused a delay, the inning would start off poorly and might mess with everyone's rhythm. My breath came quicker, and my hands started to sweat as all the repercussions hit me like one line drive after another.

"Dude." Emerson, our third baseman, elbowed me as he clapped.

Robotically, I clapped too.

"Why do you look like someone ran over your dog?"

"Fuck, is it the clip?" Kyle asked from my other side. "Did you not realize they changed it?"

Damiano looked down. "Oh shit. Who fucked with your stuff?"

"It's fine." I muttered and headed to the dugout to grab my mask. I had to get over this. Stomping down the steps, I glowered at everyone within five feet of me and swiped up my hat and face mask.

"Samson." Her voice caressed my consciousness as I stepped back onto the grass from the dugout.

I spun to where she sat with Liam. A pair of sunglasses rested just in front of the knot of curls on the top of her head. A few red tendrils fell around her pale neck. My jersey was knotted above her white cut-offs. She looked perfect. "Love that the D will get to snuggle up to your ass when you squat."

What? I couldn't help but laugh even if I had no idea what she was talking about. This woman was ridiculous, and I loved it.

"The white D on your sock." She pointed.

I tucked my chin, still unsure of what she was referring to. Then I saw it. The clip that had been sending me into a panic. I took it in again, from her perspective. It was more like a rectangle with rounded corners, but I could see the D she was talking about. And yes, when I squatted that clip did rest right against my ass.

"I guess the universe decided that if I was wearing your name, you'd wear mine too. And we know your ass is my favorite." She hit me with a smile that sucked the breath from my lungs.

"Ma." Liam flopped into the chair and crossed his arms, glaring at her, then me. "Please make her stop."

With a chuckle, I shrugged. Like I had any control over his mother. She liked seeing her initial on my leg. As if she wanted to be claimed by me. I'd take it. It was a baby step, but we were moving in the right direction.

She giggled. Liam sighed again. And my shoulders relaxed.

To me, this change in my gear had presented as a problem, a deviation from my routine. But everything about Dylan had been a deviation from my routine. Yet not one bit of it had been bad.

Her initial on my calf.

I let out a breath.

I could live with this, especially since she loved it. Maybe we really were on our way to becoming something more than two people having a baby together. And that idea made my entire night.

Dylan

32

Cortney moved to the plate, his demeanor completely changed. His body was rigid during the anthem, the tension swirling around him. I could almost feel it even though I was more than twenty feet away. Then two of his teammates were pointing at his leg, and that's when I noticed the difference between his right shin protector and the left. He'd been open about how important his routine was. Everything from his lucky socks to the color of his gear, from the order he put each piece on to the time he arrived at the stadium for games. Even the white button-down.

His tendency to stress, even about the little things, hurt my heart. Maybe I could help him understand that the universe had plans. That they were amazing rather than things to worry about or overthink. Plus, I liked the idea that the universe put my name on his ass.

"I keep waiting for him to get fed up and walk away. I've been as much of a dick as I could be. Believe me, I've tried everything."

"What?" I asked.

Liam waved me off. "It's pointless. It's like he's immune to my asshole tendencies and your weirdness." He sank so low in his seat it was like he was wishing it would swallow him.

"Weirdness?" I frowned at him.

"Ma, you realize you just yelled across the field about the guy's ass?" He crossed his arms over his new jersey. My number 8 jersey was navy, and Liam's was white with navy pinstripes. When I gave Liam his gift from Cortney, I worried that I'd have to force him to wear it, but he came upstairs wearing it without any prodding. And even if he still frowned about anything involving Cortney, I could see that thick shell slowly cracking. He was starting to like the guy.

Cortney's forearms flexed as he adjusted his hair and settled the hat and mask on his head. He lowered to a squat and shook out his broad shoulders. Yeah. Cortney Miller behind the plate was the world's best view. A quick snap of his head, and his blue eyes burned into mine. With a grin he winked.

Liam fake gagged. "You two need to be less gross."

"Liam, life lesson moment here." I tucked a leg under myself on the plastic seat and pulled my sunglasses off the top of my head. Settling them on my face, I said, "It's my job as a parent to embarrass you for the rest of your life."

He groaned.

"Could be worse, we could have brought all the moms." I pulled out a cherry Jolly rancher and slipped it between my teeth.

"Ha-ha." He rolled his eyes but quickly settled in to watch the game.

I'd been to a few baseball games with Liam over the years, and even one Revs game in June, but knowing one of the players made the experience completely different. Cortney during a game was hot. As much as I joked that I was here for the view, it was his control that amazed me. His ability to settle the young pitcher and joke around with the guys at bat. How fast he could run from second base at the end of an inning to get behind the plate and start the next one. He was incredible at what he did, and that pulled weird in my chest.

The game ended on a strike in the top of the ninth with the Revs leading by two. Cortney lifted his mask and fist bumped the pitcher before heading our way.

"Liam." He called to my son from the grass and tossed the ball. Liam's eyes widened, but he caught it. With another wink, Cortney disappeared down into the dugout.

"I can't believe he just gave me the game ball!" Liam beamed.

"Dylan?" Hannah stood in the aisle, motioning to us. "Beckett asked me to bring you to the team room."

"Do you think some of the guys would sign this?" Liam hopped up and followed Hannah, and I shuffled out of the row behind them.

"I'm sure they will. Let me grab Tom Wilson's daughter from the box, and we'll head down, okay?" Hannah said, barely turning back to us. The woman was always moving. She reminded me a lot of Liv. So efficient.

We grabbed the head coach's daughter, and by the time we made it to the team room, the post-game food was already set out. A few of the guys that hadn't played were milling around.

"Can we eat?" Liam asked.

"Dude, we each had two hot dogs and ice cream already." So far, I hadn't been hit with morning sickness or extreme fatigue, but bloating was the current bane of my existence, and if I ate any more, my already snug shorts wouldn't button.

"What? Third dinner is a thing." Liam laughed.

"I'll walk over with you." Beside him, Avery, Tom Wilson's daughter, smiled.

My son's face turned scarlet. The twenty-five-year-old blond was gorgeous, and clearly Liam wasn't oblivious to this fact.

"Sure." Liam swallowed audibly and followed her.

"Hey."

One of Cortney's teammates sidled up beside me, smiling. He held his hand out. "Christian Damiano."

"Dragon?" I asked, trying to place the man into the stories Cortney had told me.

He laughed. "'Cause I throw the fire." Though he was facing me as we chatted, his eyes slipped over my head to the food table multiple times. Just like Liam, this guy seemed to have a thing for Avery Wilson.

"She's pretty."

His eyes snapped back to me. "What?" He shook his head. "Oh, no. She's just…" With his warmer complexion, the flush was subtle, but it was still there. He cleared his throat.

I got a strong whiff of Cortney's cologne as he came up behind me. "Hi, Firefly," he said, moving in close to me. "Dragon." He tipped his head, unknowingly saving his friend from having to explain his fascination with his head coach's daughter. "You hungry?"

I shook my head. "I ate."

"Let me guess." He chuckled and angled in closer, his hair tickling my temple. "Hot dogs and ice cream again?"

"Dinner of champions."

"So, are you two…?" Christian pointed his finger from me to Cortney and back again.

I wasn't sure what exactly Cortney had told his teammates, but I didn't want to put him on the spot.

"Friends," I said quickly.

Beside me, Cortney jerked. I peeked up at him, but his face was blank, and his gaze was fixed on something across the room.

"Oh." Christian nodded. "Cool."

"Let's get Liam. I want to head home." Without waiting for a response, Cortney strode toward my son. *Friends* was clearly the wrong answer.

"Nice meeting you." I waved and followed my suddenly grumpy... I didn't even know what to call him. Baby daddy wasn't it. It didn't even begin to describe what he meant to me. I thought *friend* worked. That term meant something to me. Very few people held that title in my life, and lately, he was becoming one of my favorite friends. One of my favorite people. But from his response, it was clear that label had insulted him.

Cortney chatted with Liam on the drive, smiling and laughing about the game. It wasn't until Liam headed into his room and we were alone that the grump returned.

"I'm going to change. You can go to sleep." He yanked the drawer open and pulled out sweats and a shirt, then stormed out.

Alone in my room, I adjusted the crystals on the studs-turned-bookshelf and dresser, hoping to cleanse the angry energy that Cortney had left in his wake. We needed to talk. The question was whether we should do it tonight or before his game tomorrow. I slipped into my pajamas and readjusted my crystals again. Nervousness was a foreign sensation to me. I couldn't think of the last time I was truly nervous about something.

It might have been when I met Brett's parents. My spine stiffened at just the thought of them. Dammit. Now I was adding to the negative energy in the room.

The door shut, startling me, and I whipped around.

I sucked in a hard breath and my eyes widened.

His blond hair brushed his bare shoulder. His bulging arms and chiseled chest were on full display, along with a twelve-pack —was that a thing?—of abs. I couldn't tear my focus away from his body. I was hypnotized. Trapping my bottom lip between my teeth, I gave him a thorough once-over. Somehow, the smooth, hairless chest only made him hotter. Even his hairless legs were sexy—his tight quads and sleek calves.

The Batman boxer briefs were so on-par for him. The sight actually soothed me.

What I wasn't used to was the scowl marring his gorgeous face.

"I'm too tired to deal with being overheated tonight." He tossed his clothes into a heap on the floor.

"You're mad at me." I didn't know how else to start, so I dove in headfirst.

He sank onto the bed, his entire being deflating with the motion. He ran his hand through his hair, pushing it away from his face, and pinned me with his intense blue stare. "I'm frustrated. We are *not* friends." He huffed and dropped his forearms to his knees.

I flinched at the stabbing pain that struck my chest. Because despite the limbo we were in, I thought we had that. I shifted on my bare feet. "Why?"

He snapped up and was standing in front of me before I even blinked. "Because being this close to you?" His breathing was ragged and his thick chest was heaving. "Right this minute?" He scanned my face, then locked eyes with me. "I feel alive in a way I never knew existed."

He took one step closer, and his bare chest brushed against me. With one hand, he cupped my neck. My body broke out in goose bumps at the contact. Anything between us would be complicated, and it would probably be safest to focus on co-parenting, but I wasn't sure I cared about complications anymore.

"Do you feel this? This current between us?" Dropping his forehead to rest against mine, he let out a groan.

My body throbbed with every hot breath that escaped his lips. I needed his mouth on mine. I needed his callused hands on my skin. His weight above me. I wet my lips, suddenly parched, and he zeroed in on my mouth. Then he had one arm snaked around me and he was pulling me into the wall of his chest. Every warm swell of muscle pressed tight into me. His erection pressed hard into my hip, making my core clench.

"How can you feel this, Firefly, and say we're just friends?"

"I never said *just*."

I gave in then, closing the inch of space between his lips and mine.

Cortney

33

The second her mouth touched mine, fucking fireworks ignited inside me. The taste I'd been dying to have on my tongue exploded. The soft, plush lips moving against me were both not enough and overwhelming. It was the moment I'd been anticipating for weeks. Dylan in my arms. Her breath mingling with mine as I tucked her against my bare chest. I coaxed and toyed with her until she opened her mouth and let me in. She looped her arms around my neck and tangled her fingers in my hair.

Goddamn. She was everything I wanted, and I needed to be inside her.

I was dying to rip off the cropped shirt so I could get my hands on the beautiful breasts that I'd been dreaming of for weeks. But as I slipped my fingers under the material and brushed the underside of her breast, she pulled back.

"What are we doing?" she whispered, her eyes wide and searching.

The question was a reminder that I should be clear about where I stood before we went any further. The last time we'd had a talk like this, we were in agreement that it was a one-time thing. But now, she needed to understand that I wanted more.

"How about we give us a try?" Gently, I cupped her face with both hands. "I don't know if it will work, but fuck, do I want it to. I'm so sick of acting like I don't want the real thing with you."

The gold flecks in her eyes sparkled as she surveyed me. For several long seconds, she didn't respond. During the silence, my anxiety crept back in, and just as I'd convinced myself that she'd say no, she nodded. Then she pressed her lips against my sternum. My abs clenched as she slowly, torturously, kissed *down* my stomach and inched toward my boxers.

My cock jumped and strained against the thin material as she pressed an open-mouthed kiss above my belly button. She did it again, and my knees wobbled.

Fuck.

I wanted her mouth on me. For weeks I'd dreamed of her full pink lips wrapped around my dick. My hand knotted in her hair, holding her while I fucked her mouth so deep she gagged.

The tips of her fingers brushed against the skin just above my waistband, making my hips jerk. Then she was pulling down my boxers.

My cock sprang free, desperate for attention.

On her knees, she peered up at me, her cheeks flushed and her eyes glassy with desire. My heart raced in my chest, and I swore my dick wept as she slowly wet her lips.

"Please," I croaked.

Without taking her eyes off mine, she swirled her tongue over the tip. I groaned and fisted her hair, gently guiding her until her lips were around me. She sucked me into her warm mouth. Damn, it took all my willpower to resist thrusting deep. She braced herself with one hand on my thigh, and she wrapped the fingers of her other hand tightly around my shaft and pulled me in.

"Fuck." I groaned and tightened my grip on her hair when my tip hit the back of her throat. "You look so good with your pretty lips wrapped around my cock."

Her moan vibrated around me, and this time, I couldn't hold back. I thrust my hips.

"You're going to make me come."

She picked up the pace and sucked harder. *Fuck.* My knees started to shake. She slid her other hand down my thigh and toward her pussy.

Jerking back, I growled, "Don't you dare." Tonight, I would own her pleasure. With my hands, my tongue, my dick. I'd been dreaming about this moment for close to two months, and now I'd make up for every moment I'd missed.

She whimpered as I pulled back and grasped her under her arms. Yanking her to me, I slammed my lips to hers. Then I fucking owned her mouth with my tongue, just like my dick was about to own her pussy. In the next second, her shorts were off and her bare ass was in my hands. I loved the feel of her weight in my arms. Squeezing, I relished the way my fingers bit into her cheeks.

"Cortney, I need you."

"Damn straight you do." With my lips still on hers, I moved forward until her back met a flat surface. Thank fuck it was a wall still covered in sheetrock. I was pretty sure if we'd found the wall of studs only, we wouldn't have stopped. A burning need for the woman in my arms owned my every thought, and she was just as consumed with me.

My cock throbbed, begging for her.

"Put me inside you," I panted against her lips.

Shifting, she pulled back a fraction, gripped my dick, and pumped me slowly. I had to lock my knees so they didn't give out. With her eyes fixed on mine, she lined me up.

Holy shit. The heat of her made it impossible not to sink into her as deeply as I could. Damn, I swore she was tighter—hotter —than I remembered.

"Fuck me, Cortney," she whispered into my ear. "Hard."

I groaned at the demand. Damn, I loved her assertiveness.

So I obeyed, thrusting into her pussy with abandon. Every stroke was better than the one before. The way she gripped me, sucked me into her, was like nothing else.

Arching back so I could watch her reaction, I pulled out and slammed home again and again. Her back hit the wall with every drive. Her nails dug into my shoulders, and her breath came faster.

"Oh, don't stop," she said. "Harder, *please.*"

"I fucking love it when you beg." I thrust again and again until she shattered in my arms, her pussy milking me with every stroke.

"Dylan." Her name left my lips in a shuddering breath as I exploded inside her. With her still in my arms, I spun and leaned into the wall, needing the extra support as my arms and legs trembled. I tipped my head low and buried my face in her hair.

"You're good at hugs, but damn, you're perfection at making me come."

I chuckled. "Remember what I said about hugs? Same rule applies. Anytime you need an orgasm, I'm yours."

She shifted slightly to smile at me.

Slowly and begrudgingly, I pulled out of her. Without releasing her, I scooped up the T-shirt I'd intended to wear to bed and used it to clean us both up. Once I'd tossed the shirt into the hamper, I shuffled to the bed, keeping her wrapped in my hold. Each night so far, she'd turned her back on me, but tonight she snuggled into my chest. For the first time in weeks, my body truly relaxed. Because in this moment, the pieces were coming together beautifully, and a clear image of what our future could look like formed in my mind.

If only the team weren't heading out on a road stretch tomorrow. Because time apart could erase the progress I'd made with Dylan.

Dylan

34

Shay: Someone finally gave in and let that amazing man rock her world

Delia: She did? How do you know?

Shay: We share a wall. Thank God she doesn't share that wall with Kai and Liam.

Me: true liam would have been unhappy but yes cortney and I decided we might as well use our time together to be happy

Shay: I think it's more than that.

Me: you've said that all along

Shay: And I'll be happy when I'm right.

Liv: Well I'm happy.

Me: did becks make you come three times too

Liv: That wasn't what I meant but...

Shay: I hate you both

Delia: You have plenty of toys, Shay. Trust me, they're as good, if not better, than a man

Me: we really need to find you a man who knows what he's doing

Liv: I second that.

Delia: Just because you two have found unicorns doesn't mean the rest of us will.

Delia: Plus, we said no more men moving in!

Cortney
35

Me: How are my girls doing?

Firefly: perfect just tired and glad you'll be home tomorrow night

Me: I can't wait. The offer to hire someone to watch the kids still stands.

Firefly: never it's a privilege to help raise my friends kids plus I'd be bored without my preschool

Me: Are you wanting to open a location in Boston?

Firefly: we talked about it but with the baby not yet

Me: Well, if you need me to do anything...

Firefly: anything?

Firefly: GIF of an eyebrow raise

Me: I'm currently on a flight to Atlanta with the entire team, so no phone sex tonight.

Firefly: GIF of a crowd booing

Me: Last night was the last time. I warned you.

Firefly: I know so you'll have to make up for it tomorrow

Me: Oh, trust me, I have plans.

Dylan

36

"I've been thinking about it a lot. It might be the way I go."

The sound of Cortney's voice pulled me from sleep. He'd gotten in late last night from a six-game road stretch. It was after two when he finally crawled into bed and pulled me close. Now, though, he was no longer right beside me. He was lying on his stomach halfway down the bed with one hand on my hip and an elbow propped on the mattress. His cheek rested against his palm, and a curtain of blond hair fell over his face. From here, it didn't look like he was on the phone, but he was talking to someone.

"While I was gone, I read all about you." He brushed a thumb along the elastic of my shorts. "I know you can't really hear me yet, but I want to start now so that when we hit twenty-four weeks and you *can* hear my voice, I'll be better at this."

My heart clenched. Damn, this man was incredible.

"Plus, Mama can sense that you're a girl. If you're anything like her, which I hope you are, then you can probably sense me here too."

I forced my lungs to breathe evenly so as not to disturb him. I was intruding, but this was probably the sweetest thing I'd ever witnessed. I didn't want him to stop.

"I'm hanging out with your big brother today. I'll let you know how it goes. I think by the time you come along, he and I will be friends. But even if we're not, you'll be lucky to have Liam around. He's going to love you so much."

I tried to fight the smile but failed.

"Your mama is no longer pretending to be asleep, so I'm going to give her a little attention." He tipped forward and pressed his lips to the strip of skin between my shorts and shirt. "Love you."

The words whispered against my skin caused a lump to form in my throat and a torrent of emotions to rush through me. For both my daughter and the man who was becoming the best partner I could have asked for. He had seamlessly entered my life and jumped right into the role of a friend, supporter, and now lover, and it left me wanting more. It frightened me too, when I considered what would happen when he finally told his parents about the baby.

Cortney was going to be the best dad, no matter how his parents reacted. Willow—I was testing out the name—was going to be a lucky girl.

I pushed my fears away as he scooted up next to me.

"Her energy is really starting to like Willow."

He smiled. "That's my favorite too. How's Willow's mama doing this morning? Feeling rested? You were exhausted last night."

"Sorry." I snuggled into the bare skin at the crook of his shoulder. "I know I said I'd get up, but I was worn out."

I was almost twelve weeks. From the looks of things, the upcoming second trimester might kick my butt. Sleep had become my bestie. I'd hardly been able to stay up to talk to Cortney after his games. Most nights, once dinner was over, I pretty much crashed.

"Don't be sorry. You *need* the rest. I'm just happy to have you next to me for a couple of days. I have to head out for another nine-game road stretch on Thursday." He pressed his lips against the top of my head. Then he turned us so I was flat on my back and he was hovering over me. "Need me to stay home and help with the kids today instead of working on the Charger?"

"Liam would kill me." Liam had talked about working on the car nonstop for the entire week Cortney had been gone. And if I kept Cortney here on babysitting duty, my son would pout for days.

"I know, but I'm gone a lot, and I worry about you."

He'd had two games at home after the all-star break, then he'd left for a week. This week, he was home for three days before he'd leave for nine. Even with Liv and Beckett traveling with the team sometimes, I hadn't fully grasped how much Cortney would be gone until this last week. But instead of stressing about it, I chose to enjoy the time we had.

I brushed his hair back from his face and gave him a reassuring smile. "It's Delia's night for dinner, so once everyone is home, you and I can get cherry Slurpees, then Netflix and chill."

Cortney waggled his brows and leaned in to press a kiss along my neck. "Netflix and chill, huh?" he mumbled against my skin. "Mmm. I love that idea."

So did I. These days, after I'd experienced several Cortney-induced orgasms, no vibrator would cut it.

"*Dylan!*" Liv called from upstairs. "Ten-minute warning, sleepyhead."

Cortney groaned into my neck. Too bad Liv and Beckett weren't off on the same days their players were.

"I'm going to shower. I'll be right up." He flopped back onto the pillows and released me.

"No fair. You can't use your hands on you and not me." I sulked.

He laughed, and his blue eyes danced in the morning light. "Not that type of shower, Firefly."

DELIA HAD DROPPED the three bigger girls off at satellite camp on her way to work. Finn and Kai were happily playing *Mario 3D World* on the Switch in Kai's room while Liam moaned about the volume from under the covers of his bed. I'd love to help the kid out—more and more, I understood his desire to sleep half the day away—but the rule was simple: from eight thirty to eight thirty, there were no volume rules in the brownstone.

"What do you want to do today, Adeline?" I asked as I set her in the middle of my bed.

My phone buzzed in my pocket, so I pulled it out to check the notification.

> Becks: Don't worry. It washes out.

I read it twice and shrugged, dropping the phone to the comforter. If I didn't know what he meant, it probably didn't matter. Before Adeline and I could come up with a plan, Cortney walked in wearing gym shorts, rendering me speechless. Damn. Broad, smooth, and tan. The man was perfect.

I wet my lips and ogled his chest. My hormones were for sure surging. I didn't know whether to blame pregnancy hormones or Cortney himself.

"Did Liam say what time he wanted to head over to the garage?" He rubbed the gray towel against his wet hair.

I stood up and turned to him. The sight pulled a gasp from me, and my stomach sank.

"Boo." Adeline pointed at him.

"Boo?" Cortney asked, tossing the towel onto the bed.

"Holy shit." My heart rate surged. This wasn't good. *Oh, Liam. What did you do?*

"What's the matter?" Cortney frowned, scanning the room.

"Your—" I swallowed, reining in my composure, but it was no use. I couldn't hold back the grin. "Your hair."

He paled. "Is there a ducking spider in my hair again?" he snatched the towel off the bed and smacked his head with it.

I hurried around the bed and took the towel from him.

"No bugs, Samson."

"Boo," Adeline said again.

And now I couldn't hold in the giggles. "Yes, Addie, it's definitely blue."

"What?" Cortney asked, his eyes huge.

The boys peeked around the doorframe, Finn down low, then Kai above him, then Liam, like the damn Three Stooges.

"We got him!" Finn darted into the doorway, jumping up and down with his fists in the air.

"I didn't think it would work, but Bossman was right." Kai laughed.

"Holy shit." Liam gaped, his eyes saucers. "This was *not* me, I swear, but it's really, really, blue."

"What the duck is blue?" Cortney stormed into the bathroom.

A second later, he shouted. Even over the fits of laughter in the hallway, his words were clear.

"He's dead. I'm going to kill Beckett."

Cortney
37

"How many times did you wash it?" Liam called from under the Charger, which was lifted a good seven feet in the air.

"Three." I turned the wrench, working to loosen one of the bolts holding the muffler in place.

He moved out from under the car and shrugged. "It's not that bad anymore."

With a huff, I forced my shoulders to relax yet again. Two hours ago, my hair had been neon blue. Now that I had tossed my purple shampoo into the trash and used Dylan's, it held only a bluish tinge. Almost as if, instead of turning green in a chlorinated pool, my blond hair had gone aqua. I would need to come up with a good prank to repay Beckett for this one. Plotting with Liam was definitely part of the plan for today.

"Want to loosen these last two?" I handed Liam the wrench. "I'm going to grab the muffler."

"That thing is going to be sick. It's so straight the rumble is going to make windows shake."

I wasn't sure how much Liam knew about cars until I casually showed him my top three picks for the new muffler a week ago. After one conversation, it was obvious that he didn't just like cars. The kid was totally locked in.

"I'm really excited about the pop back."

"Hell yeah," he agreed. "Is this your first Charger, or have you had others before?" he asked when I slipped back under with the metal pipe in my hand.

"I picked up this Hellcat a year ago, but I have two others in my parents' garage."

"Which years?" he asked, helping me lower the old muffler to the ground.

"1978 and 2008."

"Nice." Liam nodded. "The Chargers are tight, but my goal is to buy an Audi e-tron GT someday."

"So you like the sleek rides." Respect. It was a good car. It wasn't the muscle I liked, but I could see it for Liam.

"The curves are beautiful, and supposedly, she handles like a dream."

"We could test drive one if you want."

Liam froze and his eyes widened, but half a second later, they narrowed on me. "I don't need to be bribed, so don't bother with the rich asshole shit."

Ah. It was time that he and I broached this subject. "I try not to act like a rich asshole."

He scoffed. "No shit. You share a house that's falling down with twelve other people. You carpool to work. The only things I've ever seen you splurge on are dugout seats for Mom and me and her DoorDash bill."

I raised my brow, feeling simultaneously relieved and more on edge, if that was possible. "We're working in the garage I bought for the sole purpose of playing around with my one-of-a-kind Hellcat."

Liam chuckled and shook his head. "I guess."

"The test drive idea wasn't a bribe." I shrugged. "Figured it would be fun to do together, so if you change your mind, let me know."

Liam studied me intently, his green eyes filled with a mix of hope and distrust, as I positioned the muffler.

"Going to help?" I asked.

An hour later, the new mufflers had been installed and the car was on the ground again.

"You actually don't suck at car stuff." Liam picked up his can of Coke from the workbench and brought it to his lips.

"Neither do you." I sat beside him and uncapped my water. The garage was rigged with AC, but the place wasn't insulated well enough to keep it more than marginally comfortable on hot days like this. The good news was that I would need another shower when we got home, so maybe the blue shit in my hair would lighten a little more.

As much as I wanted him to enjoy today, I had an ulterior motive when I invited him. I wanted some time with just him so we could have a real talk.

"I know we're doing better, but man would it be nice to not live in fear that you'll turn against me. So I wanna make sure that from here on out, you and I are good."

His green eyes narrowed. "We're good."

"Are we?"

He sighed and took a long sip of his Coke. Wiping his mouth with his wrist, he surveyed me. "I love my mom, but you know she's *weird*, right?"

"Weird?" That wasn't the word I'd use to describe Dylan.

He tipped his head, flinging the red hair out of his eyes. "This is what I was afraid of." Frowning, he held up a finger. "My mom says whatever pops into her head." He added a second finger to the first. "She believes crystals have the power to answer questions." A third finger joined the group. "She thinks she can see colors around people that give her clues about who they are." He lifts a fourth finger. "She claims to sense things."

And finally the fifth. "She believes in this grand universal plan. One where we just float through life happy to be a part of it."

Every one of Dylan's flaws, according to Liam, were things I loved about her. She was refreshingly different. And confident. She radiated this peaceful assurance that I'd never experienced until I met her.

He cocked a brow. "I got kicked out of my last two schools for fighting with kids who were making fun of her."

That I wasn't expecting. Dylan had mentioned Liam's issues at a previous school, and I knew that she homeschooled him, but I hadn't asked about the root cause of his issues.

My chest went tight, making it hard to breathe, and fury rushed through my veins. "I'm sorry, what?"

"Yeah. People think she's weird and mock her." He said the words slowly, maybe to give them time to sink in or maybe because he no longer had faith in my intelligence. "If you don't know her and understand how great she is, how, so many times, the crazy things she says are also right, then yeah, you're going to laugh at her."

"I would never." And I'd pummel anyone who made fun of her.

"You wouldn't." He shook his head. "At first, I thought you'd be easy to get rid of. Figured that you'd leave no matter what, so I wanted it to happen before anyone got attached."

"I'm not going anywhere," I promised.

"Yeah, I'm getting that sense." Liam shrugged. "It's cool that you bring us to games and around your friends and team. And that you make it clear to everyone that you're super obsessed with her."

I dropped my elbows to my knees and leaned forward, bracing for the *but* I knew was coming.

"But you're a Miller. There are tons of people in your life who *will* think she's weird, and they'll judge her. Don't be naïve. Ma and I have already been down that road with my birth father.

We know to be careful. But I worry that Ma has forgotten that."
He lowered his chin and let out a sigh.

I wanted to deny all of it. I wanted to claim that the people I associated with were better than what Liam expected. But could I? Maybe not. Unfortunately, my world consisted of plenty of assholes I didn't like. Regardless, I knew one thing for sure.

"You know your mom calls me Samson, right?"

"Yeah, another weird thing." He rolled his eyes and took a sip of soda.

"I didn't get it at first either." I chuckled. "I eventually figured it out. There's this story about this huge, handsome guy who's really strong."

"Is he modest too?" Liam smirked.

Grinning, I shook my head. "My point is that he had long hair. And his power came from his hair."

"Is this the dude that couldn't get a haircut?"

I nodded. "Yup. Like I said, all the magic was in his hair. The first time I met your mom, I wanted to blow out my hair before we went out for a drink. People always talk about it. It's my thing, right?"

"So your power comes from your hair?"

"That's what she teases me about." I pulled out my bun and let my blueish hair fall around my shoulders.

"You're saying she's wrong?"

"I know she's wrong. The story is about a man who trades his power because he loves a woman and he trusts her. He doesn't need his hair. Although I like my hair, I don't need it either. I feel the most powerful when your mom is smiling at me. So if anyone calls your mom weird again, you get me." I flexed my fist.

"You two really need to be less gross." Liam rolled his eyes, but the corner of his mouth twitched like he was fighting a smile.

"Want to test out the sound?" I tipped my head to the car.

"Hell yes." He jumped to his feet like he was a little boy and it was Christmas morning.

It was exactly as loud as we hoped it would be. So much so that we got a few glares from people on the way home. We made a pitstop for a bag of Jolly Ranchers for Dylan, and we had just gotten back to the house when my phone buzzed in my pocket.

When I checked the display, I winced. Not because I didn't like talking to my mom, but because I still needed to talk to her about Dylan, and I'd been hoping for a little time to prepare first.

"Hey, Cort. Your dad's on the line too."

Oh, my lucky day. If they were both taking the time to call, then they definitely wanted something.

"What's up?" I rested the phone on my shoulder and headed down the steps to Dylan's room.

"We wanted to go over details about the benefit. We're only two weeks out." My mom dove into a detailed account of the family color scheme that she and my sister had decided on, but I tuned her out. I hardly ever attended events, and I could give a shit what color palette my family wore to them.

Dylan wasn't in our room when I stepped through the door. Shutting it behind me, I pulled in a deep breath, then let it out slowly. I dropped onto the bed, knowing I couldn't hang up without telling them about Dylan and the baby.

"We've added silver, because Taylor's right—she'd never pull off the gold. But since you haven't confirmed who you're bringing, I didn't know if that would be enough."

"What?" I asked.

"I told you he forgot," my dad mumbled. He hadn't spoken a word since the conversation began.

My mother sighed. "It's the ribbon-cutting. Construction on the hospital is two months behind, but we've been planning this party for eighteen months and we can't possibly push it back." Her words were clipped. I had no doubt she was annoyed with the delay, and I could picture the exact expression she wore at that moment. "Regardless, you've had this marked on your calendar for months."

I grimaced. She wasn't wrong, and the Revs had honored the schedule requests New York had granted before the trade, but I had forgotten about the gala.

"You didn't make other plans, did you?" my father cut in. These two supported each other in all things, so telling them I'd forgotten about the party would put me on both their shit lists. Their partnership was an example to all of us. And exactly what I wanted someday.

"No, no, not at all," I lied.

"Great. Do you want Taylor to set you up with a date? I'm sure she could find a brunette who would look wonderful in gold."

I had used my sister's friends as escorts plenty of times over the years, but things were different now. This was my opening, so I took a deep breath and started from the beginning. Twenty minutes later, unsure of whether it had gone better or worse than I expected, I hung up the phone and went upstairs.

Delia was at the stove, stirring the contents of a stockpot, while Dylan sat at the counter.

"Where are the kids?" I shuffled up behind her and rubbed her shoulders. She let out a small groan and sank into the chair.

"That feels so good. Can you stand there like that forever?"

"His hand would eventually cramp." Delia turned back to us. "We're going to get noise complaints because of your car. You know that, right?"

Dylan moaned again. She was relaxing more by the second.

"You going to take care of those complaints for me, or should I hire a lawyer?" I smirked at Delia.

She shook her head and turned back to the stove. "You're an idiot."

"So where are the kids?" I asked again, dropping a kiss to the crown of Dylan's head.

"Liv and Beckett took theirs to the park. Liam went to the comic book store, and Kai and my girls are working on Bobbie's spine," Delia said over her shoulder.

I shuffled to the dining room doorway and took in the open books and tiny bones spread out on the folding table between the kids.

Now that Dylan was practically goo in her seat, I made my way back to her and whispered, "Hey, Firefly." Her curls tickeled my jaw. "I need a favor."

"If you do this for another five minutes, I'll definitely give you a blow job."

A low laugh rumbled up my chest. "That wasn't what I meant, but I'd never say no to an offer like that."

She spun in her seat, so I dropped my hands to my sides. "If it includes helping with these pranks you and Beckett have the kids all excited about, I'm out."

"No, I'm good with the pranks." Liam had already helped me with that. We ordered shoes identical to several pairs of Beckett's, but half a size smaller. Before our road trip, Liam, Finn, and Kai would trade them out for me. So during the nine days we'd be gone, Beckett would have sore feet. "My parents are hosting a little party in New York next Friday. It's for the hospital—"

"You did not just call the Miller Gala a little party." Delia spun around, holding the huge spoon dripping with red sauce aloft, interrupting me.

I clenched my jaw and shot her a glare, silently willing her to shut up. "My parents want to meet you, so I wondered what you thought about being my date."

"That's going to be New York's social event of the season. You're not selling this right," Delia continued. Clearly silent communication wasn't her strong suit.

I was "selling this," as she claimed, as what the event meant *to me*, not what it was to New York's high-society social climbers.

After shooting one more figurative dagger at Delia, I tucked my chin and took Dylan in. Shit. Her face had gone pale.

"Your parents want me to come?" she almost whispered.

"Of course they do." In fact, they insisted she be there. So, although I was posing this as an option, it wasn't. Not according to them. "And I'd really love it if you were my date."

Tilting her head back, she just stared at me. Her eyes were wide and her face was almost white. Liam's words from this afternoon played in my head again. Then my parents' comments. I needed her to trust me to do this. To support her. She clasped the crystal around her neck and ran it back and forth along the chain.

Finally, she nodded, and I let out a breath I hadn't realized I was holding.

"Okay, I'll go." She rested her palms on the green counters and pushed to her feet. "I'm going to lay down."

I watched her walk out of the room before I turned to Delia. "Will you help me make this easy for her?"

Delia's ponytail flicked over her shoulder as she tipped her head. "Dammit. I was going to say I didn't have enough time to deal with making your death look like an accident this week, but you had to go be all sweet."

"So tell me what to do." Because if Dylan was brave enough to give my family a chance, then I knew they'd love her. And everyone else could fuck off.

Cortney
38

Beckett: Why do my feet hurt?

Me: Is there a reason you think I might know?

Beckett: Very few people have the money and access to replace all my shoes.

Me: GIF of a weird guy shrugging

Beckett: GIF of a man pointing two fingers to his eyes and then forward

Me: I'm dying right now. You're in plastic flip-flops on the plane.

Beckett: Sleep with one eye open.

Me: GIF of a man laughing hysterically and slapping a table

Dylan

39

"**D**on't run toward the spinning blades," I yelled at Liam over the thumping.

He shot me an "I'm not five" look over his shoulder but didn't slow his pace.

"You'll have fun," Liv assured me as Beckett and Liam put the bags in the helicopter currently sitting in the Revs' stadium parking lot.

"I'm just nervous." I had agreed to do this dinner-gala-party thing with Cortney, but he'd been gone all week. The helicopter had landed here, and Beckett and Liv had hopped out. Now it was preparing to take Liam and me to New York. None of this was anywhere near my comfort zone.

But Cortney didn't want us driving the four hours alone, and he'd insisted on this so we could spend our extra time in New York with my dad. Cortney had arranged for Liam to spend Friday and Saturday with my dad in Brooklyn since we were going to be in the city, and he'd made it all happen mostly on his own. My only mission this week had been to try on dresses with Delia. And borrow a pair of heels from her that would definitely make my feet cry.

"Don't be nervous." Liv wrapped her arm around my shoulder and pulled me close. "They're going to love you."

I gave her a single nod, but no part of me believed that. I couldn't let myself hope that I could fit into his world. I'd only be crushed when I didn't, and I no longer allowed myself to be crushed. I hadn't in a long time.

I glanced at the time on the Apple Watch Cortney had given me a few weeks back.

"Yes, you better go." Liv nudged me.

Reluctantly, I shuffled toward the helicopter, my hair whipping around in the wind.

Once I'd climbed in, I followed the pilot's instructions about the headphones and seat belt.

"This is so freaking cool," Liam said, his voice coming through the com system as we lifted off the ground.

I wanted to agree, but the ball of awful sat heavy in my stomach, tamping down any excitement. Cortney was wonderful, and I'd enjoyed every minute with him, but meeting his parents?

My heart ached at the possibilities of how this trip would go. Slumping against the leather seat behind me, I pulled a Jolly Rancher out of my pocket, hoping to settle my stomach.

I wasn't trained for formal functions. I didn't see tonight concluding in any way other than this: Cortney's parents insisting I had no place in the Miller family. They'd make their demands to him, and that would end us. I grasped the quartz dangling around my neck and channeled its soothing energy. Regardless of my expectations for the type of reception I'd receive from the Millers, Cortney had been great with my friends. He'd made a genuine effort to bond with each of them. So I'd do everything I could to make a good impression, even if I had no idea how.

An hour later, the chopper landed on the roof of one of the many skyscrapers that dotted the New York skyline, and Cortney came into view. My heart lurched at just the sight of him. He looked like a statue on display in the Parthenon. Impossibly tall, broad, and intimidating. His outer appearance was totally at odds with the soft and sweet blues of his aura.

Once we were on the ground, he ducked under the spinning blades and held out a hand to me. His blond hair whipped around his face, finally free of the temporary dye from two weeks ago. As soon as we were away from the helicopter. He leaned in and kissed me.

My heart stuttered as his soft lips moved against mine. The way this man kissed made me want to dive right into him and never come back out.

"Hmm, cherry is my new favorite taste," he whispered.

"Jeez." Liam groaned. "At least wait until you leave me with Grampa before you maul each other."

Cortney chuckled against my lips. A black car waited for us at the curb, and as we approached, the driver opened the back door. Cortney ushered me in, then let Liam sit in the front.

"How are Willow and her mama today?" He palmed my lower stomach and rubbed soothing circles. "I know it's a few weeks away, but I can't wait until I can feel her move."

"We've named her and we've bought pink stuff, but we still don't actually know that she's a *she*," Liam muttered from the front seat.

"Stop being so practical," I said.

"One of us needs to be, and it's never going to be you two." Liam slumped into his seat with a *humph*.

"I started a 529 account for her. That's pretty practical," Cortney threw out. "And one for you too."

My breath caught in my lungs at that admission. He hadn't mentioned a thing about it, but as he gave my hand a hard squeeze, I relaxed. Setting up a college fund for Liam without so much as a word was completely on brand for the man next to me.

"What?" Liam sputtered, spinning in his seat.

"Aren't you planning on college?" Cortney asked, tilting his head to one side.

"Yeah." Liam nodded, his irises sparkling.

"That's what I thought. See? I can be practical."

My son gave Cortney his signature eye roll, but he couldn't fight the smile that split his face.

"He likes you," I promised once Liam had turned around again.

"The feeling's mutual," Cortney answered.

Having the stress of Liam and Cortney's relationship behind us was huge. But tonight loomed on the horizon, making it impossible for me to sit back and rest on the ride to my dad's house.

"Holy shit," Cortney sputtered twenty minutes later. "Is that a '69 Camaro?"

"Yeah. Grampa is like you. He'll trade the curves for the muscle too." Liam hopped out and took off toward the Camaro.

After helping me out of the car, Cortney was right behind him, geeking out alongside my son over my dad's perfectly restored classic.

Shaking my head at their excitement, I rounded the back of the car to the trunk.

"Should I take your bags in?" the driver asked.

"Totally not needed." Liam had packed a duffel, Cortney had a garment bag, and I'd brought a small suitcase. I could carry it.

The front door slammed, snagging my attention. And there, under the red- and white-striped plastic overhang, stood my dad, arms crossed and glowering. "Is someone going to help my pregnant daughter with the luggage, or did you expect her to do all the heavy lifting on this trip?"

Cortney's spine went ramrod straight and he whipped around to my dad. "Sorry, sir." Without another word, he hurried to me.

My dad trotted down the steps and stopped in front of me.

Looping my arms around his thin frame, I said, "He's normally all over this kind of stuff, but he was distracted by your favorite child."

My father beamed at the car. We all teased him about loving it more than any of us. "She's a beaut, isn't she?"

Forgetting about the luggage, Cortney lifted his fist to his mouth and inspected the car again. "Damn, those black stripes on that white body."

My dad slapped his back and grinned. "Thank God the idiot who knocked up my daughter can at least appreciate a good car."

With that, they wandered back to the Camaro, forgetting about me once more.

My brother stepped out the front door. The sun bounced off his auburn hair as he shook his head. I'd always envied it. Brian had lucked out and inherited Dad's darker hair color rather than Mom's vibrant red.

"Don't," he called when I bent for the bags. He jogged down the steps and slung Liam's duffel over one shoulder. "This is not giving me much hope." With Cortney's garment bag in one arm and my suitcase in the other, he tipped his head toward the guys.

"It should give you all the hope." Because three of my favorite men were crowded together and laughing, sharing in a common interest. If I got along half as well with Cortney's family tonight, then maybe we could pull this off. "Seems to me like the universe has a plan."

My brother threw his head back and groaned. "On another note, there's some woman inside who claims to be your hair and makeup person."

Delia had set that up for me. Never in my life had I considered something like this, but when Delia mentioned having someone do my makeup, I agreed. Tonight was a big night, and I wanted to make a good impression, so I deferred to her on the matter.

"Someone getting awful big for their britches?" my brother joked.

"Says the big shot attorney. Didn't you just handle that all-star quarterback's divorce?"

Brian tipped his head, gesturing for me to climb the porch steps first, then followed me into my dad's one-story house. He had lived in this fifteen-hundred-square-foot ranch since he married my mom when they were nineteen. The second I crossed the threshold, I was hit with the scent of home.

"Exactly." My brother cleared his throat and stepped up beside me. "My family law expertise puts me in the perfect position to draw up an agreement for child support and a parenting plan for you."

"You promised to get to know Cortney, not harass him," I said, pinning him with a glare.

"I won't let you be trapped in the position you were last time. This time, we'll plan ahead." Brian dropped the bags by the stairs.

"Hi!" A perky pink haired woman in her twenties popped into the living room. "I'm Sadi. Are you ready for hair and makeup? I have a cherry Slurpee and a hot dog waiting for you, as requested."

My heart fluttered and a smile teased at my lips. Looked as though Cortney was involved with this after all. "One minute." Dropping the smile, I turned back to my brother and pointed a finger at his chest. "I have to get ready. I refuse to be the reason we're late. But you told me you were coming over today to get to know Cortney. Nothing more. That's why I agreed."

"I know what I said." He stuffed his hands in his pockets and rocked back on his heels.

"So?" I crossed my arms.

"So I lied. I'll set up an agreement that will ensure you and your child are cared for." Brian glared right back. "I flew across the country to help you out with Liam when he was a baby, but

Dyl, this time, I'm already here. I demand that you're prepared and taken care of."

Slumping, I let out a sigh. My brother had already given up so much to help me. "You're so practical. Just be nice."

"I promise to get it taken care of."

That wasn't at all what I said.

Cortney
40

"Frank, this car is impressive." I climbed out of the passenger seat and pulled it forward so Liam could hop out.

When Frank suggested a quick ride, I hadn't expected to be gone a full hour, but it had given us time to chat. To my relief, Frank had that same light that his daughter possessed. Whatever it was, it made a person feel at ease in his presence.

"Next time you're in the city, I want a spin in the '78 Charger." Frank slammed his door shut.

"Deal," I agreed with a nod.

"Are you getting ready here too?" Liam asked.

With a nod, I followed him up the front steps. All I had to do was change into my tux, so that was the plan. Crossing the threshold into the living room was like stepping into 1990. The space was immaculate and covered in framed photos. Stuffing my hands in my pockets, I perused those closest to the door. In one, Dylan was about thirteen. I could see so much of Liam in her. In another, she was wearing a cap and gown. Then there was an image of her holding a redheaded baby. Their eyes were bright as they smiled at the camera.

"She's been my joy her whole life." Her dad took the photo of her and Liam out of my hand.

"I can see exactly why."

Frank's eyes met mine. "Yeah, I sensed that. As much as I try to stay out of my daughter's business, I have to admit that I think you're good for her."

"Thank you." Genuinely humbled by his compliment, I held out my hand.

He pushed it away and wrapped me in a hug instead.

"I'll take care of her. And Liam and Willow."

Her father chuckled as he pulled away. "So you believe her theory that it's a girl?"

My heart sinking just a little, I frowned. "Do you doubt it?"

"I never doubt my Dylan."

Instantly, the tension that had started to creep up eased. He and I could agree on that.

Eyeing my bag hung on the back of the sofa, I asked, "Is there somewhere I can change?"

He pointed across the room to a small half bath. Once I'd locked the door behind me, I traded my jeans for a navy tux with a thin gold tie that my sister had left with the hotel concierge. I had checked into our room before I picked Dylan and Liam up from the top of the Miller Estate's building. After I'd thrown my jeans and tee into the bag, I shut off the light and stepped out, glancing down the hall at the sound of Dylan's laugh.

Someone coughed behind me, startling me. My heart thumped against my ribcage as I spun.

A man about my age with dark hair stood in the middle of the living room, frowning at me. "I'm Dylan's brother. Brian." He held out his hand. "I wanted to go over some stuff with you."

He resembled both Dylan and Frank in subtle ways. The golden eyes like Dylan's and the brown hair with just a reddish tint like Frank. Yet something about him was entirely different.

Dylan would probably call it his energy or aura. His presence wasn't relaxing or peaceful. Not like Dylan's and her father's.

"Could we talk in the kitchen for a minute?" He waved toward the back of the house.

With a nod, I followed him into the outdated kitchen and folded my jacket over the back of the wooden chair before I settled into the seat across from him.

"Dylan's probably mentioned that I'm an attorney." He pushed a business card across the table.

Machon & Murphy. Brian Machon. Family Law.

I ran my tongue over my teeth. No, Dylan hadn't mentioned it. "Okay."

"You're aware of the issues with Liam's father, correct? How, for eighteen months after Liam was born, his grandparents put Dylan through the wringer. How they forced her to jump through hoop after hoop in order to get a simple DNA test to prove Brett was his father. Did you know they refused to allow Brett to help support his own son? Not that he would have anyway."

My stomach bottomed out and anger simmered just below my skin, like it did every time I thought about that piece of shit.

"She dropped out of school to raise him. Every day was a struggle for them."

When he was finished, I took a deep breath through my nose. "I'm aware that Liam's dad is an ass."

Brian waved me off. "Liam's dad is a wimp who jumped when his parents waved an AmEx black card under his nose."

I wasn't sure if that was worse or better.

"However, that will not happen to Dylan again."

Damn right it wouldn't. I agreed with him completely on that front, but the implication only made my blood boil. "And?" I raised a brow.

"And I'm here, as Dylan's attorney, to come to an agreement."

I jerked back. His words were like a punch to the gut. "Dylan asked for this?"

"No." He frowned down at the table. "Dylan doesn't plan the same way other people do. She tends to let life happen to her."

Though his assessment of Dylan didn't seem fair, my shoulders relaxed a little. I could handle this fucking conversation if it stemmed from Brian.

"Let's start with what your thoughts are about time with your child. How you want to deal with child support. Holidays. That sort of thing. This way we can work out an agreement that will hopefully suit you both. You know, so we can get on the same page." He leaned back in his seat, eyeing me.

I growled. "Same page? How about we start with this: I am not her ex."

Brian held out a hand, as if he was going to smooth things over, but I didn't stop. Yes, he was her brother and I hoped he wouldn't become an enemy, but he needed to understand who I was.

"I will sign whatever fucking paper you want me to sign, but know this: My plan for parenting time includes being with my child every single day I'm not with the Revs. Cooking dinner. Tucking her into bed. Helping with homework. All that." I flung my arm out. "My plan for child support? I'll buy Willow *and Dylan and Liam* anything they need. And probably most of the shit they want. Holidays? I'll be with them. For every single one. Full stop. So write up your plan. But just know it's a waste of fucking time, because I'm not going anywhere."

Brian blinked, his mouth agape.

From the doorjamb, Frank cleared his throat. "Brian, I appreciate that you want to take care of your sister. But you just insulted a good man. You own him an apology." Frank's gold eyes, so much like his daughter's, narrowed at his son. "We don't judge people by the actions of others. I taught you better than that. Give Cortney a chance to show us who he is. Personally,

I'm glad he fell for your sister. This family needs more car people."

He grinned at me, and I couldn't help but smile right back.

"Fine. I didn't mean to insult you." With a scoff, Brian rolled his eyes. Ah. *That* was where Liam had picked up his attitude. Clearly the kid and his uncle were cut from the same cloth. A jaded and cranky one.

Dipping my chin, I responded. "I appreciate everyone who is watching out for Dylan, and in the end, I know you are." I held out my hand.

He sighed and took it. "I'm sorry for assuming you were going to be a deadbeat."

I shrugged.

"But." He narrowed his eyes on me again. "I will be watching, and I guarantee that if you hurt my sister or her children, I will make your life a living hell in family court."

I smiled. "Good. If I hurt Dylan, then I deserve it."

Finally, that got a laugh out of him. "Jeez, you're so good intentioned it's hard to threaten you."

"See? I told you," Liam yelled from the other room. "Also, Mom's ready."

Standing, I slid my tux jacket off the chair behind me and slipped it on, anxious for an escape after our heavy conversation. I strode out of the kitchen but froze in the doorway to the living room. Behind me, Brian crashed into my back with an *umph*.

"Sorry," I muttered, but my eyes were glued to Dylan.

Every minute of every day, she was beautiful. First thing in the morning, with crazy hair and pillow creases on her face, I was blown away by how gorgeous she was. At the end of a long day, when she had to drag herself to our room and would fall face-first onto the bed, I was in awe of her. But this woman standing here had me swallowing my tongue.

The sleek dress clung to every one of her curves. Her hair fell over her shoulders in fat curls. Her eyes, flanked by long lashes, popped. Every fleck of gold was brought out by the fabric of her dress. Her full lips were painted a dark red. She was sexy, she was stunning. She was *mine.*

"You clean up all right," Brian joked.

Over my shoulder, I growled. When he took a step back and raised his hands, I turned back to my woman. In three strides, I was across the room with my arms wrapped around her. My palm hit the bare skin of her back as I tucked her close.

"You're perfect," I murmured.

Tonight, this woman, who was always self-assured and free and at ease, was wound up tight. I could feel it in the stiffness of her posture and see it in the uncertain expression she wore.

Tipping my chin, I looked to the hollow of her neck, expecting to see her fingers wrapped around the crystal she never took off, but the space was empty. "Where is your rose quartz?"

She lifted her black clutch. "I don't want to mess up the gold color thing."

My chest constricted at the way she rubbed her lips together nervously. Dammit. I wanted Dylan to be comfortable, and I wanted her to be herself. I pulled the bag from her hand and removed the silver necklace she never took off. With a soft smile, I gripped her upper arms and turned her. Then I carefully clipped her beloved necklace below her curls.

She turned back, worrying her bottom lip. "It won't look right. It's not gold."

"It's perfect. The colors are silver and gold." And I'd be damned if she didn't wear what she wanted.

"You're sure?" She grasped it, and instantly, the tension coursing through her eased, if only a little.

"My family is going to love it *and* you."

Dylan
41

Walking into the West Edge with Cortney was like nothing I'd ever done before. Cameras clicked and flashed around us as we stepped out of the limo. With every one, Cortney pulled me close and smiled, then chatted with the photographers. He gave them my name and called me his girlfriend without hesitation. The normal worry that hovered around him was nowhere to be seen.

Probably because it had taken up residence inside me. What would his family think of me? Did they know about Liam? Were they secretly upset about the pregnancy? Luckily, my dress, although fitted, wasn't so tight that my tiny baby bump was visible.

As soon as we stepped inside the building, Cortney's name was being hollered from the other side of the room. He towered over everyone, making him hard to miss. A moment later, a guy about my height with a two-inch silver spiked Mohawk slapped him on the back and pulled him in for a hug.

"Clint." Cortney laughed. "Nice win last week. Got another in ya?"

"I always got one more race in me." The man turned to me then. Grasping my elbows gently, he angled in and kissed me on both cheeks. "You are my new favorite person."

I blinked in confusion, and beside me, Cortney growled.

"Oh please, caveman. She's gorgeous but"—Clint stepped back and crossed his arms over his silver suit—"she has none of the right equipment. Plus, your brother is more than enough for any one person."

His brother?

"But you're making me an uncle." He clapped. "I can't wait to spoil this little one."

A deep throat cleared behind me, and I spun, only to find a smaller version of Cortney. He was just shy of six feet and nowhere near as broad, but decked out in a navy suit, he was Cortney's mini me. This man, though, had his blond hair pulled back in a low ponytail.

"Don't scare the piss out of Cort's girl before she gets to know us. You're a bit much. Give her some time to warm up." The man slipped over to Clint, shaking his head. But he settled his hand on the back of Clint's silver suit. "I'm Jamie, Cortney's brother, and this is my husband, Clint Miller."

"Otherwise known as the best driver in stock car."

Jamie and Cortney snorted in unison.

"He's humble too." Jamie rolled his brown eyes.

Before I had time to process the interaction, a high-pitched voice was shouting my man's name.

"Cort!" called a stunning older woman. Her arms and torso were covered in gold lace, and at the waistline, the dress flared in waterfalls of satin. Her bright blue eyes stood out in contrast.

"Mom." He turned and greeted his mother with a peck on the cheek. "This is Dylan." He held his hand out to me.

I swallowed back my apprehension as her eyes tracked over me.

"Cort, you didn't describe her well at all," she chided.

My stomach bottomed out as she frowned and stepped around him to me. Whatever she said, I would take and smile. I had no doubt heard worse before.

"You're stunning." Before the words could register, she shocked me by pulling me into a tight hug. "Absolutely stunning. I cannot believe you're thirteen weeks pregnant. You're like a rail." She yanked back and glared at her son. "Are you making sure she's eating enough, or shall I send our chef to stay with you?"

"Let's not start nagging so early in the evening, Evelyn." An older man with the same blond hair as his sons stepped up beside Mrs. Miller. "If you flit across a room and leave me alone with pompous idiots again, I won't be able to hold my tongue."

"You've never held your tongue well anyway." She rolled her eyes and linked arms with me. "I'm Evelyn, and this is my husband, Craig. We were so happy when Cortney told us about you."

Scanning the group around us, I couldn't help but giggle. Cortney's eyes twinkled as he looked down at me from around his mother.

"I told you not to worry," he mouthed.

"Cort, get a water for Dylan. We must keep her hydrated." Mrs. Miller waved a hand to her son.

"Whatever you say, Mom." He met my eye, silently asking if I'd be okay without him for a moment.

I gave him a nod. His family might be the brightest group of yellows and blues I'd ever seen. I loved them all already.

"Cort hasn't told us much. We know you live in Boston and you have a fifteen-year-old, but I'd love to know more about you. Let's sit." She tugged me by the arm, gently leading me toward a set of closed doors. "Being in charge gives me perks, one of which is that I don't have to stand in these awful heels for hours."

"I feel you with that. My feet hurt already." I smiled.

With a nod, the server manning the door opened it for us. The ballroom was decked out in beautiful flowers and gold silk drapings. The waitstaff was filling water glasses, and only a handful of people were milling around.

"Mother." A blond in a studded silver dress chided as she deserted the man she had been speaking to and hurried toward us. This had to be Taylor, Cortney's sister. Even if she hadn't just yelled for her mother, the height and features screamed Miller. But instead of greeting me with a smile like the rest of her family, this woman was scowling. "I told you I would deal with Little Fingers. Did you think I couldn't do it?"

My heart sank a little in my chest, and confusion swamped me. What did my preschool have to do with anything?

"What are you talking about?" Evelyn asked, tilting her head.

Taylor sighed and surveyed me. "I'm not sure how my mother got you here tonight. You are truly impossible to get a hold of."

"I'm awful about keeping track of my cell phone." I'd made a conscious effort to be better about it recently, especially since most of the time I tried to wear my Apple Watch, but I rarely responded to anyone besides Liam and Cortney and my best friends in Boston.

"I've been trying to get a good phone number for you or Zoey, but I keep getting stonewalled." Taylor turned to her mother and frowned. "I had no idea my mother would go to this length to help me."

I followed her line of sight to Evelyn, whose brow was creased and whose lips were pulled into a tight line.

"Taylor, what the hell are you talking about? Have you met Cortney's girlfriend?"

Taylor's eyes darted to me and widened, and she cupped a hand over her mouth. "Oh my gosh."

"What did you say now, Taylor?" Cortney settled a hand on

my hip and held out a stemmed glass of something that was definitely not water.

Her features went stony as she focused on her brother. "You're dating Dylan Machon and you never told me?"

He stood to his full height and went rigid beside me. "*Why* would that be a problem?" he bit out through gritted teeth.

She threw both arms in the air. "It's *not*. But I've been whining to you about getting a preschool and daycare facility set up in our corporate building. My executive assistant Layla raves about Little Fingers."

Oh. The trepidation running through me eased, and I smiled. "Layla Robins? I love her girls."

"Yes." Taylor homed in on me again. "We're moving offices, so Miller Estates and the Miller Foundation will be in one building. I will literally do anything to get a satellite of Little Fingers in that office."

The details were starting to sound familiar now. Just before I moved to Boston, Zoey brought up the idea of opening a Little Fingers in a corporate building, but before we could really look into it, I left and we decided to expand closer to me. She was running the four Jersey locations alone, and at the time, her plate was too full to consider another location. I had forgotten the idea even existed.

"Enough." Evelyn slapped her hands against her dress. "You know my rules about talking business at my events."

"But this preschool is the highest rated in Jersey, and I'm standing with her—"

Evelyn's glare ripped through her daughter.

"Fine."

I angled closer to Taylor. "I'll have Cortney text you Zoey's number. I'm sure we can figure something out."

She threw her arms around me. "You're my new favorite person."

Evelyn rolled her eyes, and I had to bite back a smile at the bickering.

"What is this?" I asked Cortney as I finally took the sparkling pink drink with two maraschino cherries at the bottom.

"It's a cherry mom-osa," he said, his voice soft. "It's made with sparkling grape juice, so it's safe for Willow."

"What happened to water?" Evelyn asked, cocking a brow at her son.

Cortney shrugged. "My girl has a cherry craving."

I took a sip, and little bubbles danced across my tongue. "I like this."

"I knew you would." He rubbed circles around my lower back and gave me a warm smile. Then he backed up and pulled out a chair at his family's table. "You should sit."

I obeyed, and Evelyn and Taylor claimed the seats on either side of me, firing off one question after another until the doors opened and the first of the nine hundred and fifty guests made their way to their tables. Craig stopped by to drop off glasses of white wine for his daughter and wife, then he pulled Cortney away to chat with a group of men in tuxes.

"I can't imagine having to plan every detail of this," I said, taking in the crowd. "How do you choose where everyone sits?"

"That's all social politics." Taylor laughed. "Mom, of course, is at the head table with us and anyone we invited." She tipped her chin up and searched the room. "Shit, I lost Casey." She waved a hand. "Oh well. He's been my escort enough to know I won't babysit him. He'll find me eventually. Anyway, from there it's all about donations and people my mom likes. The closer a person is to the front of the room, the better their standing." She rolled her brown eyes. "No one wants to be in the back corner, because all year, everyone else will remember and know it meant my mom hated them."

"It's why the four tables in the back are always empty."

Evelyn lifted her wineglass. "But you'll need to find Casey before the welcome. All eight of us are supposed to be out on the floor."

"I better run to the bathroom. My bladder will not make it through a long welcome." I pushed my chair back and winced as I once again had to balance on these awful strappy heels. *How did Delia do this all day?*

"You okay?" Evelyn looked up at me wearing a frown of concern reminiscent of the one her son gave me often.

"I'm good. You know how it is. Pregnancy and sore feet go hand in hand." With that, I hustled in the direction of the restroom.

I hadn't made it five feet before I crashed into one of the few people I'd hoped to never see again.

"Dylan?" Miriam's voice was high-pitched, and her expression was one of pure horrification.

"Hello, Mrs. Channing." I tried to sidestep her, but she latched on to my arm, digging her long nails into my skin.

"I've warned you not to use our name to get into these types of events," she seethed. "Have you forgotten what we told you would happen if you revealed anything about the *situation*?" That was how she referred to the grandson she'd never met. *A situation.* "Are you really prepared to repay the lump sum you received?"

This was one of many reasons Liam shared my last name and not Brett's. They'd been adamant since day one that I not do anything that could link me to their family, going as far as to require me to sign an NDA.

Although Brett did see Liam a few times a year, it was always away from his family and kept top secret.

"No one knows anything," I assured her, trying to subtly remove my arm from her clutches.

She had bought my silence with two hundred thousand

dollars. It had given me the ability to support Liam after that first eighteen months and had allowed me to start Little Fingers.

"Are you here representing your little school venture?" She shot me a glare, her dark eyes swimming with hatred. "We're sitting here." She waved to a table nearby. "Please tell me you're not seated with us. I have no interest in explaining how we know one another."

I glanced down at the seats one table away from mine and swallowed past the lump in my throat.

"No one knows anything about our connection, Mrs. Channing. You've made sure of that." This time I successfully yanked my arm from her grasp. But her nails bit into my skin, leaving a line of red welts.

"Miriam?" Evelyn called from behind me.

Mrs. Channing plastered on a fake-ass smile and turned to Cortney's mother. I used the distraction to slip away without another word. My hands shook and my knees trembled as I hurried away.

I made it past one more table before strong fingers wrapped around my wrist. I flinched and my heart leapt into my throat.

"Firefly, what the fuck?" Cortney loomed over me, his eyes focused on the scratches down my arm. His jaw locked and the hand around my wrist shook. He was barely holding back his fury. "What the hell just happened?"

"Nothing. I'm fine," I assured him, not wanting to make things worse. But I winced as a stabbing pain shot up my foot with my next step. Damn, my feet hurt. And now my arm throbbed too. Tears welled in my eyes. I couldn't deal with Brett's parents right now. Or ever. I just wanted to escape.

"Baby." Cortney's anger seemed to wash away as he pulled me into his arms.

I yelped as he lifted me and strode easily past the last few tables and out into the hallway. He set me down on the bench outside the bathroom and crouched in front of me.

"It hurts me to look at your feet. Take them off."

"I can't." I shook my head, running my fingers along my crystal and stealing its settling energy.

Ignoring my argument, he flicked the straps around my heels and pulled the shoes off one at a time. From his position below me, he tilted his chin and scrutinized me. "Tell me who that woman was and what the fuck she said to you."

I sighed and slumped forward. "She's Brett's mother."

Cortney sucked in a breath, and his blue eyes, eyes usually full of so much warmth, went icy.

"It's not a big deal. But part of our agreement was that I would never try to enter their social circle. The NDA I signed has this stupid clause that says I owe them a lot of money if I try to use their name to further my social status in any way."

Cortney's jaw locked, and his chest heaved so quickly I was afraid he would hyperventilate.

I caressed his cheek and tipped his chin up. "Don't worry. She has no idea why I'm here. I'll stay out of the way."

He took a deep breath in through his nose, then another. "Why don't you go to the bathroom? I'll be here when you get out."

I pressed my lips together and tilted my head. "It's really fine."

"Oh, it will be." He popped up and kissed me lightly. "Go to the bathroom so we can get back out for my mom's thing."

With a nod, I stood. I felt so much better without the damn shoes. When I came out of the restroom, though, Cortney was nowhere to be seen. I scanned one end of the hall, then the other, but I was alone.

Just as I was ready to park myself on a bench and wait, the door to the ballroom pushed open and Cortney appeared, empty-handed.

"Where are my shoes?" I asked.

"The trash. Anything that hurts you needs to be gotten rid of, so I threw them out." He reached for my hand. "Come on, Mom is waiting for us."

With his fingers wrapped around mine, he pulled me through the doors into the grand dining room. The guests were all in their seats, and a few members of the waitstaff were bustling around the table one away from ours.

"I took care of the shoes, but my mother took care of the other trash." Cortney tipped his head to the back of the room, where the empty tables Evelyn had mentioned were set up. I gasped as my stomach jumped into my throat. Because there, in the far corner, sat Miriam Channing and her husband.

Cortney didn't slow or stop. He just dragged me to the stage.

My heart sank, and I tugged on his hand. "I can't go up there barefoot."

"Why?" he asked, turning to me.

Dammit. This man didn't understand. I had just begun to feel like maybe I could fit in with his family, but if he dragged me up there, I'd embarrass them. I waved a hand at the stage, ready to explain that to him, and that's when I noticed. The rest of his family was already up there. Clint was clad in green socks emblazoned with the number 24. Next to him, Jamie wore brown socks. His sister's bright teal toenails peeked out from under her silver dress. Her date's black socks clashed with his navy suit, and Mr. Miller stood tall in his brown socks for all to see. His mother's feet weren't visible under her dress, but I didn't have to see them to know she wasn't wearing shoes either. I glanced down then and took in Cortney's socks.

My eyes welled with tears. I blinked them away furiously as we moved to stand with the group. Taylor gave me a big smile and Clint waggled his brows. Even Jamie's mouth seemed to lift a bit as he glanced at us. And beyond just standing with them, I truly felt welcomed into their family. Cortney held my hand tightly through his mother's welcome, and when she invited the crowd to the dance floor for the first dance, he escorted me down from the stage and wrapped his arms around me.

He was so much more than I ever expected, and at that moment, everything I'd been fighting crashed through me. I loved him. So I popped up on my toes and kissed him. I was done fighting my feelings for this man. A man who was dancing at a formal event wearing a pair of firefly socks.

Cortney

42

Her plush lips pressed against mine, and the burning rage that had been racing through me since I saw that woman yanking on Dylan's arm finally settled. My girl had so seamlessly become my peace of mind, my soft place to land, my everything, and I hoped after tonight, she realized it. I hoped that maybe I'd become that for her too.

I pulled back and scanned her face. "You okay?"

She nodded silently and rested her head on my chest. Soaking up the warmth of her, I squeezed her a little tighter and surveyed the room. Although I'd ask my mother to throw the Channings out, she'd suggested a harsher punishment.

There, at a table in the back corner, Miriam Channing glared at me.

Witnessing my mother's calm explanation about adjusting the Channings' seating based on feedback she'd received regarding Miriam's wish to not move in the same circles as my mother's darling Dylan had been the highlight of my year. Watching Miriam sputter, wide-eyed, and then be escorted to one of the four back tables my mother had always left empty told me without words how much my parents approved of Dylan's place in my life. And it effectively announced to every member of New York's high society that Miriam Channing was officially a social pariah.

Normally I got no pleasure out of these events. I couldn't care less who was in and who was out, but tonight, I reveled in the knowledge that the Channings were out. So I finished the dance with my girl in my arms and my family clearly in my corner.

"Can I get another cherry mom-osa?" Dylan asked as we made our way back to the table.

"Anything you want." And not just when it came to the drink.

After I got her settled in her seat, I headed for the bar, only to be stopped by the sound of my brother's voice.

"The bigger they are, the harder they fall."

Sticking my hands in my pockets, I raised a brow.

"Are you going to deny it? I've been waiting for the day you met your match."

I shook my head and dropped an elbow to the bar. "My world has become very small." All that mattered to me was directly related to the woman I couldn't take my eyes off. Still seated at my family's table, she was leaning to one side, laughing along with Clint.

"It's funny how love does that. It clocks you in the head, and for a while, you can't see anything but it." Jamie ordered a drink for himself and one for Clint, and while the bartender worked, we turned back to the room. Clint was holding his hand out to Dylan. She placed her palm against his and popped back to her feet. "They're going to become besties."

I snorted.

"Clint's words, not mine." Jamie shook his head.

"I hope they do," I admitted.

Jamie smiled and gave my shoulder an easy punch. "Me fucking too. Clint has been dying for you to settle down and give him a sister-in-law. And I'm much happier when that man is smiling."

Ducking my head, I chuckled. My brother was a tough-as-nails asshole until his husband was involved.

Jamie brought his whiskey to his mouth. "Have you told her you love her yet?"

My heart stuttered in my chest, and I whipped my head toward him so quickly it spun.

With a shrug, he swallowed audibly. "You and I aren't the best at words. But I can tell you from experience that our partners need them sometimes. You can never go wrong by showing her, but don't forget to tell her too."

I hadn't said those three little words to Dylan, but not because I didn't feel them. Oh, I did. My love for her had become such a big part of me I wasn't sure I could exist anymore without it. But saying the words aloud? That was a bridge I hadn't crossed. So many times, I'd thought them, but I didn't think she was ready to hear them just yet. And if I confessed the depth of my feelings and she wasn't in a place to accept them, then where would that leave us?

"Tell her." My brother slapped my back and sauntered to our table with a glass of whiskey in each hand.

I grabbed Dylan's drink and followed him.

The rest of the night was a blur of her smiles as Dylan chatted and laughed with my family. Every one of them loved her.

Hours later, I closed the hotel room door behind me and reached for her wrist. I spun her, pinning her against the door, and pressed the length of my body against hers.

When her lips parted in a gasp, I claimed them, relishing in the shock of lust that always rocked through me when I kissed her. Never had a kiss pulled me in, calmed me down, and revved me up, the way every one of Dylan's did. I could spend my life just kissing her and never get bored.

Her body arched into me as I cupped her face, letting my tongue dominate her mouth. Owning it, like she owned me. Slowly, I trailed my fingers along the column of her neck, over her shoulder, down the smooth bare skin of her back to her zipper. Once I'd lowered it, the two straps of material were easy to push off her shoulders. And then she was standing in front of me in nothing but a lace thong. Her breasts were full—and getting more so every day—with pretty rosy nipples. The tiny bump of her abdomen had me swallowing past the lump in my throat. Not only did this woman challenge me, turn me on, and bring out emotions in me I didn't know I was capable of, but she spent every day protecting our child. Her body literally sacrificed itself moment by moment to take care of our little girl.

"Do you know how perfect you are?" I asked, my voice hoarse. Dropping to my knees, I pressed my lips against the place where our baby rested. Then I lifted back to my feet. I wanted Dylan to understand that my next words were meant for her. "I love you."

Her eyes widened, then a smile broke across her face. "I love you too." Her words were barely audible, but they rushed through me like a sonic boom. Never had a whisper been so loud.

The intense need to worship her body, to show her how much I loved her, pulsed in every fiber of my being. I dropped my lips to hers at the same time I lifted her.

She wrapped her arms around my neck and hooked her ankles just above my ass, all while meeting my tongue stroke for stroke.

Shuffling back, I stopped when my legs hit the bed, then dropped onto the mattress, keeping her in my lap. Pulling back, her eyes sparkling and her lip pulled between her teeth, she got to work unhooking the gold studs that held my shirt together. With my hand in her hair, I spun so she was flat on her back and I could get the fuck out of my clothes.

"In a hurry?" she chuckled as I almost tripped trying to kick off my boxers.

I lost my breath as I reached out to caress her smooth cheek.

"Couldn't wait any longer to feel your soft skin against mine. Damn, I have this burning need to be close to you." I climbed onto the bed beside her and pressed my mouth to her plush lips.

Shifting onto her knees, she pressed a hand to my chest, guiding me down until I was flat on my back. The heat of her hand and the way her smile knocked the air from my lungs had me feeling like the luckiest bastard in the entire world. She straddled me, and even through the lace of her panties, I could feel how wet her pussy was. My cock jumped at the contact, desperate to be inside her. With my hands splayed on either side of her ribcage, I brushed my thumbs against the underside of her breasts and rubbed myself against her wet heat.

Above me, she shuddered in response.

"Kiss me," I ordered.

Leaning over me with her hair falling around us, she did as I commanded. Because she was where I belonged, I disappeared into her. Only she remained, the coconut scent of her hair blanketing me, the feel of her soft skin against me, the taste of her tongue teasing mine. This was heaven.

And yet none of it was enough. I lifted her and yanked at the lace barrier between us. Her breasts swayed above me, tempting me to tease her nipples as she shimmied out of her panties. When she straddled me once more, with nothing between us, her skin was so soft and warm and her pussy so wet against my cock.

But still, it wasn't enough.

I rolled her onto her back and hovered over her, ghosting my lips over her forehead, down her nose, and to her mouth. I only lingered a moment before continuing my journey, needing to taste all of her. Her neck, her shoulder, her collarbone, my favorite spot between her breasts. Her stomach and belly button.

I swirled my tongue there for a moment, then kissed both sides of her pelvis.

In response, her hips rocked up off the bed, begging me for attention. I could not deny her. Enraptured by her, I ran my tongue up and down her slit, teasing her, tormenting her.

With a moan, she grasped my hair and directed my movements, writhing below my lips, her hand twisting in my hair.

"Cortney, I'm so close, right there." She whimpered.

Obediently, I sucked her clit into my mouth.

"*Yes.*"

That was all it took to have her coming on my tongue. My cock throbbed, desperate to be on the receiving end too. I needed to own every drop of her pleasure. Once her orgasm had ebbed and she sank back into the bed, I lifted her arms and pinned them over her head.

Below me, her lips were swollen. Her cheeks were flushed and her eyes were blazing with a need that matched my own.

I nudged her legs apart and lined myself up with her opening. My cock throbbed against her, begging me to slam into her and chase my own desire. I resisted, resolved to take my time with her. Painstakingly slowly, I entered her, groaning at the sensation of her soft, wet heat surrounding my sensitive head. The breath left my body as I pulled out slowly. Then I pushed in again, farther this time, until I was finally locked inside her.

It still wasn't enough.

Rocking into her, I focused on the way her muscles tightened around me, watching the pleasure roll over her face and her pupils dilate as she got closer to release. Intertwining our fingers above her head, I dipped low and took her mouth with mine. I couldn't get close enough to this woman. Fuck, I wanted to crawl into her body and truly become one with her. I pulsed inside her, my own pleasure building.

Pulling back, I continued my slow movements, watching her expression. Her hair was splayed out on the pillow. Her cheeks were rosy with excitement, and her eyes swam with desire and love and desperation. All the emotions that whirled inside me. She was my other half. The person my soul had been waiting for my entire life.

"Oh, God, Cortney," she cried, her eyes drifting closed and her pussy spasming around me.

"Look at me," I demanded through gritted teeth.

She obeyed, and as I looked into her eyes, I saw my entire being in her. I let go then, filling her with a part of me. My body shook as my release pulsed through me. Until finally I rolled onto my back, pulling her tightly into the crook of my arm.

"Wow," she mumbled against me.

"Yeah," I said, my chest still heaving.

"That was—"

"Everything."

She was my everything.

Dylan

43

"It's okay to FaceTime him, right?" I asked as the ultrasound tech pulled the bottle of goo out of the warmer.

"Sure, people do it all the time. He's probably upset he's missing this." The goo warmed my stomach as she spread it across my skin.

Fourteen weeks was an odd time for an ultrasound, but since I was measuring small, my doctor wanted to check the baby's size and fluid levels. We'd scheduled it for today because it was Cortney's only day off for two weeks.

But massive thunderstorms had not only canceled the Revs game in inning four last night, but they'd also grounded their plane in San Francisco until early this morning. Instead of sitting next to me, Cortney was probably somewhere over New York.

The FaceTime ringtone sounded once before he picked up.

"How did it go? Done already? That was quick. Is something wrong with Willow?" Cortney's questions came out rapid fire as soon as his face appeared. "It's her kidneys, isn't it? Okay, I've done the research. There is a doctor in New York—"

"Chill, Samson," I cut him off. "We haven't done anything yet. I'm sure everything is fine." Though he'd been more at ease lately, his panic response was still high. "We're just about to start."

The tech moved the wand across my stomach, and a black and white image appeared on the screen in front of us.

"One sec." I flipped the camera view so he could see the computer screen.

"Oh my God. There's a head. And arms." He blinked several times rapidly. "Firefly, that's a baby."

The ultrasound tech fought a smile, and I had a lump in my throat. I wasn't normally overly emotional, but between seeing our little girl and hearing the love in her dad's voice, it yanked hard on my heartstrings.

"I wish I was there. She's perfect." He took a breath. "Wait, she's perfect, right?"

Now I smiled. There was my big old worrier.

"I didn't think you'd gone over blood test results with the doctor yet..." the tech said.

I shook my head. "No, but I know it's a girl." Our souls connected about it weeks ago.

"Oh, okay. I didn't want to give anything away if you wanted it to be a surprise." She moved the wand across my stomach, and my full bladder screamed. "But yes, she looks great."

Cortney let out a deep sigh, and the tight lines around his mouth disappeared. Now that he'd seen her and had received confirmation that she looked great, he would worry less.

"Whoa, is that a baby, Shammy?" I wasn't sure which teammate it was until Kyle Bosco came on the screen.

"It's my little girl." The phone shifted. "Look at her."

There was a rush of commotion, and one face after another appeared on the screen as they passed it around.

"Dude, we need to get her a jersey," Christian Damiano said.

"I bet Daddy already took care of that," Kyle teased. "He's kind of possessive about his girls wearing his shirts."

"Hell yes I am. Give me back the phone." Cortney's blue eyes reappeared and focused on Willow again.

"I need to take a few more measurements, but first, you might like this." The woman pushed a button, and a whomping rush filled the room.

"That's her heartbeat." Cortney's eyes sparkled with each thump of our little girl's heart. "She's perfect."

"She is."

The tech was still moving the wand around, snapping photos and taking measurements, but everything about her energy told me there were no issues.

"Flip the phone. I want to see Mama for a minute."

I hit the button and smiled at him.

"Thank you." He swallowed hard and blinked rapidly again.

My heart squeezed at the sight. God, our little girl made this big, strong man tear up.

"Thank you so much. For giving me her and Liam. For loving me. All of it. Damn, I hate that I can't kiss you right now."

I cleared my throat. "I'll collect when you get home."

He smiled. "We're landing in about thirty. You sure you don't want to meet me and Dad for a late lunch?"

"I'm still going to pass."

As much as I enjoyed Cortney's family, and although most of them had been texting me regularly since the gala, Cortney needed to do this alone. Evelyn had clear boundaries when it came to family time and business talk. So although Cortney and his dad had some work to discuss, they hadn't had the chance yet. Cortney had asked his father to come up for lunch so he could make it clear that he was staying in Boston permanently and that Miller Estates wasn't in his future.

"Okay, text me after you talk to the doctor."

"These are for Mom." The tech handed me a line of black and white photos and then wiped the gel from my stomach.

I met with the doctor next. Just like I suspected, Willow looked great. She was measuring perfectly and my fluid levels were adequate. After I sent a quick update to Cortney, I headed out of the office. My phone rang the second I stepped out onto the sidewalk.

"I told you it went great." I laughed.

"What did?" Zoey, my partner at Little Fingers, asked.

"Oh, I thought you were Cortney. The ultrasound went well. Willow looks perfect."

"Amazing. I just wanted to go over the details that Taylor sent over."

For the next several minutes, Zoey laid out the proposal she and Taylor had worked up for Little Fingers.

"Utilities will be included since we'll be housed in their building, and we'll be covered under their umbrella policy. They can all but guarantee full classes because they have a daycare waitlist already. Plus they will make the space exactly what we want, including outdoor access with a playground and grassy area."

"And you think you can handle it along with the other four you're overseeing?" I balanced my phone between my cheek and my shoulder and pulled a Jolly Rancher from my pocket.

"Now? Absolutely. The directors at our existing locations do most of the heavy lifting. That'll give me time to focus here." Zoey sounded excited, so that sealed it for me.

"Then I'm in. Let's do it."

"Perfect. And maybe in a year or so, when Willow is a little older, we can find a situation like this in Boston. Partnering with the company means so much less work for us."

"We'll see." I was focused on the here and now. We could revisit that idea when the time came. "But send the paperwork over and I'll get it all signed."

"Thanks. I'm glad it went well this morning."

I hung up just as I turned onto our street.

"No, I'm done. You can't micromanage a project when you know nothing about construction work." The contractor Delia hired last week stormed down the steps and slammed the door of his pickup truck.

Delia stood on the porch with her hands on her hips and her ponytail falling over her shoulder, wrapped in a thick blanket of rage.

"Another one bites the dust, huh?" I stopped on the landing next to her.

"He suggested we not bother pulling permits with the city for the electrical work to avoid the 'hassle.' Can you believe that?"

"I take it that's a bad thing?"

Cortney was going to lose it soon if the walls in my room weren't finished. He wanted the living room and kitchen finished and baby safe too. Plus, the electrical was making him nuts. I figured it was PTSD from the spider incident. But regardless, he wouldn't be happy that we were once again contractor shopping.

"*Delia*," Beckett called from inside the house. For once, the frustrated tone wasn't directed at me.

With a huff, Delia stomped back inside. "It's my house and I will fire any idiot who doesn't make muster."

"I've had a day. I don't ducking need this." Beckett crossed his arms and scowled. "Livy! We need a new list of names." He stormed into the kitchen, ranting, with Delia and me right behind him.

"I was afraid it would come to that. But I agree with Delia. The wiring should be inspected by the city. That's the last place we should be cutting corners here." Liv turned to me and gave me a soft smile. "How did the doctor go?"

"Perfect." I shrugged. "It's twins."

Liv's mouth fell open.

Beckett choked, and his face went red. "What?"

I laughed. "Kidding."

"Duck, you scared me. Though it would have explained the

whole thing with Cortney." He rubbed his chest and turned to unzip his briefcase. "Do me a favor. I have the contract I drew up when he and I renegotiated terms so that he'd move into this hell hole…"

Words kept coming, but my brain froze. "*What?*"

"You know." Beckett tossed a stack of papers at least an inch thick onto the green counter. "The bonus stuff I agreed to as long as he moved in with you."

"*Excuse me?*" Liv's hand hit the counter with a deafening smack. "*What* did you do?"

Beckett turned his attention back to his briefcase. "It wasn't a big deal."

They continued back and forth, but I wasn't listening. With a shaking hand, I picked up the stack of papers on the counter. The dates all matched. Beckett had bribed Cortney to get him to move in with us.

My stomach sank and my breathing went ragged. Like someone knocked the wind out of me. His words from that night on the roof replayed in my brain.

"You swear this suggestion to move in has nothing to do with Beckett?"

"It's about you."

But that had been a lie.

Cortney

44

"Sorry I'm late, Dad." I dropped into the chair across from my father.

"No problem." He set his phone on the table and waved a hand, probably to signal the server to bring whatever he'd ordered for us. "Before I forget, this is from your mom." He reached into the pocket inside his suit jacket and handed me a small box.

I tucked it into my pants pocket. "Thanks."

"I will forever be your mother's errand boy." He chuckled. "So what do you want to discuss?"

I hadn't planned this to be a bomb drop when I asked Dad to fly up for lunch. But this morning had changed everything. Missing out on Dylan's ultrasound today solidified the decision I'd been waffling about for weeks.

"I talked to my agent today. He's going to let Revs management know that I'm not going to take the contract extension. I'm retiring at the end of the season."

My father's brown eyes widened and he sat back slowly. "Oh." He let out a breath. "This wasn't expected. But in light of Dylan and the baby, I can't say it's the wrong decision."

"Exactly. I don't want to spend the first eight months of Willow's life only seeing her through FaceTime. She won't even know me. That doesn't work for me."

The corner of my dad's mouth lifted, and he pressed his hands together in a prayer pose in front of him.

Examining me, he asked, "When will you and Dylan move back to New York? October? We won't be in the new building until spring, but I'm certain we can shift some people and get you an office—"

"Dad." I shook my head and swallowed past the lump in my throat. "I'm not leaving Boston."

His brows rose. "Oh."

Here it went. I sucked in a deep breath and let it out. "This is me telling you that, although I'm retiring, I won't be working for Miller Estates, or the Miller Foundation."

He tapped his fingers on the tabletop and shrugged. "With your love of cars and your analytical brain, the racing side wouldn't be the worst place for you. I'm sure Clint would love it."

I sighed. "I know nothing about stock cars or racing. And I'm not helping Mom with her events either."

Now he frowned. "Then what are you doing? Are you saying you want to do *nothing*?"

I shook my head. "I'll do something. I'm not sure what yet, but I'm going to do my own thing. I love you and Mom and all you've built, but I don't intend to jump into any of the family's businesses."

Tapping his fingers again, he ducked his head, thinking, worrying, problem-solving, no doubt. But honestly, this wasn't a problem. He'd eventually get that.

My phone buzzed on the table in front of me. Beckett. I figured he'd freak out when he got the news about my retirement, but I was ignoring him. He and I could talk face-to-face when I got home. But only *after* I talked to Dylan.

"Baseball." My dad took a deep breath and nodded.

"What?"

"You need to be in baseball."

"Maybe." I could probably work with the analytics team or maybe do some scouting. I didn't want to coach. But if there was a place for me in the front office, that would be the best of both worlds. I could work with the team and also be home every night. Or I could put feelers out with the colleges around Boston.

"Well." My father picked up his phone. "Convincing Langfield to let go of the Revs won't be easy, but we can make it happen."

"What?"

"You need a baseball team, and you want to stay in Boston." He pursed his lips. "Hmm. Maybe we could buy a team and move it to Boston. I can get a team researching Massachusetts's ability to support two pro baseball teams."

I scoffed. "Dad, don't be ridiculous."

"I'm completely serious," he said, leaning forward. "Why would you think I wouldn't help you the way I help your siblings?" He reached across the table and placed his hand over mine. "Just because you went your own way with baseball doesn't mean I won't do whatever it takes to help you grow and succeed."

I patted my dad's hand and smiled. Damn, my heart squeezed in my chest at the realization that my family would do anything to support me. Even if their need to hover drove me insane sometimes. "I know that, Dad. And if I need a baseball team, you'll be the first to know." But I really wanted to figure out my own stuff.

"It would be a lovely wedding present." He smiled. "And we could rename the team. Call it the Fireflies. Honor Dylan with it so she'd feel like she was part of it."

Chuckling, I shook my head. "We'll see."

"Also, I need to know which schools Liam's looking at so we

can make sure we're up to date on our donations. We don't want to hold him back."

"Right." I rolled my eyes. "I'll ask him, but he does have a few years before college."

"Can't plan too early, and we want to help."

An idea popped into my head. "Happen to know the name of a good contractor?"

"Of course. What's it for?"

The waiter dropped off our steaks, and I dove into an explanation about the brownstone and its state as we ate. After Dad promised to have Jamie send me some names, the conversation shifted to talk of Clint's race the following week, then to a deal Jamie had just closed. My dad even happily raved about Dylan's preschool partnering with the company. He was proud of all of his kids, and the way he and Mom had embraced Dylan and Liam so easily made me happy.

My phone buzzed three more times with messages from Beckett during lunch. The man was persistent, that was for sure. If it had been Dylan, or any of the moms, really, I'd be worried that something was wrong. But no one would leave Beckett in charge of breaking important news after the way he'd dropped Dylan's pregnancy news without her permission. Beckett was going to have to wait. Before I got into details with him, I needed to hash out my retirement plans with Dylan.

With Dad's blessing when it came to forging my own path and his promise of any support I wanted, I headed home to Dylan. Not stressing about my dad and his plans felt like a weight off my back. Or maybe it was the knowledge that I wouldn't miss so much next year because I would be in Boston full time. That, and the way everything had fallen into place in a single day.

Turning the corner, I grinned. The tree was lit up with orange lights tonight, making the orange dick on the window stand out.

The lights were on in every window but the foyer, and the

gutter was still teetering on the edge of the roof. It was ridiculous that I was so thrilled to call this place home.

I hadn't even stepped across the threshold when Beckett appeared in front of me.

"Where the duck have you been? You're in so much trouble."

Liam stepped up behind him. "You promised never to make Ma cry."

What the fuck was going on?

Cortney

45

"Tell me this is a terrible practical joke?" I snapped at Beckett.

The fucker's only response was to shake his head.

"Why in God's name did you tell her you bribed me to move in? That wasn't even remotely what happened," I gritted out through clenched teeth.

"How was I supposed to know you hadn't told her the story?" Beckett shrugged.

I ran my hand through my hair. "Where is she?" I spun and searched the family room, then stormed into the kitchen. But only the kids were around. "Where is she?"

He pursed his lips and ducked his head. "I'm not sure I'm supposed to say."

"Now?" I smacked the counter so hard the vibration of it radiated all the way up to my shoulder. "*Now* you decide you care about what you should or shouldn't say?"

"Liv says I have to figure it out someday." He chuckled.

The sound had my blood boiling. Right then, I wanted nothing more than to clock this asshole and lay him out on the hideous kitchen floor.

"Seriously, Beckett? Do you hate her that much?" Lacing my hands through my hair, I tugged on it. I had to find her.

"Hate her?" He frowned. "Why would you think I hate her?"

I took a deep breath through my nose, reminding myself that killing my boss would only land me in prison.

"Listen, Man Bun, I love Dylan." He shook his head. "Not in the way you do, obviously. But like an annoying little sister. I want the best for her. So I paid a fortune—way more than you're worth, in my opinion—and gave up four good prospects to get you to my team."

I dropped my hands back to my sides, my head swimming in confusion.

"And do you know why? Because I knew you were perfect for her, and I wanted her to be happy."

That was why the trade had come out of the blue? All I could do was gape and try to wrap my brain around what he was saying.

"My ducking GM and upper management just let me do it too. Bunch of yes-men who all need to go." He frowned and knocked his knuckles on the counter. "I need to deal with that as soon as the season is over."

I sighed, my chest still so damn tight I could barely breathe. I didn't fucking care about Revs management when my girl was upset and I had no clue where to find her.

"Right." He looked me up and down. "Not the point, but I got you to Boston and stole those nasty socks to get you to the house. And boom." Beckett tossed his hand in the air. "One meeting, and she's pregnant. Then I got you to move into the house. And boom, you're a goner. I set it all up, and every detail fell into place perfectly. You're both happy. So you're welcome."

A small part of me wanted to thank him, but mostly I just wanted to throttle him.

"We're happy? Right now? Do I look happy? How about

Dylan? How did she look the last time you saw her? Where. Is. She?" I gritted the words out.

He scowled, but he didn't give up the information.

"The moms are all on the roof," Liam said from behind me.

Without another word, I spun and headed for the stairs, but the kid stepped into the doorway, blocking my exit.

His eyes cut through me, and he tipped his chin up. "You're fixing this?"

Unblinkingly, I met his eye. "Your mom is magic. She came into my life at the exact moment I needed her. She's brightened every detail, every experience, and she's opened my eyes to all the best parts of the world. I love her, and there is no way in hell I'll ever let her go."

Liam smiled and stepped aside. With a slap to his shoulder, I raced up the stairs. At the top, I threw the door open and darted out onto the roof.

Four heads snapped my way and too many voices piped up at once. Yet not one of the voices belonged to Dylan. She just tipped sideways on the sofa, holding a bright green Slurpee cup with one hand. Her other hand lifted to her crystal. Dammit. I hated that I was causing her stress. I had to fix this.

"You." Delia propped her hands on her hips and glowered at me.

Dylan set her Slurpee on the table and wrapped her arms around her legs. I wanted to run to her, but Delia stalked toward me and blocked my path. Apparently, I had to get past these three women first. Although I appreciated that my girl was surrounded by so much love and support, at the moment, I wanted them all out of the way.

"I almost trusted you, but I should have known better. In the end, you were only after money."

Huffing, I tossed my arms in the air. "Delia, the money in my contract isn't even a drop in the bucket to me. I could never make another dime and live an extravagant life until the day I die."

Delia rolled her eyes in response, and I swore she puffed up more to keep me from making my way to Dylan.

I stepped to the left, trying to see around her, but she shifted with me.

Straightening, I looked her in the eye, praying she could see how much I meant these next words. "I will sign everything I own over to Dylan tomorrow if that makes her happy. She can have full control of all of it. I don't give a shit about money."

Almost imperceptibly, Delia's mouth lifted at the corner. Or maybe it was just wishful thinking.

I stepped to the right, but this time Liv crossed her arms over her chest to stop me. She was wearing the mask she normally reserved for work. The fierce expression was intimidating, even when accompanied by her leggings and messy bun.

"Can I please—"

"Did you do it so you could play longer?" Liv cut me off. "Was baseball the most important factor here?"

Had Liv not bothered to check in at work all day? Dammit. I'd already proved where baseball fell on my priority list. "I love the game, but it will always come second to my family. Check your email if you don't believe me."

"Your family?" Shay jumped in, tucking her hair behind her ear and glaring. "I thought I could trust you to put Dylan above the Miller name."

I gritted my teeth. She had taken my words totally out of context. "Let me be clear. When I say *family*, I mean Dylan, Willow, and Liam. And for the record, my parents and siblings love them all."

Shay almost smiled.

"Th—" Delia and Liv both opened their mouths, surely to spew more accusations, but I was done.

"*Enough*," I yelled.

All three women went silent. I shuffled back to the door to the house and held it open. "I accept and appreciate how much you all love and support each other. But I need to talk to my girl-friend, so with all due respect, if your name is not Dylan, get the duck off this roof."

Delia crossed her arms like she had no intention of budging. "Out."

All three glared at me, but they reluctantly filed past. Once they were headed down the stairs, I shut the door and turned to the most important thing in my life.

Dylan

46

His hair stuck out all over his head, and his blue eyes swam with desperation as he rushed across the roof.

What the hell had Beckett said to him? The man truly had no idea when to shut up.

Hearing that Cortney had lied and had been bribed to stay with me sent me spiraling. Without my permission, my thoughts had diverted to the past, and all those old aches and insecurities had held me in their clutches. But that wasn't fair to Cortney. He had already done more than any person should to prove to me how he felt. His actions were always just as loud as his words. And although my besties wanted to test him, prove he would fight for me, I did not doubt him.

"Look at me." He dropped onto the sofa next to me and cupped my face. The warmth of his palms pressing against me soothed me. "Look at me. See *me*. Not the catcher for the Revs. Not a Miller. Not Beckett's employee. I'm just a man. A man who worries about too many things. A man who's terrified of spiders and snakes. Who spends too much time working on puzzles and loves cars and a good prank." His irises deepened to a vibrant blue, and his voice dropped. "And a man so *totally* in love with you that the rest is just noise." He ran his thumbs along my cheeks. "Look at *me*. And tell me you have doubts about how completely committed to you and our family I am."

I swallowed the lump in my throat and pressed a hand over one of his where it still lay on my cheek. "I don't have doubts. Love filled up the cracks where doubt could get in."

"Marry me."

His words hit me with a fierceness that left me speechless. Before I could muster up any type of argument about the idiocy of jumping into marriage just because he thought I was upset with him, he shifted and pulled a ring from his pocket. Pinched between his massive fingers, it looked so delicate. Thin silver vines wove around each small diamond on the band before meeting in an Asscher-cut diamond with a halo around it. The vintage style was breathtaking.

"I didn't plan on doing this today. I had a few ideas in mind when I asked my mother for my grandmother's ring weeks ago. But we don't need fanfare. All we need is each other and our kids. So I'm asking now. Marry me, Dylan. Because I can't imagine a day in my life without you in it."

I blinked, still shocked, though a warmth was rushing through my chest. If I accepted, then I could keep this amazing man forever.

"Yes." I smiled, never more grateful to the universe and its plans than I was at this moment.

"We can go to Connecticut tomorrow morning and be married by ten o'clock." He looked serious, like he'd go to the ends of the earth to prove his feelings to me.

"Or," I said, because although I loved his willingness to be spontaneous, that idea didn't feel quite right, "we could plan a time when all the family can be there. All the people we love should be there to witness the best day of our lives, right?"

"Whatever you want. As long as you're happy, I'm in." He slipped the ring onto my finger and kissed my knuckles.

"It's beautiful," I said, splaying my fingers to get a good look at his grandmother's ring.

"Only half as beautiful as the woman wearing it." Leaning in, he pressed a chaste kiss to my lips, then rested his forehead against mine. With his eyes closed, he took a long breath, but his hands trembled as he held my face between his palms. Slowly, he opened his eyes and pulled me into his lap.

"I'm not letting you go. Ever. And I swear to you, no one had to bribe me to spend a single second with you." He tightened his hold on me. "I'm sorry I didn't tell you about all the details of my conversation with Beckett."

"It's okay."

"It's not. We don't have secrets."

"Samson, we don't have secrets now." I rested my head on my shoulder. "You signed that contract what, two months ago? We were hardly anything then. You had no obligation to tell me at that point. I've read the contract. Beckett didn't bribe you to move in. Honestly, it looks like you reworked your contract so it would screw him over if you left Boston."

His entire body relaxed around me and his hand skimmed down to rest on my lower stomach. "Once I found out about Willow, I refused to let anyone have the power to keep me away from you or her."

"I understand. You might not have given me the specifics, but I see it. I know you weren't lying when you said it was about Willow and me."

He shook his head. "From the second you tossed my shamrock socks across the sidewalk at me, everything has been about you."

I ran my hand along his jaw, smiling at the way his blond five-o'clock shadow tickled my palm. "I want it to be about us. You, me, Willow, and Liam."

"It always will be," he promised, brushing his lips against

mine once more. "Which is why I'm retiring at the end of the season."

Gasping, I jerked back. "Wait." That wasn't what I meant. I'd never forgive myself if he left baseball because of me.

He shook his head. "If I don't retire, then I'll be at spring training on your due date. What if I don't make it home in time? I'll spend the first eight months of her life on the road more than I'm home. I won't be there to help you if she's awake all night. There's a good chance I'll miss her first smiles, her first word. That's not enough. I want her to know me. I want to know her. From day one. And I want to be around to keep building a relationship with Liam and to be there for you."

I pressed my teeth into my lip to keep it from wobbling as he angled in and nuzzled against my neck.

"I want you snuggled next to me at night," he said, breathing in the scent of my hair. "And I want to wake up in your arms in the morning. I want us. I've had years of baseball. I'm ready for something more."

"I'd love that. But only if you're sure you won't feel like you're missing out. I would never ask you to give up something you love so passionately."

"I felt like I was missing out today. Stuck on a plane instead of at your side during the ultrasound. Having to listen to her heartbeat through the phone. Unable to hold your hand as we counted her little fingers and toes. That forced me to admit what I wanted next year to look like: Me here with you. All the time I can get with Willow. More time bonding with Liam. There are so many kids in this house, so if this means we have a stay-at-home mom and a stay-at-home dad, it won't hurt."

I laughed. No way was he staying home. He'd stress that everyone would die on a daily basis. The poor man would go insane in a week. "I think it's pretty well written in the stars that you'll work for Beckett."

"I just said I'm retiring."

God, men were so blind sometimes.

"You're retiring from the game. But you're Beckett's work wife. There is no way he'll survive if he can't toss a folder at you and debate the stats and the future of players. You two are kindred spirits."

Cortney huffed. "We are not."

"You'll see." It was obvious the day I met him. His aura meshed perfectly with Beckett's.

He pulled back and brushed his hand through his hair. "So if you weren't upset with me, then why did everyone else think so? Why was I read the riot act five times before I made it to you?"

Resting my cheek against his chest again, I linked my fingers with his. "At first, I cried. So everyone freaked out."

Cortney stiffened behind me.

Humming, I nuzzled into him. "It's okay."

He sighed and relaxed just a fraction. "I want to be the reason you smile. I never want to be the cause of your tears. The idea of that guts me."

I tilted my head up and squeezed his hand. "Samson." When he looked down at me, I continued. "We're going to fight. I'm going to cry or get mad, and sometimes I'm going to piss you off. That's life. But working through our issues, apologizing, and letting our souls reconnect will make us stronger."

He brought my hand to his lips and pressed a kiss to the ring he'd just put on my finger. "I love you."

"I love you too. But the rest of our family here? They needed to hear what I already knew."

"Hmm?" His brow creased.

"Delia had to see that you'd fight for me."

He held me even closer, if that was possible. "I'd burn the world down for you if that's what you needed," he whispered against my ear.

"I know." And that knowledge felt incredible. Now that I had them, I couldn't imagine living without Cortney's love, care, and protection.

"So everyone went along with Delia's plan?"

"Liv thought Beckett needed a lesson on running his mouth and meddling, so she let him think I was upset. Shay was pissed about some hockey game she's taking Kai to for his birthday. So we had a rant-at-the-world, throw-everything-into-the-fire moment."

He peeked over my head at the fire pit on the table in front of us. The flames were still flickering in the evening air. "Do you actually put stuff in there? You know that's a fire hazard, right?"

I giggled. He didn't need to know about the time we tossed our clothes into the fire. "Don't worry."

"As long as you're around to help me with that, we'll be okay."

Cortney
47

"Where the duck is he?" Beckett paced in front of the bar at the clubhouse.

Today was going to be interesting if he didn't chill out.

"Didn't you say you were teeing off at eight? Jamie is never late." Shoving his hands into the pockets of his suit pants, he huffed. The man was wearing a suit to play golf, but that wasn't my problem.

He was right that my brother was never late. But I was working really hard not to stress. This introduction had to go well. The safety of our family depended on it.

The door opened, and any hope I had faded at the sight of a neon green mohawk and the smiling face of my brother-in-law.

"Clint." Beckett scowled and crossed his arms.

"Cort and Beckett. Two of my faves." The best way to describe Clint's energy was *two-year-old who had been given a pound of chocolate.* "Cort, congrats on the engagement. Mom is already planning the perfect wedding idea to pitch to you and Dylan when you come down next week."

"Fun." I had been serious about eloping a few weeks ago, but Dylan had made it clear that she wanted a family affair. I got it.

Her dad should get the chance to give her away, and her three best friends would likely make our lives hell if they weren't invited to her wedding. Now my mom was dead set on planning the wedding of the year and not inviting any of the Channings. The whole process was going to be overwhelming, but first, we had to deal with fixing the house.

"Where's Jamie?" I asked.

"Oh, you know your brother." Clint waved me off. "Always so busy with work stuff."

"I talked to him yesterday. This was on his schedule," Beckett growled.

"That growl. If my heart didn't belong to another, I would be tempted." He shook his shoulders. "But I asked if he'd let me step in."

"Why?" Beckett demanded.

"Mom." As if that one word explained it all. "She never lets us talk business at family gatherings, and I have plans to discuss with Cort." He glanced at his watch. "I took the liberty of moving the tee time to eight forty-five—"

"Why?" Beckett cut in.

Clint cocked a brow and chuckled. "Because I would have never made it by eight. Obviously."

Beckett rubbed his temples and shot me a glare. "This pain in the side of my head was exactly how I knew Dylan would be perfect for you. She and Clint both bring it on. Every ducking time."

Clint gasped. "*You* set up Dylan and Cort? You must find someone for Taylor next. That tool she brought to the gala was awful."

"Don't give him any ideas." I shook my head. The girls were all actively trying to get Beckett to stop meddling. "Did you tell Enzo about the time change?"

We'd asked Enzo to meet us to play eighteen holes after Beckett and I had chosen him from the list of contractors my father had given us. We needed to schmooze him and get him on board with our project. The house had to be done before Willow was born if I had any hope of holding on to my sanity. Dylan and I still didn't have a wall in our room, and it was starting to give me chest pain, even if the love of my life wasn't worried. She firmly believed the universe was going to provide someone. I, on the other hand, was talking to realtors about the other brownstones on the street. Because maybe I could get her to move if it was only a house away.

No one could explain why the property values were skyrocketing in our neighborhood. In the last few weeks, two houses that hadn't even gone on the market had sold for outrageous prices. Even with us as neighbors. With our constant noise complaints, the tacky decorations, half a skeleton hanging from the front porch, and a dick painted on the window, we seemed like terrible neighbors. Yeah, we weren't the reason the market was booming.

"Enzo will be here at eight thirty so we have"—he glanced at his watch again—"sixteen minutes to talk business."

"What business?"

"There's a position available at Miller Racing."

Dropping my head back, I sighed. Clint was as uninterested in working with me as I was with him, so who knew what this was.

"Don't huff and puff. It's not like working for Jamie." Clint slid his hands into his pockets. "I know Dad has people doing research about Boston and its ability to support a second baseball team—"

Beckett sputtered, choking on air.

"Arms up." Clint wrenched one of Beckett's arms up and whacked his back. "Mmm. Such good muscles you have."

Beckett jerked away from him. "What second baseball team?"

"Don't listen to him." I was wasting my breath, because just like Dylan, Clint knew how to work Beckett up.

"My in-laws are always going above and beyond for their kids. Dad is set on giving Cort a team to run." Clint shrugged.

All I could do was sigh. My father and I had been through this already.

Beckett glared at me. "I have plans."

"Do you?" Clint clapped. "Are you moving your team? Because Jamie has been looking for a place to house our new stadium."

My brother was not.

Clint grinned. "And *I'm* working on colors and logos."

Oh shit. That better not be true.

Beckett was wide-eyed and sweating all of a sudden. He shook his head and scowled. "Boston can't support two teams."

Clint shrugged. "I don't run numbers, so who knows."

Red-faced, Beckett scoffed, but he was pulling at the collar of his shirt and his eyes were darting all over the place.

I was about to call enough when Beckett whirled on me.

"I need a GM starting next season. Someone smart, analytical, and willing to tell me no when they think I'm acting like a moron."

I nodded. "I agree." That would help the future of his team for sure.

"You don't officially retire until after the world series, so I can't approach you yet. But ducking duck, my plan is to offer you the GM position."

"Why?" Dylan had been saying I should work for him, but what the hell did I know about being a GM?

"You know every player in the league. You know how to build a team that meshes. You're smart, you're driven, and you're obsessed with the game. You have no issues disagreeing and speaking your mind. You back up your opinions with so much data I'm overwhelmed. And most importantly, I trust you." Beckett rolled his eyes. "I can teach you anything you don't know. You want to stay in Boston, so this would ensure no travel. I had a plan and a contract and a speech, but duckity duck, every time I have a plan that involves you, you make a hard turn left. Don't buy a team. Come build the best team in the league *with me*."

Wow. "Okay. I'll talk to Dylan."

Clint blinked and tapped his pointer finger against his chin. "This prank took a weird turn."

"What?" Beckett rounded on him, still huffing and puffing.

He shrugged. "Liam and two little guys called me. They wanted my help pranking you both. You were supposed to freak out."

"I did," Beckett snapped.

"Oh, good. They'll adore that." Clint beamed. "Next topic—the house. My niece and nephew can't live in that place. Their house needs to have all the things." He waved his hands like he was showing us a banner. "I'm thinking gold-plated fixtures."

For the love of God. I just wanted walls.

Beckett sighed hard and signaled to the bartender to bring him a glass of whiskey. "We're getting nowhere with this meeting."

"We have eighteen holes to figure it out," I reminded him.

Beckett shook his head. "I'm not actually playing golf. I have to work." When I raised my brow, he added. "Hockey season's about to start."

I shrugged. At least the suit made sense. But this news was going to make the eighteen holes interesting. My gaze ran over my brother-in-law.

He smirked. "I see your brain going. Don't worry, Jamie's out on the putting green. I promised him I'd stay out of your meeting with Enzo, but Jamie will play with us." Clint patted my shoulder and almost skipped out of the bar just as Enzo walked in.

Khaki pants, golf shoes, and a polo. But it was tension he wore like a second skin.

"Typical Italian pretty boy," Beckett muttered, sidling up next to me.

"I wouldn't underestimate him. You've heard the same things I have. This is gonna be a hard sell." Enzo Di Luca was business savvy and extremely successful. He'd grown his family's company from a dime-a-dozen construction company to the type my father had on his short list.

"Good thing we have an ace in our pocket." Beckett almost smiled as we walked over to meet the man.

But fifteen minutes later, Beckett was smiling because, although Enzo wasn't thrilled, he was on board.

"Now we just need to get Delia to agree." Beckett shook his head.

"Dylan's got it covered. When I told her I was worried about that, she told me and I quote, *Delia will agree because the universe has a plan. You'll see.*"

"Hopefully the universe's plans go more smoothly than mine tend to."

Dylan
48

"I know you think it's poison, but Willow loves high-fructose corn syrup and red dye number 12. Who am I to deny my child?" I shrugged, sucking on the cherry candy.

A buzzer sounded, and the arena broke out in cheers. Hockey wasn't my thing, but today was Kai's birthday, and more than anything, he wanted to spend it here. Shay had been stressing about it for weeks, but in the end, she couldn't deny him. Beckett had arranged for us to attend one of his team's preseason games, and Shay realized that if she pushed too hard against hockey, she risked encouraging Kai to rebel.

"But you could have a juice smoothie," Shay rambled on.

I didn't want a smoothie, so I stopped listening. She was my bestie and I loved her forever and always, but the woman needed to chill about what I ate.

"You know," Delia interrupted from my other side, "I think I'm with Dylan about the baseball men."

"What?" Shay asked, leaning forward so she could see Delia.

"She's talking about the great asses in tight pants. I couldn't agree more. Especially Cortney's." As of the end of September, he was officially retired. Damn, I was going to miss the view of him squatted behind the plate. "The Boston Bolts look like marshmallow men."

Beckett raised a brow at me a few seats down.

"Don't worry, Becks. The only person I ogle obnoxiously from across stadiums is Cortney."

Behind us, Cortney and Liam walked in, each carrying a tray.

I hopped up when they set them on the high-top table in the suite.

"What about me?" Cort asked, pulling me in for a hug.

"Oh, just that you have a great ass. Everyone enjoys looking at it." I wrapped an arm around his back and gave it a quick pat. "But only I get to truly enjoy it."

"Two-way street, Firefly." He slid his hands down my back and into the pockets of my maternity jeans.

Liam sighed. "Are you two ever going to stop being gross?"

"Probably not." I shrugged.

"Hot dog, burger, nachos, soft pretzel, ice cream, slushie." Cortney pointed out each. "And a fruit cup and a water."

"Thank you for being an amazing hunter-gatherer."

"You are so weird. We just went to the concession stand." Liam flicked his hair out of his eyes and dropped into the seat next to Kai.

Cortney gave me a quick kiss. "I'm always happy to get you what you want, as long as you balance it with food that won't cause gestational diabetes."

"It's all about balance." I snagged the fruit cup from the tray and took a sip of the slushie.

He pulled out his phone and broke into a smile.

"Did you get it?"

My fiancé flipped his iPhone so I could see the picture of the beat-up 1963 Porsche 356 sitting in his garage across town.

"Liam is gonna die when he sees it."

He glanced over his shoulder to make sure my son wasn't

paying attention. Cortney was hoping to surprise Liam with it one day this week. "It's going to be fun fixing it up with him."

I popped a nacho into my mouth and chewed. "I'm not sure a sixteen-year-old needs a perfectly restored classic car to drive on day one."

With a shrug, Cortney propped himself up against the barstool by the table and pulled me between his thighs. "We're adding safety features, and if he wrecks, that means we'll get to work on it again."

"That's an interesting take on an expensive project." I chuckled and grabbed another nacho.

"Firefly, what's the point of having money if I can't spoil you and our kids with it?" Cortney leaned down and pressed his lips against my neck. "Get used to it. I'm at my best when you and Liam are smiling."

I shivered as his warm breath hit my neck. The universe had blessed me with the best soon-to-be husband and father I could ask for.

"Dyl!" Shay called from across the room, her nose wrinkled. "Do you know how many nitrates that hotdog contains? It's emulsified meat glued together with all sorts of disgusting chemicals."

I didn't know what emulsified meant, but I did know that I loved hot dogs. I took a big bite of the one in my hand. "The universe told me to give the baby what she wants. And what she wants is nitrates."

Cortney chuckled and rested his chin on my shoulder as Shay launched into another lecture on the benefits of smoothies. I mumbled a nonanswer at her, because the girl needed a hobby that didn't involve feeding me.

Beckett headed our way and swiped a nacho off the plate. "I want to talk to you about the draft ideas I emailed you."

Cortney's chin wiggled on my shoulder as he shook his head.

"Not until after the world series, Bossman. I have a few more weeks of peace."

Beckett crossed his arms and shot him a glare but was quickly distracted by Shay, who was blatantly checking out some hockey player on the ice. Her aura was suddenly tinged with passion-y orange. I couldn't tell who'd caused the reaction—all the marshmallow men looked the same to me—but Beckett broke out into a smile. It dropped almost as quickly, though, and his expression turned contemplative.

"Oh, Becks," I chided. "You should not meddle with whoever Shay is eye-fucking."

"I have no idea what you're talking about. You're the only one around here who goes on about hot players."

"Hey!" Cortney scoffed.

"None of them are as hot as you, Samson. Don't worry."

He pressed a kiss to my neck. Over his head, I watched Beckett, though, because the man had that twinkle in his eye.

"Your wife is going to leave you with blue balls for a month if you meddle with the love life of another one of her besties," I warned.

"I have no idea what you're talking about, Dippy Do." He smirked.

Yes, he did.

Cortney laughed into my hair. "This one won't cost as much. Parker already plays for a Langfield team." His lips brushed the shell of my ear. "Here we go again, Firefly."

But if Shay ended up as happy as I was with Cortney, then who was I to get in the way?

"We'll see."

MOTHER PUCKER SNEAK PEEK

Chapter 1
Shay

I look at my watch for the fourth time in the past half hour, begging for time to speed up. There's so much I could be doing right now, rather than watching a bunch of overgrown barbarians on ice skates dash around after a tiny puck.

Even if they are a bunch of gorgeous, overgrown barbarians with nice asses . . .

It's a brutal game, and even in the short time I've been here, it seems like someone is always getting hurt. Why would anyone willingly play something so dangerous when there are so many more civilized sports like golf, or track, or . . . I don't know, egg throwing?

Sighing, I rummage for my phone inside my purse. I might as well make my weekly grocery list while I have the time.

My hand wraps around the thick G-spot wand I carry in my purse, brushing over the indentation before I find my phone and pull it out.

I have a collection of such toys nestled in the back of my

nightstand drawer, but this purse-sized one always stays with me. It's a little overused and has seen better days, but it's reliable, effective, and practical. What more could I ask for?

"Chicken," I mumble, typing into my text app. "Flaxseed, Ezekiel bread, quinoa–"

I'm jostled, almost losing my grip on my phone, when my son Kai and the man–or rather, manchild–Beckett Langfield fist bump each other across my body.

"Did you see him score, Bossman?" my nine-year-old yells over the din of the crowd, using the nickname all the kids call Beckett. He's such a quiet kid in general, so I'm always a little taken aback whenever I hear his voice teeter over its normal soft volume. "Rowan 'Slick' Parker is going to be the greatest defenseman of all time. I just know it! That play was ducking fantastic!"

"Language." I eye my son before scowling at Beckett. Kai may not have actually cursed, but I know he meant to. He thought about it. Another teaching my best friend, Liv's, gazillionaire husband has so graciously bestowed upon my son.

I hear an 'oof' slide out of Beckett's mouth, indicating my best friend has likely elbowed him in the ribs from his other side. He pointedly looks at my son and repeats, "Yeah. Language, IceMan." He uses the nickname he gave my son when he moved into the Boston brownstone with me and my best friends, and Kai smiles.

I shake my head, tucking the long side of my asymmetrical bob behind my ear before going back to my phone, ignoring the chatter between my best friends and their kids. We're all standing in Beckett Langfield's private owner box at the arena, watching the Bolts play a preseason game. Well, technically, his brother owns the team, but tomatoes, to-mah-tos.

"Now, what else did I need to add to this list?" I mutter to myself, looking down at my list.

It's wild to think that only nine months ago, me and Kai were adjusting to our lives without Ajay–from a family of three to a permanent family of two–and now, we're living with not one, but thirteen other people in the same house. My best friends–all single moms, like me, and women I couldn't survive without–their kids, and more recently, Beckett and Cortney. Cortney is my other best friend, Dylan's, fiancé, who also happens to be the catcher for the Boston Revs.

Many people might call us crazy for taking a part in what seems like an outlandish social experiment, but one of the best decisions I ever made was during our last girls' trip when we all resolved to move into Delia's enormous, but dilapidated, brownstone in Boston and do what we always planned to do ever since college–raise our kids together.

Men were never a part of the original pact, but since Liv actually fell in love with her then fake-husband, Beckett, and Dylan fell for her baby-daddy-to-be Cortney, we've just added to our brood.

It's been one wild and crazy ride over the past few months–a far cry from my and Kai's quiet, albeit lonely, life in California–but I can't say I've ever had as much fun.

"Asparagus and kale." I twist my lips as I type into my phone.

I have no interest in ice hockey, or any contact sport for that matter. I'd much rather be sitting at home, reading a book or researching the negative effects of high fructose corn syrup. But since Beckett promised to take Kai to the Boston Bolts's game as a gift for his ninth birthday, and insisted we all make a night of it, I'm stuck in this overfilled arena, with obnoxious and drunk fans–who all look like they might have been on their way to a frat party but mistakenly ended up at a sporting event.

If it wasn't for the fact that it was Kai's birthday present, we would never be here. He and his dad may have watched the Bolts religiously on TV, but I have no interest in condoning such a dangerous sport to my son.

He could break a bone, or worse . . .

And though he's been relentless in begging me–with his soft voice and those downturned, puppy-dog eyes, reminiscent of my late husband's–to let him learn hockey, I've been adamant about not giving in.

Though, I did give in to that large Slushie in his hands, full of all sorts of terrible sugars, artificial food coloring, and who the hell knows what else. I wouldn't have, but the kid used those puppy-dog eyes to Jedi mind trick me into breaking my resolve.

I let it go just this once, but I'll have to detox his body of all that nastiness with wholesome, healthier foods all week.

Come to think of it, I should add sardines, liver, and Brussel sprouts to my list.

I turn to look at Dylan behind me. She mindlessly smooths a hand over her pregnant belly before taking a bite of what I can only assume is a hotdog.

My nose wrinkles. "Dyl, do you know how many nitrates that hot dog contains? It's emulsified meat glued together with all sorts of disgusting chemicals."

Dylan's eyes glitter in my direction, speaking around her mouthful. "The universe told me to give the baby what she wants. And what she wants are nitrates!"

I roll my eyes, adding another essential item to my list. This one specifically for Dylan's detox. "I'm going to make you that oatmeal, turnip, and turmeric smoothie again. I know how much you loved it last time."

Dylan responds with something that sounds strangely like, " . . . loved it about as much as I love eating compost," but the sound of the buzzer and the crowd going absolutely berserk drowns out some of her words.

The Bolts have scored another goal, and while the players glide effortlessly over the ice, my gaze snags on the defenseman with the number sixteen and the name Parker written on his jersey. Even from where I stand, it's clear he towers over the players, both in height and presence.

I'd seen images of him on TV, since both my late husband and our son were crazy about him, but seeing him in real life today . . . he's like a gravitational force all on his own.

The man is well over six feet, with dark hair and golden, sun-kissed skin, despite the fact that he likely sees more ice than the sun most days. And from my incredibly unreliable recollection of his screen image, that skin is complemented with a golden-green gaze, thick eyelashes and brows, and plump, smooth lips that may have had me involuntarily licking my own.

But again, that was from my incredibly unreliable recollection.

My eyes trail him like slutty jersey chasers, watching his swift movements and complete focus. There's an assurance and decisiveness in the way he moves, guiding the puck with the precision of a surgeon, making me wonder if he applies the same sureness and control to everything else he does with those large hands . . . and that sculpted body.

And thinking about what he might do with his hands off the rink has me swiping my bottom lip with my tongue and clearing my throat unnecessarily. Annoyingly, I catch Beckett's eyes and his stupid knowing smile peering my way.

I don't know what that smug grin on his gazillionaire face is all about, but if he doesn't drop it, I'm going to smack it right off him. I quickly drop my eyes to my phone, wishing my short hair could hide my burning ears.

I just need to get laid again.

It's the only reason I was gawking at a man almost a decade younger than me, and envisioning what his stick would feel like between my–

"Holy shh!"

"Oh, no!"

A collective gasp shifts the entire atmosphere in the arena and has me lifting my head to see what I missed.

I get up on my toes to get a better glimpse, catching Beckett swearing under his breath. "Duck! That doesn't look good."

"What happened?" I ask, my brows furrowed as I watch Rowan Parker shuffle to stand back up on the ice. He's limping on his skates, clearly not putting pressure on one leg as he walks over to the bench, but it's hard to tell how hurt he is.

"Something happened when he shot to make the goal, and he fell," Kai answers. "Didn't you see it, Mom?"

I shake my head in answer as Beckett fills in more details. "He lost his balance somehow when he swung, but my worry is, he fu–" Beckett catches himself, knowing all the kids are hanging on to his words, "ducked up his leg."

He takes his phone out and calls someone, likely his brother or the physician. "Hey, what's happening? How badly hurt is he?"

Liv and I exchange a concerned glance before I peer at Kai next to me, his previously bright eyes now veiled with worry. I place my hand on his dark hair, scratching the back of his head. "He's going to be okay, sweetheart. Don't wor–"

"I'm bringing my wife's best friend over to him now," Beckett states on the phone, cutting off my words and getting a glare from me. I really hope he's not talking about me. "Her name is Shayla Kumar, and she's a physical therapist. We'll have her assess him."

"Wha–" I say with a start.

What the hell is he talking about? Has he lost his mind? Why the hell is he volunteering me? Doesn't the NHL have their own doctors and athletic trainers?

"She'll be there in a minute," he decides, hanging up the phone.

"Beckett . . ." Liv says, seeming just as confused. "What the heck are you doing?"

"I just talked to the team's physician. He's still stitching up Sanders, and the head trainer and athletic trainers are with other players. They could use someone to help take a look at Parker."

Beckett turns to me and I swear, if I didn't know better, I'd say there's a glint in his eyes. A fucking glint! What is this guy up to?

I shake my head vigorously. "I'm a physical therapist, not a physician or an orthopedist. If he's hurt, he'll need to get looked at by–"

"And he will," Beckett cuts in. "But right now, for the sake of the team, the physician could use another pair of hands."

I put my hands on my hips, recalling the all too observant smile he gave me earlier when he caught me ogling the muscle-bound stallion in skates. "Is that what the physician told you? That he needs another pair of hands? Because that seems highly unlikely, not to mention something that could get me into legal trouble." I look down at Kai to ensure he isn't paying attention, before I continue in a hushed tone, "Or is this another one of your ploys?"

Beckett reels back. "Ploys for what?"

"To get me to date one of the guys on your team again?" He's been trying to set me up with random people in his network for the past few weeks, and I've been thwarting all his efforts.

I don't have the time or energy to date. Not when I have goals and responsibilities. Like raising my son, running my business, and growing old with my best friends. I don't need more.

Beckett gapes at me animatedly. "I would never take advantage of a situation as serious as this to find you a suitable man. That you could even think I was capable of such low-handed tactics, only so I could get you hitched and out of the ridiculous pact you and your best friends, including my beautiful wife, made is beyond hurtful."

He groans when Liv elbows him again, and my squint gets squintier. "You're a lying piece of–"

"Language," he interrupts me before I can finish, gesturing toward the exit. "Come on. I'll take you there myself. And as for legal repercussions, need I remind you my family owns the team?"

I take a breath before looking at Liv to see if she'll come to my defense. Instead, she shrugs, covering the side of her mouth to stage-whisper to me, "I mean, there are worse things than having to examine the man who's said to melt the ice just by being on it."

—-

Five minutes later, and after letting Kai know I'll be back shortly, I'm standing outside the team's locker room, adjusting the strap of my purse unnecessarily over my shoulder. I don't know what Beckett said to everyone when he went inside ahead of me, but a minute later, everyone has shuffled out, except for the defensemen I'm here to see.

Beckett swings his head in the direction of the entrance, giving me the signal to go inside.

"Wait." I furrow my brows. "You aren't staying?"

He shakes his head. "I've gotta check on Liv and the kids. You've got this."

I give him another knowing look before he takes off with a barely suppressed smile. The man always has something up his sleeve.

Clearing my throat, I place my mask of professionalism on before stepping into the locker room. Truth be told, the mask no longer feels like one. The only people I let my hair down around are my best friends, but even they call me the "ball of nevers" for a reason. Because I tend to say no first, and then perhaps come around to saying yes, but only if I'm compelled to do so.

Sure, I've shown that silly side to my son when we're having pillow fights or when I'm tickling him to get him to laugh, but otherwise, the fun-loving, carefree girl I used to be stays buried–and that's exactly where she ought to be.

To the rest of the world, I'm a bit on the rigid side. Some may even call me anal, bordering on obsessive. While I wouldn't say I'm ritualistic, I am regimented.

I try to eat only healthy, organic food, limiting my intake of anything processed. I'll have a glass or two of organic wine occasionally–and one other little vice I refuse to acknowledge at this moment–but I consider that a reward for being "good" throughout the week. I try to sleep at least seven hours a night, workout at least five times a week, and get all my annual exams done on time.

Because sometimes a missed annual exam can mean the difference between life or death.

I wasn't always a "ball of nevers".

My best friends know that better than anyone else. I was the crazy one of our group in college–staying out until the sun came up, drinking until Delia could wiggle the cocktail glass from my grasp. I was the girl who rolled into physics wearing pajama bottoms and a sweatshirt, smelling like last night's bad decisions and minty toothpaste.

It all changed after I met my late husband, Ajay. And though I still miss his presence in my and my son's life, I've finally come to accept his loss after three years. I've also come to accept that our marriage was far from perfect, and that somewhere in the middle of it all, I became less of the person I used to be and more of the person he wanted me to be. Somewhere in the middle of it all, I forgot how to have fun.

But despite the fact that I've come as far as I have through therapy and the support of my best friends, neither they nor Beckett Langfield can convince me to take a leap for love again.

Not after what I endured right along with Ajay. Not after the way I watched him lose his battle with the C-word I've sworn to eliminate from my vocabulary. Not when I know the universe doesn't give second chances, despite what my astrologically-inclined best friend Dylan believes.

That's not to say I haven't had a casual hook-up here or there.

I don't use the Tinder app on my phone often, but when the need arises and all I want is to feel a stranger between my legs for a night–instead of my collection of hand-operated toys, one of which is sitting in the safety of my purse right now–I haven't shied away from finding someone on there.

But emotion and attachment? Commitment and love? Those are words from my past that I don't plan to reinstate into my current dictionary. Not when my son needs me more than ever, not when he's my only reason and focus.

I take another step forward when my eyes fall on a stretch of sun-kissed skin. The sinewy muscles in his bare back flex and strain like they're both uncomfortable and content at the same time. He keeps his tattooed forearm above his head, leaning on it while keeping the weight off his injured leg.

Noting a glint of silver from his necklace, my eyes caress his broad back once more before trailing down to his tapered waist. Have I ever seen a more beautiful ass on a man? I honestly can't recall.

He's one hell of a prototype for physical human perfection. A colossus amongst ants. Sheer strength and beauty wrapped into one enormous form. And if my heart is galloping this fast from just ogling his back, then I might be in danger of heart failure when he turns around.

"You like what you see, Doc?"

The rumble of his voice hits me square in the ribs before my body jolts back to reality, as if his voice had an electrical charge. How did he know I was checking him out?

I'm not one to be flustered easily, but I'm finding myself at a loss for words. "Shit. Um . . ."

At my mumbled attempt to regain my composure, Rowan 'Slick' Parker turns around to study me with hooded eyes. A smug grin plays over his ridiculously plump lips while his eyes stay fixed on mine.

He holds up his phone, showing me that it's on camera mode. "Watched you walk in and check me out like you were fixin' to make me your next meal." His smile grows before he slicks his lips with his tongue. "And while I'm usually the one to do the eating, I'm not entirely against being offered up on a platter for you, Doc."

ALSO BY JENNI BARA

Want more of Cortney and Dylan?

The Rev's baseball fun continues in my new series

The Boston Revs Three Outs

Pre-Order Christina Damiano, the Revs

hot headed pitcher and the coach's daughter's story

The Fall Out

Curious about the baseball boys from the NY Metros

NY Metros Baseball

More than the Game

More than a Story

Wishing for More

Romcoms written as Gracie York

Goldilocks and the Grumpy Bear

Tumbling Head over Heels

Along Came the Girl

Peter Pumpkined Out

Dear Reader,

First, let me just say a massive THANK YOU! Thank you for reading Mother Maker. Thank you for supporting me. It's only because readers exist writers get to live out their dreams.

Being an author, creating another world, and characters that the readers fall in love with is fun, but can be lonely. Those of you who know Britt and I, you know we never like to do alone. So a year ago we had this fun idea of writing a series together. We asked two of our author besties to join us writing a group of mom friends. And Daphen had this amazing idea of falling down brownstone. And boom the Momcom world became a thing.

Over the last year it's been so much fun meeting up, laughing on the phone and on zoom with these women as we plotted, wrote, and rewrote Liv, Dylan, Shay, and Delia's stories. Getting to put the struggles of single parenting and some of each of our quirks and strengths into the characters has made this series even better.

And I'm so excited to announce that some more Boston Revs baseball players stories will be coming out this year! The Boston Revs Three Out series will release in the spring and summer starting with The Fall Out in March.

Finally, remember: Live in your world, fall in love in mine.

Jenni

ACKNOWLEDGMENTS

A big thank you my kids who have to hear, "Hold on a second, mom is writing." Or "I have one more signing this weekend"—it takes a lot for you all to deal with my writing, but you all are awesome about it.

Thank you to my parents, who support me in all I do all the time. I couldn't get through life without you guys. Being able to count on you both all the time for help or support, or encouragement, is the best gift. Thank you for being examples I can strive to be with my kids and being the best grandparents ever.

Beth, thank you for being so flexible and understanding with this book and everything. The fact you made sure every small detail of this Momcom world matched is why these series is as good as it is! Finding you was the best thing that ever happened! I will never stop singing your praises from the rooftop. You are amazing with your edits and proofreads and checking everything twice! You are thoughtful and detailed and amazing at keeping an author's voice. More than that, you are a friend who I am so grateful to have in my life. Thank you for being the wonderful person you are.

Becca and the rest of the Author agency you all are the best. You keep up with me and always keep things under control. I'm chaos and I'm sure I make you nuts with the wait, when is the cover reveal messages, I constantly send your way.

Sara, thank you for being you. For making all the Momcom and KU stuff run smoothly and working on everything a million percent even when I try my best to distract you. Your graphics are always perfection and the fact that you can keep coming up with new ideas is a skill I wish I had. I wish I could clone you because you know when I find something I like I'm always great let's get two!

Madi we were A LOT with the cover, but you put up with us graciously and always answered my many many emails. Thank you for helping bring our vague sometimes annoyingly different idea to life.

Jeff, thank you for being the final nit-picky check to make sure everything is perfect. Becoming a romance reader wasn't on your to do list, but I'm grateful you did it anyway!

Britt, you are my bestie, my travel buddy, my partner in crime, and my work wife. I love that every time we are together the laughs don't stop. Thank you for all your help making this story work and for adding into yours all the stuff I threw your way. Your ability to create the perfect story and characters is something that amazes me. You rock this author thing every day and inspire me by how hard you work. I love seeing your success! We may not have found my ghost yet but we have forever to keep trying new places, searching out cake at two am, and teaching me all the songs and shows I still don't know. PS EVERYONE if she ever asks Jenni's number is 8675309.

Daphne thank you for being not only one best friends but my teacher. The amount of knowledge and insight you have given is something I am forever grateful for. And your friendship is something I don't want to do without. No matter how busy you are and how crazy your own life is you are always checking in on me because you are simply the best. Everyone should check out the Lovewell Lumberjacks by Daphne Elliot because this woman has too much talent to not be known to every reader.

Swati, thank you for being amazing and joining us on this crazy idea. You answered a late night phone call and didn't hesitate to jump in with us on this adventure. I love your friendship and your skills as a writer. Your ability to create a anxiety tension filled world and then pivot on a dime and suddenly having us laughing. If you want an amazing read that will forever live in your thoughts you need some of Swati's Element Series.

Amy, thank you for being the Shay to my Dylan. For putting up with my chaos and my next 'fun' thing. We'd never get anything done without your organization and schedules. I'm so lucky to get to call you one of my best friends. Thank you for your help with Mother Maker and putting time into the entire series for us.

Amy Jo thank you for being a friend and an amazing talented merch maker! You always jump as soon as I need anything and a package is in the mail with amazing keychain, braclets, mini and more! Anna thank you for being a great friend and helping whenever I need beta reading or jumping in to create a new logo you always step up! Amy thank you for always betaing and making great tiktok and being an awesome person and friend.

To all my author friends and beta readers, thank you for being supportive and inspiring writers. Haley Cook, AJ Ranney, Kristin Lee, Alexandra Hale, Amanda Zook, Kat Long, Bethany Monaco Smith, Elyse Kelly, and so many, many more.

And big thank you to the rest of my friends and family who have helped me with encouragement and feedback. I love you all and am so thankful for your support.

ABOUT THE AUTHORS

Two years ago, the four of us met as new author's just starting our writing careers. This year we took a leap and decided to write together and what fun it was!

Made in the USA
Las Vegas, NV
25 April 2024

89134280R00184